The Little Key
of Solomon

Lemegeton Clavicula Salomonis
The Little Key of Solomon

ED. Gemma Gary

TROY BOOKS

Lemegeton Clavicula Salomonis
The Lesser Key of Solomon

This edition © Troy Books 2023
First printing in paperback August 2023

ISBN 978-1-909602-60-1

All rights reserved.
No part of this publication may be reproduced, stored within a retrieval system or transmitted in any form or by any means, electronic, mechanical, photocopying, scanning, recording or otherwise, without the prior written permission of the publisher.

Any practices or substances described within this publication are presented as items of interest. The author and the publisher accept no responsibility for any results arising from their enactment or use. Readers are self-responsible for their actions.

Published by Troy Books
www.troybooks.co.uk

Troy Books
BM Box 8003
London WC1N 3XX

Contents

Introduction	6
The Art Goetia	15
Of the 72 Infernal Spirits	15
Observations	33
Figure of the Circle	34
The Triangle	35
Solomon's Sexagonal Figure & Pentacle	36
The Secret Seal of Solomon	37
The Brazen Vessel and the Ring	38
The Other Materials	39
The Conjurations	39
The Invocation of the King	42
The Chain Curse	43
The License to Depart	45
The Art Theurgia Goetia	46
The Names, Seals & Characters of the 31 Chief Spirits etc.	48
The Conjurations	83
The Art Pauline	85
The First Hour of any Day	85
The Table of Practice	86
The Conjuration	98
The Invocation	99
The Second Part of the Art Pauline	100
The 12 Seals Attributed to the Signs & Angels	102
The Art Almadel	109
The Almadel	110
The 2nd Chora	111
The 3rd Chora	112
The 4th Chora	113
Invocation	113
The Notory Art of Solomon	115
Here beginneth the first Treatise of this Art	120
Of what Efficacy Words are	120
An Explanation of the Notary Art	121
The First Precept	121
A Spiritual Mandate of the Precedent Oration	121

The Exposition of this Oration	122
The Words of these Orations Cannot be Wholly Expounded	122
Of the Triumphal Figures	122
The Expositions of the Lunations of the Notary Art	123
He Sheweth how the Precedent Oration	123
The Oration	124
The second part of the precedent Orations	124
The third part of the precedent Oration	124
This Oration hath no Exposition in the Latine	124
Of the Efficacy of that Oration	124
Here he sheweth, in what manner those Notes differ in Art	125
The Oration	125
How this Oration is to be Said	126
Here followeth the Prayer we Spake of Before	126
Here following is the Prologue of the precedent Oration	126
Here beginneth the Prologue of this Oration	126
Here he sheweth some other Vertue of the precedent Oration	127
Here followeth an Oration of great Vertue	127
The Oration of the Physical Art	127
Another part of the same Oration	127
Here follows an efficacious Preface of an Oration	128
Here he sheweth how every Note of every Art	128
A Certain Special Precept	129
The Oration	129
The Beginning of the Oration	130
Here is also a particular Exposition of the fore-going Oration	130
The first of these Orations which we call Spiritual	131
The Election of Time	131
Here followeth the beginning of this Oration	131
This is the Beginning of the second part of that Oration	132
Then the Parts being Commemorated as is Directed	133
How the Latine Orations	133
Here he speaketh of the efficacy of all these	133
In this Chapter he sheweth the efficacy of the subsequent Oration	134
In this Chapter He Setteth Down the Time and Manner	135
No Man that is Impeded or Corrupted with any Crime	135
This is a Prologue or Exposition of the Precedent Oration	136
How Every Several Art Hath its Proper Note	137
Of the Liberal Sciences	137
He declareth what notes the three first liberal Arts have	137
Here Solomon Sheweth, how the Angel Told him Distinctly	138
The Reason why the Dialectical Art hath two Figures Onely	139
The Reason why Rhetorick hath four Figures	139
But of the other Arts and their Notes	139
How the Grammatical Notes are to be looked into in the first Moon	139
Here followeth the knowledge of the Notes	140
Of the Logical Notes	140
How the Logical Notes are to be Inspected	140

Contents

How we must Beware of Offences	140
How the Notes ought to be Inspected, at Certain Elected Times	141
How Divers Months are to be Sought Out	141
Here is made mention of the Notes of all Arts	141
Definitions of several Arts, and the Notes thereof	142
The first Oration at the beginning of the Note	142
The 3 Oration	143
The 4 Oration	143
Three Chapters to be published, before any of the Notes	146
How the Proper Notes are to be inspected	147
What dayes are to be observed in the inspection	147
Of the inspection of general Notes	147
How the three first Chapters are to be pronounced	147
How the fifth Oration of Theology ought to be rehearsed	147
How these Orations are to be said every day	149
The 7 Oration	150
Special precepts of the Notes of Theology	151
How Solomon received that ineffable Note from the Angel	151
How the precepts are to be observed in the operation of all Arts	151
These precepts are specially to be observed	152
The Experiment of the precedent work	152
For Eloquence and stability of mind	155
To Comfort the outward and inward Senses	155
This following is for the Memory	156
This following strengtheneth the interiour and exteriour Sences	156
This following giveth Eloquence, Memory and Stability	156
An Oration to recover lost wisdom	157
To obtain the grace of the Holy Spirit	157
To recover intellectual wisdom	157
Say these Orations from the first day of the month, to the fourth day	157
Hereby is increased so much Eloquence, that nothing is above it	157
The third part, the sign Lemach	159
For the memory	159
The Conclusion of the whole work	159
The Benediction of the place	160
To perform any work	162
Some other precepts to be observed in this work	163
The processe follows	163
Other precepts	164
The manner of Consecrating the Figure of Memory	165
Four dayes the Figure of Memory ought to be consecrated	166
The following Oration hath power to expell all lusts	168
For Theft	173
For Love	173
Appendix A	175
Appendix B	175

Introduction

The *Lesser Key of Solomon*, as it is popularly known, more properly *Lemegeton Clavicula Salomonis*, is a collection of magical texts brought together in compilation in the 17th Century and circulated widely among occultists and magicians since. It consists of five books, presented traditionally in the order of: *the Ars Goetia, Ars Theurgia-Goetia, Ars Paulina, Ars Almadel,* and *Ars Notoria*.

It is the first book, the *Ars Goetia*, that enjoys the greater notoriety, perhaps due to the influential edition by Samuel Liddell MacGregor Mathers and Aleister Crowley, published in 1904 as *The Book of the Goetia of Solomon the King* and embellished heavily by Crowley's hand. However, notoriety will have been imparted long before by its subject and title: *Goetia* – the black art of demon and spirit summoning – its Ancient Greek roots tangled deep within the dark fertility of witchcraft.

Here catalogued are 72 'evil' spirits, each possessed of the ability to undertake specific magical tasks, or to impart upon the magician specific powers. Provided also are the magic circle and triangle of evocation to be employed, along with the regalia and the invocations, conjurations and curses with which to summon forth and control the spirits.

Within the *Ars Theurgia Goetia*, the magician is instructed in the calling forth of a catalogue of 31 aërial spirits – which are in nature betwixt the celestial and the infernal, good and evil. The spirits are arranged hierarchically upon the compass, and seals are given for them along with those for some of the dukes and servants beneath them. They are possessed of all-encompassing, non-specific powers.

The *Ars Paulina*, a grimoire of the Pauline Art, takes its name after the apostle Paul. It is a two-part grimoire of Angelic, planetary and astrological magical invocation via the use of seals, talismans, incenses and the Table of Practice. Upon this table sits the crystal, into which the Angelic presence is conjured into visible manifestation.

The *Ars Almadel*, too, is an instruction in the art of Angelic scrying. Herein the magician learns of a method of Angelic invocation via the use of the Almadel – a carefully constructed waxen altar through which incense fumes arise from beneath.

Introduction

The *Ars Notoria* presents orations unto the Divine to impart upon the magician knowledge of the arts and sciences. The mystical images, or *notae*, from which the *Ars Notoria* takes its name, and intended to accompany the prayers, are absent however from the text.

And so, the five books of the *Lemegeton Clavicula Salomonis* represent, in order, a spectrum of spiritual magical art – from the infernal, through the aërial, the celestial, the Angelic and unto the Divine.

To make this edition of the *Lemegeton Clavicula Salomonis*, I have drawn from an intriguing, and seemingly rather rare publication. Held within a faded, once vibrant wine-mauve buckram binding is *The Little Key of Rabbi Solomon*. Its autographic text – blue-purple in colour, suggesting reproduction via the hectographic gelatine printing process – was penned by the hand of the astrologer-occultist Robert T. Cross (1850-1923), the last in a line of 19th century astrologers writing under the name 'Raphael' and whose publications were sought after by the cunning folk and fortune-tellers of the time. The first in that line was the similarly named Robert Cross Smith (1795-1832) from whom the great Welsh *dyn hysbys* Henry Harries once sought tuition in the art of spirit conjuration. His publications, under the name 'Raphael' were particularly popular with cunning folk for their practical information on astrology and fortune-telling, with the addition of charms and spells. Such books could be ordered from occult book sellers of the time – mainly in London – such as John Denley and George Bumstead who held shops, operating also by mail order.

The Robert T. Cross incarnation of 'Raphael' was also a highly regarded predictive astrologer, known to have taken students in the art. Given the nature of some of his publications however, it is likely that he would have offered tuition in the magical arts also.

His 1879 book *Raphael's Ancient Manuscript of Talismanic Magic*, drew from a Solomonic manuscript that had once belonged to Ebenezer Sibly, alongside the work of Francis Barrett and Cornelius Agrippa. Whilst better known via the later De Laurence edition, this book, like our *Little Key of Rabbi Solomon*, was a hand written manuscript, originally reproduced via hectographic reproduction. These original editions, due to the nature of the hectographic process, would have appeared only in exceedingly small print runs. Raphael's Little Key appears to have escaped a De Laurence re-issue and, to date, the only reference I have found to this book's existence is within M. J. Rudwin's 1921 anthology *Devil Stories*.

At present, the faded book in my possession appears to be the only *known* surviving copy, and now, and to my knowledge, within these pages the content of *The Little Key of Rabbi Solomon* appears in print for the first time since its original publication in 1879.

Unfortunately, at some point in its past, the pages up to page 3 were torn out. Fortunately, the 1921 *Devil Stories* reference gives the title page in full, allowing for its reproduction in the present edition. The Little Key of Rabbi Solomon consists of the *Ars Goetia* and the *Ars Almadel*, complete with drawings by Robert T. Cross of the spirit seals, the triangle of manifestation, the magic circle, the 'sexagonal' figure, the pentacle, brazen vessel, ring and seal of Solomon, and the Almadel. At the end of the book is the addition of intriguing magical operations – for theft, and for love. The operation for theft consists of 'The Mighty Oration' whilst the operations for love involve a circle, conjurations, image magic and a magical fire.

Of course, one does wonder, what source manuscript did Rober T. Cross use to write his edition of the *Lemegeton*? Sloane 3825, 3648 and 2731 for exapmle all show distinct differences, such as occasional variations of spirit and divine names which can't easily be explained as copy errors. The illustration for the magic circle, with its concentric rather than the more usual spiralling arrangement of the names, closely resembles that found in Arthur Edward Waite's *The Book of Ceremonial Magic*, first published as *The Book of Black Magic and of Pacts* in 1898. However, 'Raphael's' *The Little Key of Rabbi Solomon* pre-dates this by almost 20 years. The question of the identity of the source text/s is one that I am happy to leave to those far better acquainted with the various *Lemegeton* manuscripts and editions.

With the first couple of pages missing from *The Little Key*, I have used text drawn from the Sloane Manuscript 3825 to replace the absent text up to and including '*in the form of an old fair Man, riding upon...*' in the description for the spirit Agares, after which the text from *The Little Key* takes over. I have also taken the liberty of providing my own ink drawings of the missing spirit signs for Bael and Agares, the spirit sign drawings thereafter being those by Robert T. Cross, clarified and prepared for this edition by Jane Cox.

To make this a more traditionally 'complete' edition, I have added the *Ars Theurgia Goetia* and the *Ars Paulina*, from Sloane 3825, and the *Ars Notoria* after Robert Turner's 1657 translated edition. For this edition I have replaced the images in the *Ars Theurgia Goetia* and the *Ars Paulina* in their entirety with my own ink drawings, yet having sought to replicate as far as possible the character and charm of the imagery from these books as they appear in Sloane 3825.

Folded and pressed between the pages of my copy of *The Little Key* was an interesting little type-written note, the content of which I give below. The signature and the hand-written year are a little difficult to identify (the surname 'Skeggs' perhaps, and the year 1959 or 1989 possibly?). The note

Introduction

makes mention of the missing pages, as well as of the 'other' book. This would have been an accompanying and matching original hectographic edition of *Raphael's Ancient Manuscript of Talismanic Magic*, which was for sale alongside my copy of *The Little Key*, but sadly had already been bought by someone shortly before I acquired it.

The Little Key of Rabbi Solomon

Published c.1890, this book is of extreme interest having details of the 72 spirits, with their seals, metals, and ranks. The clear descriptions of their appearances and their commands of spirit legions, shew with clarity that the author has some very good authority to write so clearly of these mysteries. Later in the book are given some observations, with various pentacles and many powerful invocations. This book is more dangerous than the other, but it is unfortunate that pages 1&2 are missing.

Neither of the two mauve-coloured books deal with BLACK MAGIC in the sense that it is known today – that is, the worship of the Satanic Majesty, as opposed to God the Father, Son, and Holy Ghost – but rather with the ideas prevalent between 1600 and 1900, that the spirits of various lusts could be encouraged,..

In fact, of course, this boils down to the same thing, but it would be very wrong to suggest that the original owners – indeed the publishers, were practisers of the Cult.

It would be very wise to keep these well out of sight, only allowing people who understand such things to get in possession of them.

In re-publishing the content of *The Little Key of Rabbi Solomon* we are, of course, going against the note writer's advice to keep it well out of sight, however, we do believe that our readers qualify as those 'who understand such things.'

I hope that this book will provide an interesting and, in some respects, unique addition to the available editions of the *Lemegeton*. I have endeavoured to preserve the original spelling and punctuation, except in only a few places where understanding might otherwise be impeded. I have provided footnotes here and there, mostly regarding the divine and spirit names, for comparative purposes.

For both the practitioner and academic reader seeking an edition more complete with extensive and thorough comparative work to accompany the present book, I would, of course, recommend Joseph H. Peterson's excellent and definitive *The Lesser Key of Solomon*. I must recommend also *The Goetia of Dr. Rudd*, based upon the manuscript version of the *Lemegeton* by Dr. Thomas Rudd, not least for its highlighting of the importance, particularly for the practitioner, of the 72 Shem ha-Mephorash angels corresponding to the 72 Goetic demons.

Gemma Gary
Trebartha, North Hill, Cornwall.

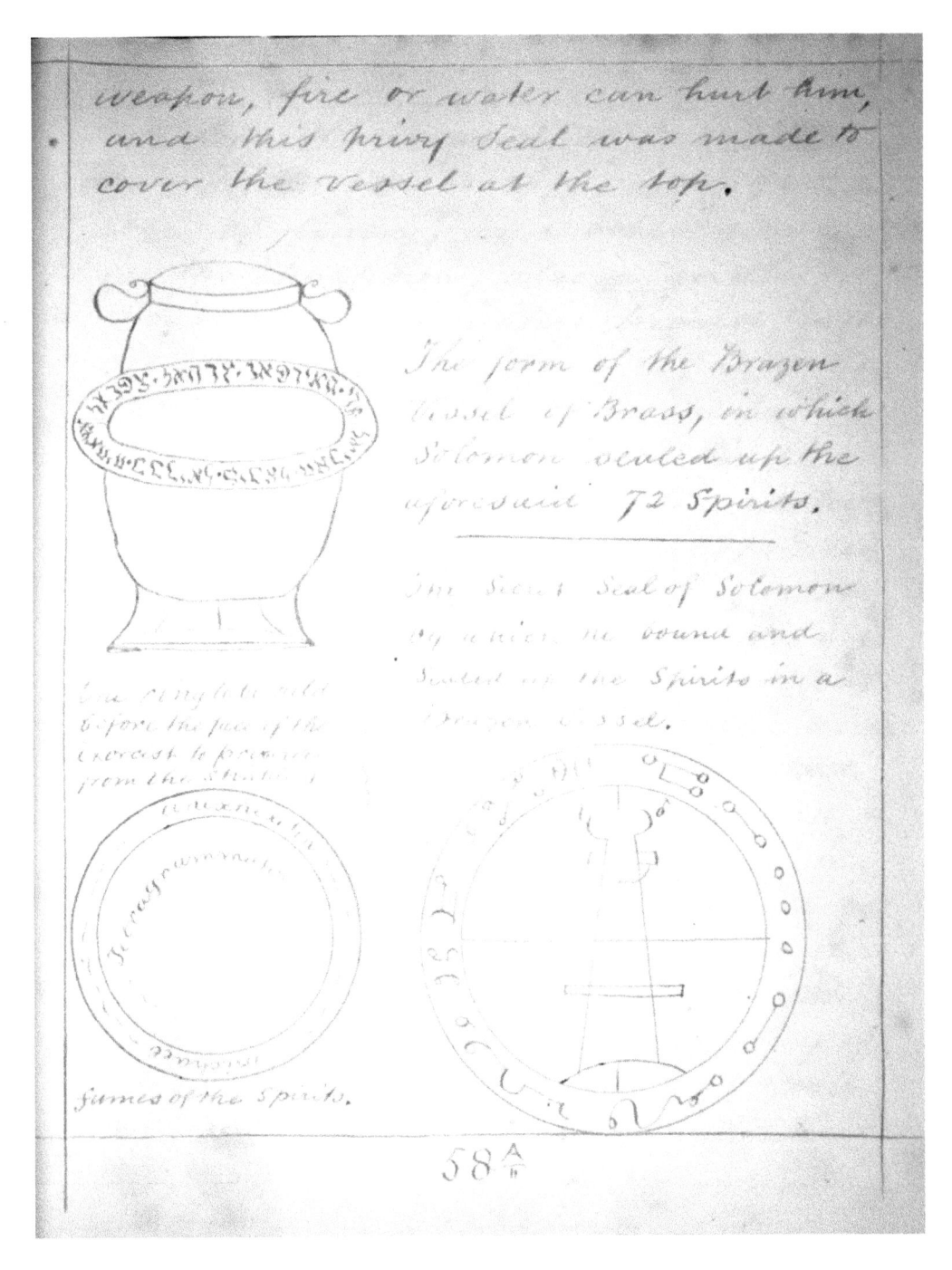

Page 58A from 'The Little Key of Rabbi Solomon' showing drawings by Robert T. Cross depicting the Brazen Vessel, the Exorcist's Ring and te Secret Seal of Solomon.

Lemegeton Clavicula Salomonis

> **Bathin Seal.**
> The 18th is called Bathin he is a mighty Duke and appeareth like a strong man, with a tail of a Serpent, setting on a bold coloured horse, he knows the virtues of herbs and precious stones, and can transport men suddenly from one Country to another, he rules over 30 legions of Spirits.
>
> **Saleos Seal.**
> The 19th is called Saleos he is a great & mighty Duke and appeareth in the form of a Gallant Soldier, riding on a Crocodile with a crown on his head, he causes the love of women to men, and men to women, he governs 30 legions of Spirits.
>
> **Purson Seal.**
> The 20th Spirit is called Purson, a Great King, he
>
> 13.

Page 13 from 'The Little Key of Rabbi Solomon' giving the seals and entries by Robert T. Cross for the Goetic spirits Bathin, Saleos, and Purson.

The Little Key of Rabbi Solomon

Containing the Names, Seals and Characters of the 72 Spirits
with whom he held converse,
also the Art Almadel of Rabbi Solomon,
carefully copied by "Raphael,"
London, 1879

title page from the "Raphael" (Robert T. Cross) manuscript

Lemegeton Clavicula Salomonis
or
Little Key of Solomon

Which contains all the names, orders and offices
of all spirits that ever he had any converse with.
With the seals or characters belonging to each spirit
and the manner of calling them forth to visible appearance.
In five parts called books

title page from Sloane 2731

Of the Seventy-Two Infernal Spirits
of the
Brazen Vessel

BAEL

The First Principal Spirit is a King ruling in the East, called Bael. He maketh thee to go Invisible. He ruleth over 66 Legions of Infernal Spirits. He appeareth in divers shapes, sometimes like a Cat, sometimes like a Toad, and sometimes like a Man, and sometimes all these forms at once. He speaketh hoarsely. This is his character which is used to be worn as a Lamen before him who calleth him forth, or else he will not do thee homage.

AGARES

The Second Spirit is a Duke called Agreas, or Agares. He is under the Power of the East, and cometh up in the form of an old fair Man, riding upon a Crocodile, very mildly, carrying a Goshawk in his hand, he makes those run that stand still, and fetch back runaways, he can teach all languages and tongues, and has power also to destroy dignities both temporal and spiritual, and causes Earthquakes, he is of the order of Virtues, and he has under his rule 31 legions, and his seal is to be worn as a lamen.

VASSAGO

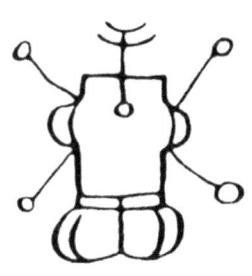

The third is a mighty Prince being of the same nature as Agares, He is called Vassago, This spirit is of a good nature and his office is to declare things present, past, and to come, and to discover all things hidden or lost. He governs 26 legions of Spirits.

Lemegeton Clavicula Salomonis

GAMIGIN[1]

The fourth Spirit is Gamigin, a great Marquess, he comes in the form of a little horse, or ass, and then in a human shape, he speaks with a hoarse voice, and teaches all Liberal Sciences and gives an a/c of dead Souls who died in sin, he rues over 30 legions of inferiors, his Seal must be worn before you.

MARBAS

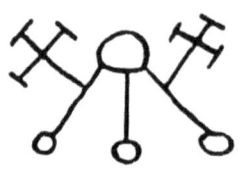

The fifth Spirit is called Marbas, he is a president and appeareth in the form of a great lion, and afterwards in the human shape, he answers truly of all things hidden or secret, he causes diseases, and cures them again. He gives great knowledge and wisdom, in machinery, and can change man into divers shapes, he governs 36 legions of Spirits.

VALEFOR

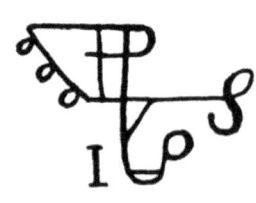

The sixth Spirit is Valefor, he is a mighty Duke, and appears in the form of a lion with many heads, he tempts those with whom he is familiar to steal, he governs 10 legions of Spirits, his Seal is to be worn constantly if you will have his familiarity.

AMON

The 7th Spirit is Amon, he is a marquess great in power and most strong, he at first appeareth like a wolf with a serpent's head, vomiting forth fire and flames, but at the command of the magician he puts on the human shape, with dog's teeth set in his head, he tells of things past and to come, and procures love, and reconciles friends and foes, he governs 40 legions of Spirits.

BARBATOS

The 8th Spirit is called Barbatos, he appeareth when the Sun is in Sagittary with four noble Kings and three companies of great troops, he giveth the understanding of all sciences, he breaks hidden treasures open, that have been laid hid by enchantment, he is of the order of Virtues, he knows all things past and to come, he reconcileth friends, and those in power, he rules over 30 legions of Spirits, his Seal must be worn before you.

---

1. The names SAMIGINA, or GAMIGN are given by Mathers/Crowley

Ars Goetia

PAIMON

The 9th Spirit in order is Paimon, a great King, and very obedient to Lucifer, he appeareth in the form of a man sitting on a dromedary with a crown on his head, there goes before him a host of Spirits like men, with trumpets, and well sounding cymbals, and all sorts of musical instruments, and his speech is such as the magician will well understand,. This Spirit can teach all arts and sciences, and all secret things, and can discover what the Earth is, and what holds it up in the Waters, and what the wind is, and where it is, or any thing you may desire to know, he gives dignities and confirmeth the same, he binds or makes men subject to the wil of the magician if he desires it, he gives good familiars, which can teach all arts, he is to be observed towards the N.W. he is of the order of Dominions, and has 200 legions of Spirits under him, one part of these is of the order of the Angels, and the other of Potestates, if you call this Spirit Paimon alone, you must make some offering to him, and then there will attend him two Kings, Beball, and Abalam, and other Spirits of the order Potestates, in his host of 25 legions, because these Spirits which are subjected to him, are not always with him, except the magician compel them.

BUER

The 10th Spirit is Buer a great President, he appeareth when the Sun is in Sagittary, he teach philosophy moral and natural, logic, and the virtues of all herbs and heals all distempers, in man, and gives good familiars, he governs 50 legions of Spirits, and this is his seal to obedience, which you must wear when you want him to appear.

GUSION

The 11th Spirit is a strong Duke called Gusion, he appeareth like Xenophilis and tells of things past, present and to come, he shows the meaning of all questions you can ask, he reconcileth friendships and gives honour and dignities, he rules over 40 legions of Spirits.

SITRI

The 12th Spirit is Sitri, he is a great Prince and he appears with a leopard's face, but at the command of the magician he takes on the human form, very beautiful, influencing men with women's love and women with men's love, he causeth them to show themselves naked, when so desired, he governs 60 legions of Spirits.

BELETH

The 13th Spirit is called Beleth, he is a mighty King, and terrible, riding on a pale horse with trumpets, and all kinds of musical instruments, playing before him, he is very furious at his first appearance, that is when the exorcist calls him up, the magician must then hold a hazel stick in his hand, stretched forth towards the East and South quarters, making a triangle, or a circle, commanding him into it by the virtue of the bonds and charms hereafter mentioned, and if he does not come into the triangle by your threats, rehearse the bonds and charms before him, and then he will yield up obedience, and go into it, and do what he is commanded by the magician, yet he must receive him very courteously, because he is a great King, and do homage to him as the Kings and Princes do, which attend him, and you must have always a silver ring on your middle finger, of your left hand, held against your face,. This great King Beleth causeth all the love that is possible to be between man and woman, He is of the order of Powers, and governs 85 legions of Spirits.

LERAJIE[2]

The 14th Spirit is called Lerajie, he is a Marquess great and powerful, shewing himself in the likeness of an archer, clad in green, carrying a bow and quiver, and causeth all great battles and contests, and the wounds to putrify that are made with arrows and archers, he belongs to sagittary, and governs 30 legions of spirits.

ELIGOR[3]

The 15th Spirit in order is called Eligor, a great duke appearing in the form of a goodly Knight, carrying a lamen, an ensign and a serpent, he discovers hidden things and causes wars, and how the soldiers shall order, he causes love and lust, and governs 60 legions of Spirits, you must wear his seal or else he will not appear or obey you.

ZEPAR

The 16th Spirit is called Zepar, he is a great Duke and appeareth in red apparel, and armed like a soldier, his office is to cause woman to love men, and he binds them in love, and also makes them barren, he governs 26 legions of spirits, his Seal is this which he obeys when he sees it.

---

2. LERAYE, or LERAJE in Sl.3825. LERAJE, or LERAIKHA in Mathers/Crowley
3. ELIGOS in Mathers/Crowley

BOTIS

The 17th Spirit is called Botis, he is a great president and an earl, he appeareth at first as an ugly vipor, then at the command of the magician, he puts on the human shape, with great teeth and two horns, carrying a sharp sword, in his hand, he tells of all things past and to come, and reconcileth friends and foes, he governs sixty legions of Spirits.

BATHIN

The 18th is called Bathin he is a mighty Duke and appeareth like a strong man, with a tail of a Serpent, sitting on a bald coloured horse, he knows the virtues of herbs and precious stones, and can transport men suddenly from one Country to another, he rules over 30 legions of Spirits.

SALLOS[4]

The 19th is called Saleos he is a great and mighty Duke and appeareth in the form of a gallant soldier, riding on a crocodile with a crown on his head, he causes the love of women to men, and men to women, he governs 30 legions of Spirits.

PURSON

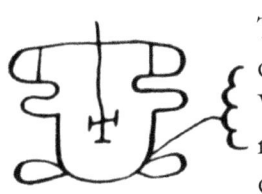

The 20th Spirit is called Purson, a great King, he appeareth commonly like a man, with a lion's face, carrying a cruel Viper in his hand and riding on a Bear, going before him, many trumpets sounding, he makes things hidden and can discover treasure, and tell all things present, past and to come, he can take a body either human or airy, and answers truly of all earthly things, wither secret or divine, and of the creation of the World, and bringeth forth good familiars, and under his government are 22 legions of Spirits, partly of the order of virtues, and partly of the order of thrones.

MORAX[5]

The 21st Spirit is called Morax, he is a great Earl and President, he comes like a great Bull with a man's face, is office is to make men very knowing in Astronomy and all other liberal sciences, he can give good familiars, and wise, which knows the virtues of all herbs, and stones which are precious, he governs 36 legions of Spirits.

---

4. SALLOS in Mathers/Crowley
5. MARAX in Mathers/Crowley

IPOS

The 22nd Spirit is called Ipos he is an Earl and a mighty Prince, and appeareth in the form of an Angel with a lion's head, and a goose's foot, and a hare's tail, he knows things past and to come, he makes men witty and bold, and governs 36 legions of Spirits.

AINI[6]

The 23rd Spirit is called Aini, a great Duke and strong, he appears in the form of a very handsome man, in body, with three heads, the first is like a Serpent, the second like a man having two stars in his forehead, the 3rd is like a cat, he rides on a viper, carrying a firebrand in his hand burning, wherewith he sets Castles, Cities, and other places on fire, he makes one witty in all manner of ways, he gives true answers on private matters, and governs 26 legions of Spirits.

NABERIUS

The 24th is called Naberius, he is a most Valiant Marquess and appears in the form of a cock crowing, and fluttering about the Circle, and when he speaks it is with a hoarse voice, he makes men cunning in all arts and sciences, and especially in the Art Rhetoric, he restores lost dignities and honors, and governs 19 legions of spirits.

GLAYA LABOLAS[7]

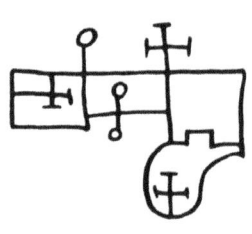

The 25th Spirit is called Glaya Labolas, he is a mighty president, and comes in the form of a Duke, with wings, like a griffin, he can teach all the Arts and Sciences in an instant, he is the author of bloodshed and manslaughter, he tells of things past and to come, and causes love of friends and foes, he can make men be invisible, and he has under his rule 36 legions of Spirits.

BUNE[8]

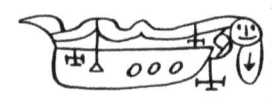

The 26th is called Bune, he is a strong, great and mighty Duke, and comes in the form of a dragon with three heads, one like a dog, one like a griffen, and the third

---

6. AIM in Sl. 3825 & in Mathers/Crowley
7. GLASAYA LABOLAS in Sl. 3825 & in Crowley/Mathers
8. BUNE, or BIMÉ in Mathers/Crowley

like a man, he speaks with a high and comely voice, he changes the places of the dead, and causes those Spirits which are in them to gather upon the sepulchre, he gives riches, and makes man wise and eloquent, he gives true answers in your demands and governs 30 legions of Spirits, this is his seal, which you must wear as a lamen.

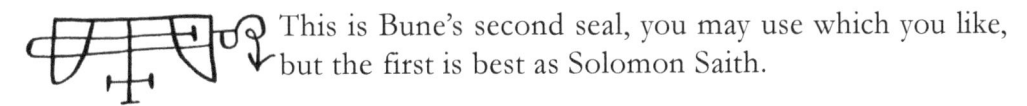

This is Bune's second seal, you may use which you like, but the first is best as Solomon Saith.

RONOBE[9]

The 27th Spirit is named Ronobe, he appeareth in the form of a monster, he teaches the Art and Rhetoric very well, he gives a good understanding, the Knowledge of tongues, the favor of friends and foes, he is a marquess and a great Earl, and their obeys him 19 legions of Spirits.

BERITH

The 28th Spirit in the order as Solomon bound them, is named Berith, he is a mighty, great and terrible Duke, he appeareth in the form of a soldier with red clothing, riding on a red horse, and a crown of gold on his head, he gives true answers of things past, present, and to come, you must use a ring as before spoken of Beleth, when you call him forth, he can turn all metals into gold, he can give dignities and confirm them, he Speaks with a clean and subtle voice, he is a great liar, and not to be trusted in giving advice. He governs 26 legions of Spirits.

ASTAROTH

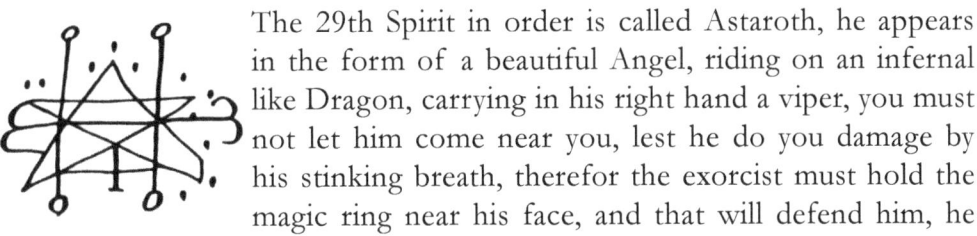

The 29th Spirit in order is called Astaroth, he appears in the form of a beautiful Angel, riding on an infernal like Dragon, carrying in his right hand a viper, you must not let him come near you, lest he do you damage by his stinking breath, therefor the exorcist must hold the magic ring near his face, and that will defend him, he gives true answers to things present past and to come, he can discover all Secrets and will declare willingly how the Spirits fell if desired, and the reason of his own fall, he makes men wonderfully knowing in all the liberal Sciences, he rules 40 legions of Spirits.

---

9. RONOVE in Sl. 3825. RONOVÉ in Mathers/Crowley

FORNEUS

The 30th Spirit is called Forneus, he is a great and mighty Marquess, he comes in the form of a great sea monster, he can teach and make men wonderfully knowing in all arts and Sciences, he causes men to have good names, and to have the understanding of tongues, he maketh one to be loved by their foes as they are by their friends, and governs 29 legions of Spirits.

FORAS

The 31st Spirit in order is called Foras, he is a mighty and great President and appeareth in the form of a strong man, he can give an understanding to man, how they can know the virtues of all herbs and precious stones, and teach them the Art of logic and Ethics in all their parts if desired, he makes men invisible, witty, and Eloquent, and to live long, he can discover things hid, and recover things lost, he rules over 29 legions of Spirits.

ASMODAY[10]

The 32nd Spirit in order is called Asmodai, he is a great King strong and powerful, and appeareth with three heads, the first is like a Bull, the second like a man, and the third like a ram with a serpent's tail, belching or vomiting forth flames of fire, out of his mouth, his feet are webbed like a goose, he sitteth on an infernal Dragon carrying a lance and a flag, he is the first and chief of the power of Amaymon, and goes before all those, when the exorcist has a mind to call him let it be abroad, and let him stand on his feet, during the time of action, and with his cap off, for if it can be Amaymon will deceive him, and cause all his doings to be wronged, As soon as the exorcist sees Asmodai in the shape as before said, he shall call him by his name, saying, Art thou Asmodai, and he will deny it, and by and bye he will bow down to the ground &c., he giveth the ring of virtues, he can teach the Art of Arithmetic, Geomancy [geometry], and all handicrafts, he gives full answers to all demands, he makes men to be invisible, and shows the place where treasures lay, and guards it, if it be among the regions of Amaymon, he governs 72 legions of Spirits.

---

10. ASMODAY in Sl. 3825 & in Mathers/Crowley

GAAP

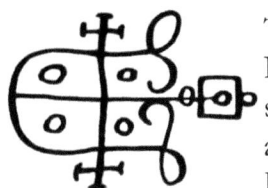

The 33rd Spirit is Gaap, he is a great President and mighty Prince, he appeareth when the Sun is in some of the Southern signs in the human shape, going before him are four great and mighty Kings, as it were to guide and conduct him along. His office is to make men Knowing in Philosophy and the liberal Sciences, he can cause love or hatred, and make men invisible, he can teach you how to consecrate those things that belong to the Divination[11] of Amaymon his King, he can deliver familiar Spirits out of the custody of other magicians, he answers truly of things past, present and to come, he can carry and recarry men most speedily from one place to another at the will of the Exorcist, he rules over 66 legions of Spirits, he is of the order of Potestates.

FURFUR[12]

The 34th Spirit is called Furfur, he is a great and mighty Earl, appearing in the form of a Hart with a fiery tail, he will not Speak until he is compelled and brought within the triangle; being forced thereinto, he will take upon him the form of an Angel; being bidden, he speaks with a hoarse voice, and can cause love between man and wife, he can raise thunder and lightning, blasts and great winds, he gives true answers of Secret and Divine things if commanded, and rules over 26 legions of Spirits.

MARCHOSIAS

The 35th Spirit is named Marchosias, he is a great and mighty Marquess and appeareth in the form of a wolf having griffin wings and a serpent's tail vomiting up fire out of his mouth, but at the command of the Exorcist, he puts on the form of a man, he is a strong fighter, he gives true answers to all questions and is very faithful to the Exorcist in doing his business, he was of the order of Dominations and governs 36 legions of spirits.

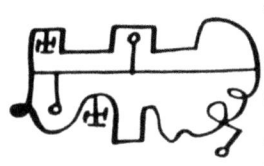

SOLAS or STOLAS[13]

The 36th Spirit is Solas or Stolas, he is a powerful prince and appeareth in the shape of a raven at first before the Exorcist, and then he takes the Image of a man, he can teach the Art of Astronomy, and the virtues of herbs and stones, he governs 26 legions of Spirits.

---

11. 'dominion' should be read here in place of 'divination'.
12. FURTUR in Sl. 3825
13. STOLAS in Sl. 3825. STOLAS, or STOLOS in Mathers/Crowley

PHENIX[14]

The 37th Spirit in order is Phenix, he is a great Marquess and appeareth like the bird Phenix, having a child's voice he sings many sweet notes before the exorcist, which he must not regard, but by and bye he must bid him put on the human shape, then he will speak marvellously of all wonderful signs [sciences] if desired, he is a great and excellent poet, and will willingly do your requests, as he hopes to return to the 7th Thrones in 1200 years, he governs 20 legions of Spirits.

HALPAS[15]

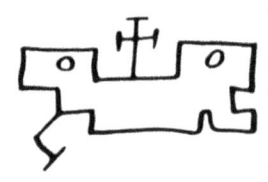

The 38th Spirit is Halpas, he is a great Earl and appeareth in the form of a Stock Dove, he Speaks with a hoarse voice, his office is to burn towns and to punish with the sword wicked men,[16] he can send men to war, and to other places appointed, he governs 26 legions of Spirits.

MALPAS[17]

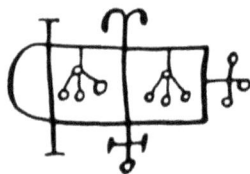

The 39th Spirit in order is called Malpas, he appeareth in form at first like a crow, but after he will put on the human form at the request of the Exorcist, he speaks with a hoarse voice, he is a mighty president and very powerful, he can build houses and high towers, he can bring quickly artificers from all parts of the world, he can destroy the enemies' desires and thoughts, he can give good familiars, and if you make him a sacrifice, he will receive it kindly and willingly, but he will deceive him who doth it, he governs 40 legions of Spirits.

RAUM

The 40th Spirit is called Raum he is a great Earl and appeareth in the form of a crow, but at the command of the Exorcist he will put on the Human shape, his office is to steal treasure, and to carry it where he is commanded, and to destroy cities and the dignities of men, and to tell of things past and what is, and what will be, he causes love between friends and foes, he is of the order of Thrones, and governs 30 legions of Spirits.

---

14. PHOENIX in Sl. 3825. PHENEX, or PHEYNIX in Mathers/Crowley
15. HALPHAS in Sl. 3825. HALPHAS, or MALTHUS in Mathers/Crowley
16. Sl. 3825 & Crowley/Mathers read: *his office is to build up Towers and to furnish them wth ammunition and weapons*
17. MALPHAS in Sl. 3825 & in Mathers/Crowley

FOCALOR

The 41st Spirit is called Focalor, he is a mighty Duke and strong, and appeareth in the form of a man with griffin wings, his office is to kill men and to drown them in the waters and to overthrow ships of war, he has power over both winds and sea but he will not hurt any man or thing, if he be commanded to the contrary by the Exorcist, he hath hope to return to the 7th Thrones in 1050 years, he governs three legions of Spirits.

SABNACK[18]

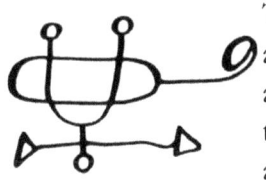

The 42nd is Sabnack,[19] he is a mighty and great Marquess, and very strong, he appeareth in the form of a soldier with a lion's head, riding on a pale coloured horse, his office is to build castles and cities and to furnish them with armour and to afflict men in many ways with wounds and rotten sores full of worms, he gives good familiars at the command of the Exorcist, and governs 30 legions of Spirits.

VEPAR

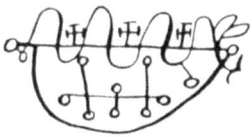

The 43rd Spirit is named Vepar,[20] he is a great and strong Duke, and appears like a mermaid, his office is to guide the waters, and the ships laden with armour thereon, and will at the request of the Exorcist cause the sea to be rough and stormy, and to cause the sea to appear full of ships, he causes men to die in three days with putrifying sores and wounds and causing worms to breed in them, he governs 29 legions of Spirits.

SHAX[21]

The 44th Spirit is called Shax, he is a great Marquess, and comes in the form of a Stock Dove speaking with a hoarse and subtle voice, his office is to take away the Sight, hearing, and understanding of any man or woman at the command of the Exorcist, and to steal money out of the King's houses, and to carry it again in 1200 years, at the command he will fetch anything but he must be commanded into the triangle first, or else he will deceive him, and tell him many lies, he can discover all things that are hidden and not kept by wicked Spirits, he gives goof familiars, and rules 30 legions of Spirits.

---

18. SABNACH in Sl. 3825. SABNOCK in Mathers/Crowley
19. The 43rd spirit in Sl. 3825 & in Mathers/Crowley
20. The 42nd spirit in Sl. 3825 & in Mathers/Crowley
21. SHAN, SHAX, SHAZ or SHASS are given in Mathers/Crowley

VINÉ

The 45th Spirit is called Vine, he is a great King and an Earl, and appeareth in the form of a monster, but at the command of the Exorcist he will put on the human shape,[22] he comes in the form of a lion, riding on a black horse with a viper in his hand, his office is to discover things hidden, witches, and things present past and to come, he, at the command of the Exorcist will build towers, and throw down great strong walls, makes waters rough, and stormy, he governs 36 legions.

BIFRONS

The 46th Spirit is called Bifrons, he is a great Earl and appears like a great monster, but after, at the will of the Exorcist, he puts on the human form, his office is to make one knowing in Astrology and geometry, and other Arts and Sciences, he teach the virtues of herbs and precious stones and woods, he changes dead bodies, and puts them in other places, and lights candles seemingly upon their graves, he governs six legions of Spirits.

VUAL[23]

The 47th Spirit is called Vual, he is a great and mighty Duke, and comes in the form of a mighty Dromedary at first, but after a while he puts on the human shape and speaks with the Egyptian tongue, his office is to procure the love of men and women, and will tell of all things past present and to come, he also procures friendship between friends and foes, he was of the order of Potestates, and governs 37 legions of Spirits.

HAGENTI[24]

The 48th Spirit is called Hagenti, he is a great President, and appears in the shape of a mighty Bull with griffin wings at first, but at the Exorcist's command he puts on the human shape, his office is to make men wise, and to instruct them into divers things, and to transmute all metals into gold and to change wine into water,[25] he commands 33 legions of Spirits.

---

22. Copied in error, possibly, from the description for Bifrons?
23. UVALL, VUAL, or VOVAL in Mathers/Crowley
24. HAAGENTI in Sl. 3825 & in Mathers/Crowley
25. Followed by *'and water into wine'* in Sl. 3825

Ars Goetia

PROCEL[26]

The 49th Spirit is named "Procel", he comes in the form of an Angel, he is a great and strong Duke speaking something mystically of hidden things, he teach the Art of Geometry and the liberal Sciences but at the command of the Exorcist he will make great noises, like the running of mighty waves, although there be none, he warms waters and distempers bath[s], and was of the order of Potestates before his fall, he governs 48 legions.

FURCAS

The 50th Spirit is called Furcas, he is a mighty Duke and appeareth in the form of a cruel old man with a long beard and hoary hair, sitting on a pale coloured horse with a sharp weapon in his hand; his office is to teach Philosophy, Astronomy, Logic, Chiromancy and Pyromancy, and in all their parts perfectly, he governs 20 legions of Spirits.

BALAM

The 51st Spirit is called Balam he is a great terrible and powerful King, with three heads, the first is like a Bull, the 2nd like a man, the third like a man with a serpent's tail and eyes flaming fire, riding upon a furious bear, carrying a goshawk in his fist, he speaks with a hoarse voice giving true answers of things past present and to come, he makes men to go invisible, and be witty and governs 40 legions of Spirits.

ALLORES[27]

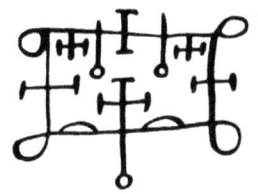

The 52nd Spirit is called Allores, he is a great and mighty strong Duke, and appears in the form of a soldier riding on a great horse and his face is like a lion's, very red, having eyes flaming fire, his speech is hoarse and very loud, his office is to teach Astronomy and all the liberal Sciences, he giveth good familiars and rules over 30 legions of Spirits.

(The mode of conjurations and diagrams of Circles, and of the brazen vessel in which Solomon bound these Spirits, will be given further on)

---

26. CROCELL or CROKEL in Mathers/Crowley
27. ALLOCES in Sl. 3825 & in Mathers/Crowley

Lemegeton Clavicula Salomonis

CAIM[28]

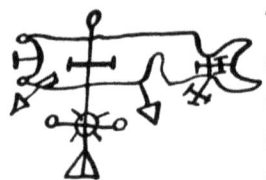

The 53rd Spirit is called Caim, and a great president and appeareth in the form of a bird called the Thrush, but after a while he puts on the human shape, like a man carrying a sharp sword in his hand, he seems to answer in burning ashes, he is a good disputor, his office is to give men the understanding of birds and the lowing of cattle, the barking of dogs and other things also the Knowledge of waters, and gives true answers of things to come, he was of the order of Angels, and now rules 30 legions of Spirits.

MURMUR[29]

The 54th Spirit is called Murmur, he is a good Duke and Earl, and appeareth in the form of a soldier riding on a griffin with a Duke's crown on his head, there goes before him two of his ministers and great trumpets sounding, his office is to teach Philosophy perfectly, and to contrain souls deceased to appear before the exorcist and to answer things that may be desired of them; he was partly of the order of Thrones and partly of Angels he rules 20 legions of Spirits.

OROBAS

The 55th Spirit is called Orobas, he is a mighty great prince appearing at first like a horse but at the command of the exorcist he puts on the human form, his office is to discover all things past, present, and to come, and he gives good dignities and palaces[30] and the favor of friends and foes, he can answer of the Creation of the World and of Divinity, and is very faithful to the Exorcist and will not let him be tempted by any spirit, he governs 26 legions of Spirits.

GEMORY[31]

The 56th Spirit is named Gemory, he is a strong and powerful Duke, and appears in the form of a Beautiful woman, with a duchess's corset[32] tied about her middle, his office is to tell of all things past present and to come and of treasures hid and where it lieth, and will procure the love of women both young and old, he governs 26 legions of Spirits.

---

28. CAMIO or CAIM inMathers/Crowley
29. MURMUR or MURMUS in Mathers/Crowley
30. *prelacies* in Mathers, Crowley
31. GREMORY, or GAMORI in Mathers/Crowley
32. *crownett* in Sloane 3825

OSE[33]

The 57th Spirit is called Ose he is a great president and appeareth like a leopard at first, but after a little time he puts on the shape of a man, his office is to make one cunning in all the liberal sciences and he gives true answers of Divine and Secret things and he can change men into any shape as the exorcist may desire, and that he that is changed will not know it, he governs 3 legions of Spirits.

AMY, or AVNAS[34]

The 58th Spirit is called Amy, he is a great president and appeareth in the shape of a great flaming fire, but after a while he puts on the shape of a man; his office is to make one wonderfully knowing in Astrology and the liberal Sciences, he gives good familiars, and can betray treasures kept by Spirits, he governs 36 legions of Spirits.

ORIAS[35]

The 59th Spirit is called Orias, and a great marquess, he appears in the form of a lion riding on a very strong horse with a Serpent's tail and holding in his right hand two great Serpents hissing; his office is to teach the virtues of the stars and the mansions of the planets, and how to understand their virtues also he transforms men, and gives dignities, prelates[36] and confirmations, and the favour of friends and foes, he governs 30 legions of Spirits.

VAPULA[37]

The 60th Spirit is called Vapula, he is a great mighty and strong Duke, appearing in the form of a lion with griffin wings, his office is to make men knowing in handicraft professions also in Philosophy and the Sciences, he rules 36 legions of Spirits.

---

33. OSÉ, or VOSO in Mathers/Crowley
34. AMY, or AVNAS in Mathers/Crowley
35. ORIAX, or ORIAS in Mathers/Crowley
36. *places* in Sl. 3825. *Prelacies* in Mathers/Crowle
37. VAPULA or NAPHULA in Mathers/Crowley

ZAGAN

The 61st Spirit in order is named Zagan, he is a great King and a president, and appears at first in the form of a Bull with griffin wings but after a while he puts on the human shape, and makes men witty and can turn water into wine, blood into wine, and wine into water, and can turn all metals into coin of that dominion, and he can make fools wise, he governs 36 legions of Spirits.

VALAC[38]

The 62nd Spirit is called Valac, he is a mighty great president, and appeareth like a little boy with Angel's wings riding on a two headed dragon, his office is to give true answers of hidden treasures, and tell where Serpents may be seen, and which he will deliver to the exorcist with his force of strength. He governs 38 legions of Spirits.

ANDRAS

The 63rd Spirit is called Andras, he is a great Marquess and comes in the form of an Angel with a head like a black night raven, riding upon a strong black wolf with a sharp bright sword flaming in his hands, his office is to sow discord, if the Exorcist have not a care he will kill him and his fellows, he governs 30 legions of Spirits.

FLAUROS[39]

The 64th Spirit is Flauros, he is a great Duke and appeareth at first like a mighty and strong leopard, but at the command of the Exorcist he puts on the shape of a man, with fiery eyes an a terrible countenance, he gives true answers of things, past, present and to come, but if he be not commanded into the triangle he will deceive the exorcist, but will gladly talk of Divinity and the creation of the world; and of his and other spirit's fall; he will destroy and burn those who are the Exorcist's enemies if he desires it, and will not suffer him to be tempted by any Spirits or otherwise, he governs 36 legions of Spirits.

---

38. VOLAC, VALAX, VALU or UALAC in Mathers/Crowley
39. HAURES, HAURAS, HAVRES or FLAUROS in Mathers/Crowley

ANDREALPHUS

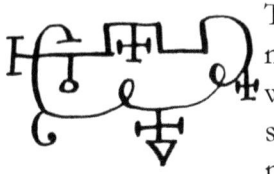

The 65th Spirit is called Andrealphus, he is a mighty marquess, and appearing at first in the shape of a peacock with great noises, but after a while he puts on the human shape, he can teach perfectly all things belonging to measurements, also Astronomy, and make men very subtle and cunning therein, he can transform men into the likeness of a bird and governs 30 legions of Spirits.

CIMEIES[40]

The 66th Spirit is called Cimeies, he is a mighty Marquess strong and powerful, appearing like a valiant soldier riding on a black horse, he rules over Spirits in parts of Africa, his office is to teach perfectly grammar, logic and rhetoric, and to discover hidden treasures and things lost, and hidden, he can make a man seem like a soldier of his own likeness, and governs 20 legions of chief Spirits and some of the inferior Spirits also.

AMDUSCIAS[41]

The 67th Spirit is called Amduscias, he is a strong and great Duke, appearing at first like a unicorn, but after at the request of the Exorcist he will stand before him in the human shape, causing trumpets and all kinds of musical instruments to be heard and not seen, also trees to fall and bend at the will of the Exorcist, he gives excellent familiars and governs 29 legions of Spirits.

BELIAL

The 68th Spirit is Belial, and he is a mighty King and powerful, and was created next after Lucifer, he appeareth in the form of a beautiful Angel sitting in a chariot of fire, speaking with a comely voice, that he fell first amongst the Angels, and worthies of a wiser sort, who went before Michael and other Heavenly Angels, his office is to distribute preferences[42] of Senatorship, and to cause favors of friends and foes, he gives excellent familiars, and governs 80 legions of Spirits, – NOTE. This King Belial must have offerings, sacrifices and gifts made to him by the Exorcist, or else he will not give true answers and then he tarries not one hour in the truth, unless he be constrained by divine power.

---

40. CIMEJES, CIMEIES or KIMARIS in Mathers/Crowley
41. AMDUSIAS or AMDUKIAS in Mathers/Crowley
42. *preferments* Sloane 3825

DECARABIA

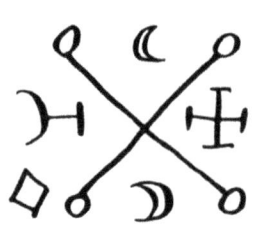

The 69th Spirit is called Decarabia, he is a Marquess, and comes in the form of a star in a pentacle ☆, but after, at the command of the Exorcist, he puts on the Image of a man, his office is to discover the virtues of birds and precious stones, and to make a similitude of all birds to fly before the Exorcist, and to tarry with him singing and eating as birds do, he governs 36 legions of Spirits.

SEERE[43]

The 70th Spirit is called Seere, he is a mighty prince and powerful under Amaymon King of the East, he appears in the form of a beautiful man riding on a strong Horse with wings, his office is to cause and give and to bring all things to pass of a sudden and to carry them any where you would have them, for he can fetch them over the whole Earth in the twinkling of an eye, he makes a true relation of all kinds of theft and several other things, he is indifferent good, or bad,[44] and will do the will of the Exorcist, He governs 26 legions of Spirits.

DANTALIAN[45]

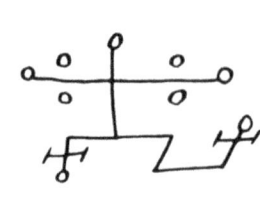

The 71st Spirit is called Dantalian, he is a great and mighty Duke appearing in the form of a man with many faces, or like men and women, and a book in his right hand, his office is to teach all arts and Sciences and to anyone, and to declare the secret councils of anyone, for he knows the thoughts of all men and women, he can change them at his will, he cause love and shows by vision the form and true similitude of anyone, let them be in what place or part of the world they will, he governs 36 legions of Spirits.

ANDROMALIUS

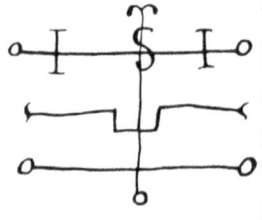

The 72nd Spirit in order is called Andromalius, he is a great Duke and mighty Earl, and appeareth in the form of a man holding a serpent in his hand, his office is to bring the good and the thief back that are stolen, and to discover all wickedness and underhand dealings, and to punish thieves, and their wickedness, and to discover treasures that are

---
43. SEERE, SEAR or SEIR in Mathers/Crowley
44. Sl. 3825 reads: *he is Indifferent good Natured*
45. DANTALION in Mathers/Crowley

hid. He governs 36 legions of Spirits. His seal as above is to be worn as a lamen when you conjure him.

These be the 72 mighty Kings and Princes , that King Solomon commanded into the vessel of Brass with their legions, of whom Beliel, Bileth, Asmodai and Gaap were chief, and it is supposed it was for their pride that Solomon never declared why he thus bound them up and sealed the vessel, he by Divine power cast them all into a deep lake or hole in Babylon, and the Babylonians wondering at seeing such a thing there, they went into the lake or hole to break the vessel open, suspecting to find a great treasure, but when they had broken it open, out flew all the chief Spirits and their legions following them, and they were restored again to their former places, but only Belial who entered into a certain image and there gave answers unto those who did offer sacrifices to him, as the Babylonians did for they did offer sacrifices, and worshipped that image as a God.

Observations

You are to observe first the Moon's age in your working, the best days are when the Moon is 2, 4, 6, 9, 10, 12 or 14 days old as Solomon says, and no other days are profitable;

The Seals of these 72 Spirits are to be made on metals; The chief Kings on Gold; Marquesses on Silver; Dukes on Copper; Prelates on Tin or Silver; Knights on Lead, and Presidents on fixed Quicksilver; and Earls on Silver and copper equally alike.

These 72 Spirits are in the power of Amaymon, Corson, Ziminar [Zimimar], and Gaap [Goap], which are those Kings ruling in the 4 quarters, E. W. N. S. and are not to be called forth (except it be on a very great occasion) but invocated and commanded to send such Spirits, as are under their rule and power as is shown in the following conjuration or invocation, –

These Chiefs may be bound from 9 to 12 O'clock Noon, and from 3 until Sunset, but Marquesses may be bound from 3 to 9 p.m. and from Sunset to Sun rising, Dukes may be bound from Sunrise to Noon in clear weather; Prelates may be bound in any hour of the day; Knights may be bound from day dawn until Sunrise, or from 4 p.m, to Sunset; Presidents may be bound in any hour of the day until twilight at night. Counts and Earls may be bound in any hour of the Day, so that it be in woods or any other place where men do not resort, nor where any noises are.

Lemegeton Clavicula Salomonis

Figure of the Circle
that Solomon made to preserve himself from the malice of those Evil Spirits.

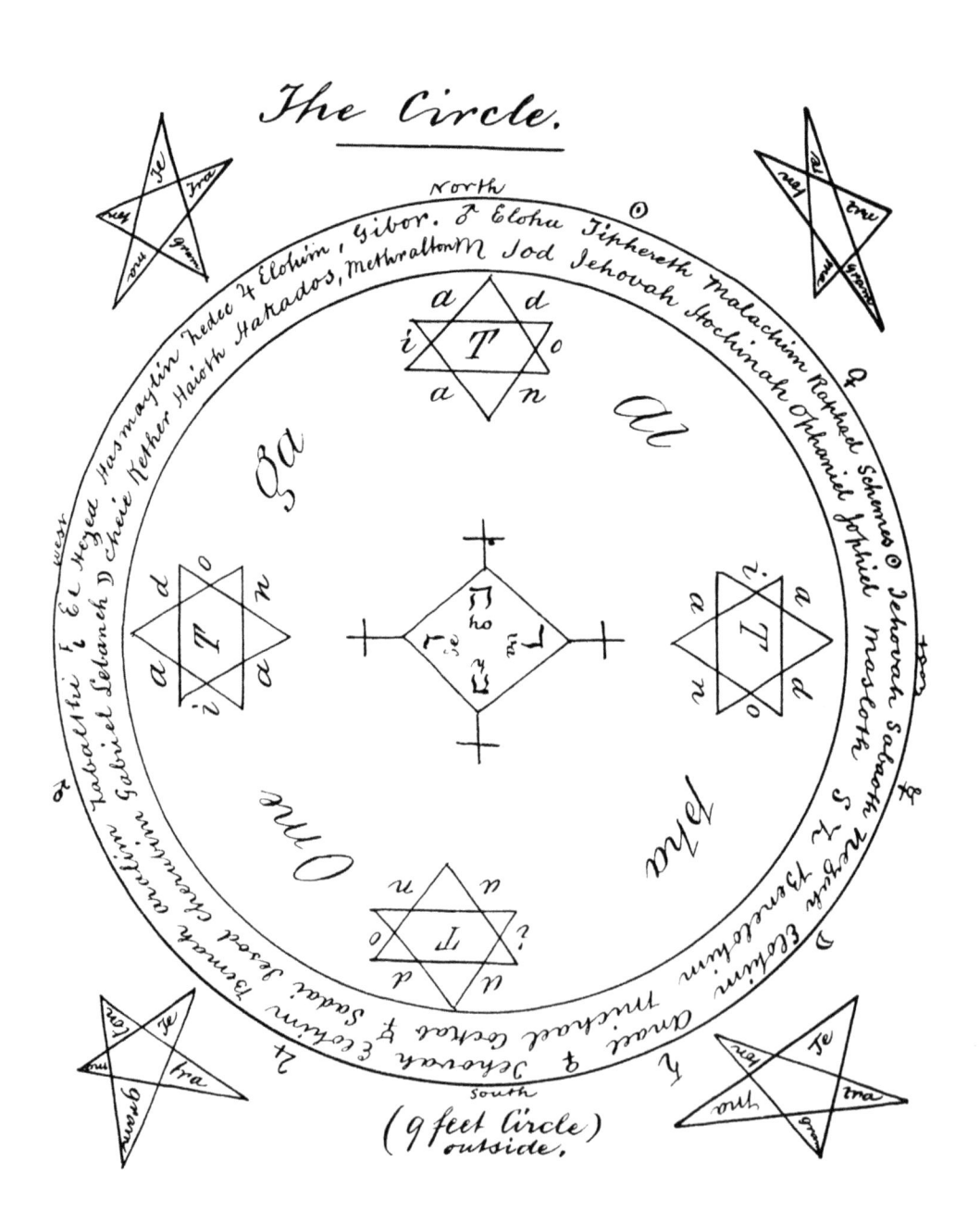

In another copy the Circle was written round thus: *Jehovah, Elohim, Binah, Aralim, Sabbatha, S.♄. El, Hesel, Hasmalin, Zeleck S.♃, ✠ Eheie, Kethor, Haioth, Hackados, Methraton, Reschith, Hagallatin, P.M. Jod, Jehoval, Hackmat, Ophanism,* S.Z. 2nd Circle: *Elohim, Gebor, Seraphim, Camael, Madim S.♂. Eloha Tetragrammaton, Raphael, Schemes, S.☉, Jehovah, Sabaoth, Neza, Elohim, Haniel, Zoza, S.♀, Elohim, Sabaoth, Hod, Ben, Elohim, Michael, Cochab, S.☿, Sadai, Jesol, Cherubim, Gabriel, Zeranah, S.☽.*

The Triangle
that Solomon commanded the disobedient spirits into

It is to be made two feet off the Circle, and 3 feet over,[46] note this circle is to be placed upon that coast the Spirit belongs to, and observe the moon when working, and that she be increasing in light.

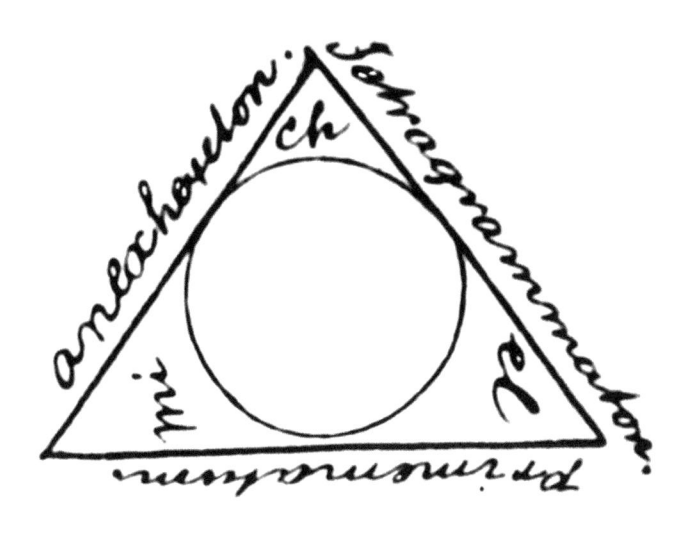

The following figures are to be made on parchment made of a calf's skin, or on gold or silver, and to [be] worn on the skirt of the robe made of white, with the seal of the spirit on one side of the cloth, and which is to be shown to the Spirits when they have appeared, that they may be compelled to be obedient, and take the human form.

46. Meaning two feet distant from the magical circle, and three feet across in width

Lemegeton Clavicula Salomonis

Solomon's Sexagonal Figure

The Pentacle of Solomon

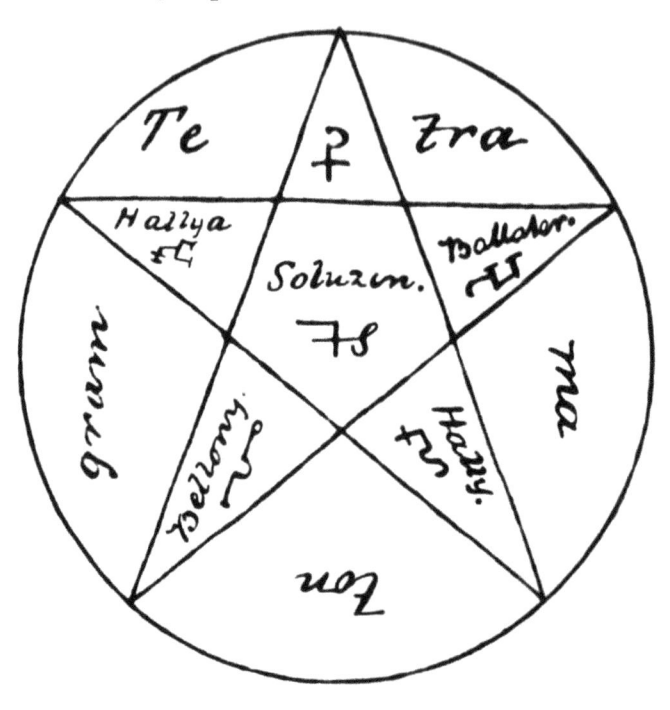

Ars Goetia

The Secret Seal of Solomon
By which he bound and sealed up the Spirits in a Brazen Vessel

This secret Seal is to be made by one that is clean both inwards and outwards, and has not defiled himself with any woman for the space of a month, and has with fasting and praying has got pardons of all his sins, it is to be made on a Tuesday or Saturday at 12 o'clock at night, written with the blood of a black cock that has never trod hen, on Virgin parchment; Note, on this night the Moon must be increasing in ♍, with it is to be burned some perfumes, made of Aloes, Rasen, Cedar and Alum, by this Seal Solomon compelled the aforesaid Spirits into a brass vessel, and sealed it up with the same; he, by it, gained the love of all manner of persons, and overcome in battle, for neither weapon, fire or water can hurt him, and this privy Seal was made to cover the vessel at the top.

Lemegeton Clavicula Salomonis

The form of the Brazen Vessel of Brass
In which Solomon sealed up the aforesaid 72 Spirits

The Ring
To be held before the face of the Exorcist
To preserve from the stinking fumes of the Spirits

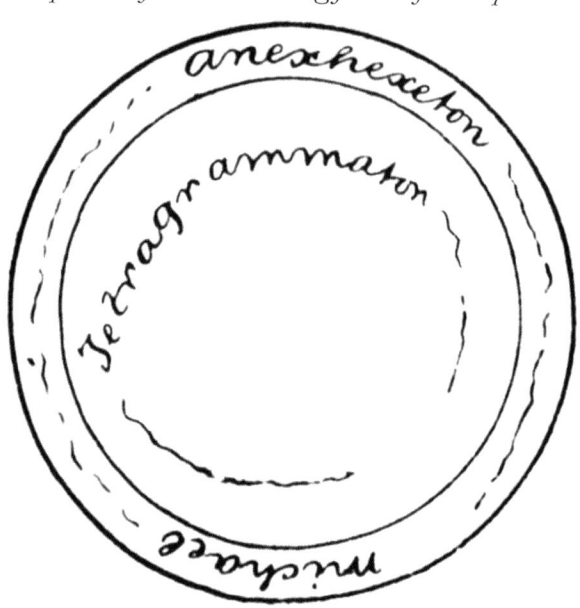

The Other Materials

The other materials are a sceptre, sword, mitre, or cap, a long white robe of linen, and other cloaks for the purpose, also a girdle of lion's skin, 3" inches broad, with all the names about it, as about the outer circle.– Also perfumes and a fire of charcoal kindled to put the fumes into to smoke and perfume the place appointed fir action, also anointing oils to anoint your temples and eyes with and clean water to wash yourself in, and in so doing you are to say as David did "Thou shalt purge me with hyssop O Lord, and I shall be clean, thou shalt wash me and I shall be whiter than snow", and at the putting on of your garments you say, "By the figurative mystery of this holy vestment, I will cloak me with the Armour of Salvation in the strength of the Highest, Ancor, Amicor,[47] Amides, Theodonias, Anitor, that my desired end be effected through thy strength Adonai to whom the praise and glory will for ever and ever belong."

After you have so done, make prayers to God, according to your work as Solomon has commanded.

Conjuration to Call Forth any of the Aforesaid Spirits

I invocate and conjure you thou Spirit N_ and being with power armed by the Supreme Majesty, I strongly command you by Baralanenses,[48] Baldachiensis, Paumachie,[49] and Apoloresedes,[50] and the most powerful Princes Genio, Liachide,[51] Ministers of the Tartarean Seat, Chief Prince of the Seat of Apologia in the 9th region, I exorcise and powerfully command you Spirit N_ in and by him who said the Word and it was done, and by the Holy and most glorious Names, Adonai El, Elohim, Elohe, Zebaoth, Elion, Escherce,[52] Jah, Tetragrammaton, Sadai, that you forthwith appear and shew yourself unto me here before this Circle in a fair and human shape without any deformity or ugly form, and forthwith and without delay do you come from all parts of the World to make rational answers to questions shall ask of you, and come ye peaceably, visibly and affably without delay and manifesting what desire

---

47. Amacor in Sl. 3825
48. Beralanensis in Sl. 3825
49. Paumachiæ in Sl. 3825
50. Apologiæ-Sedes in Sl. 3825
51. Liachidi in Sl. 3825
52. Escerchie in Sl. 3825

Lemegeton Clavicula Salomonis

being conjured by the Name of the Eternal living and true God Heliorem,[53] I conjure you by the especial and true name of your God that you owe obedience unto, and by the Name of your King which has rule over you, that forthwith you come without tarrying and fulfil my desires and demands and persist unto the End, according to my intentions, and I conjure you by him and by this ineffable Name Tetragrammaton, Jehovah, which being heard, the elements are overthrown, and the air shaken, the sea runs back, the fire is quenched, and the Earth trembles, and the whole host of Celestials, Terrestrials, and infernals do tremble and are troubled and confounded together that you visibly and affably speak unto me with a clear voice, intelligibly and without ambiguity, therefore Come ye, in the Name Adonai[54] Zebaoth, Adonai Amorani,[55] Come ye, come ye, why stay ye? Adonai Saday the King of Kings command you.

Say this often as you please and if the Spirit do not come, say as follows –

The Second Conjuration

I invocate, conjure and command you Spirit N_ to appear and show yourself visibly to me here before this Circle in fair and comely shape, without any deformity or tortuosity, by the Name of One, the Name Y & V, which Adam heard and spoke, and by the name Joth which Jacob heard from the Angel wrestling with him, and was delivered from the hands of his brother Esau, and by the Name of God Agla which Lot heard and was saved with his family, and by the Name Anehexeton[56] which Aaron [heard] and spoke and was made wise, and by the Name Schemes Amathia, which Joshua called upon and the Sun stayed his course, and by the Name Emmanuel which the 3 children Shedrach, Mashach, and Abednego sung in the midst of the fiery furnace and was delivered, and by the Name Alpha and Omega which Daniel named and destroyed Bel and the Dragon, and by the Name Zebaoth which Moses named, and all the rivers and waters in the Land of Egypt brought forth frogs and they ascended into the houses of the Egyptians destroying all things, and by the Name Escerchie Oriston which Moses named and the rivers and waters in the land of Egypt were turned into blood,[57] and by the Name Elion, which Moses

---

53. Helioren in Sl. 3825
54. The last three instances of 'Adonai' in this conjuration are given as 'Adonay' in Sl. 3825
55. Amiorem Sl. 3825
56. Anaphexaton Sl. 3825
57. This is a reversal of the phenomena ascribed to the names Zebaoth and Escerchie Oriston. In Sl. 3825, for example, it reads: *and by the name Zebaoth which Moses named and all the Rivers and waters in the land of Egypt were turned into blood and by the name Escerchie Oriston, which Moses named and all the Rivers Brought forth froggs, and they went into ye houses of ye Egyptians, Distroying all things.*

Ars Goetia

called, and there was great hail such as never was seen since the creation of the World, and by the name Adonai[58] which Moses named and there came up locusts over all the land of Egypt, and devoured all that the hail ad left, and by the name Hagios, and by the Seal Adonai and by Otheos, Jetros,[59] Athenoros,[60] Paracletus, and by the three Holy and Secret names Agla, On, Tetragrammaton, and by the dreadful day of judgement, and by the uncertain sea of glass which is before the face of the Divine Majesty, mighty and powerful, and by the four beasts before the throne having eyes before and behind, and by the fire round about the throne, and by the Holy Angels of Heaven and by the mighty wisdom of God, and by the Seal of Basdathea,[61] and by this name Primematum,[62] which Moses named and the Earth opened and swallowed up Corah; Dathan and Abiram, that you make faithful answers to all my demands, and perform all my desire, so far as in your office you are capable of performing, therefore come ye peaceably and affably, visibly and without delay to manifest what I desire, speaking with a clear and intelligible voice, and to my understanding.

If they come not at the rehearsing of the two former conjurations, (as without doubt they will) say on as follows, it being a constraint –

I conjure you Spirit N._ by all the most glorious and efficacious names of the most great and Incomprehensible Lord, God of Hosts that you come quickly without delay from all places and parts of the World wherever you are and make rational answers to my demands, and then visibly and affably speaking with the voice intelligibly to my understanding as aforesaid,

I conjure and constrain you spirit N._ by the aforesaid and by these seven names which wise Salomon bound thee and thy fellows in the brazen vessel of Brass, Adonai,[63] Prayai,[64] Tetragrammaton, Anexhexeton,[65] Inessensatoal,[66] Pathunion[67] and Itemon, that you appear here before this circle to fulfil my will in all things, that may seem good unto me, and if you be disobedient and refuse to come I will in the power of the supreme being and Everlasting Lord, God, who created both you and me and all the World in 6 days, and What is contained in it, Eye, Saray, and by the power of these names Primematum,[68]

---

58. Both instances of 'Adonai' in this conjuration are given as 'Adonay' in Sl. 3825
59. Iscyros Sl. 3825
60. Athenatos Sl. 3825
61. Baldachia Sl. 3825
62. Primeumaton Sl. 3825
63. All instances of 'Adonai' in this conjuration are given as 'Adonay' in Sl. 3825
64. Prerai in Sl. 3825
65. Anephexeton in Sl. 3825
66. Inessenfatall Sl. 3825
67. Pathatumon Sl. 3825
68. Primeumaton Sl. 3825

which commands the whole host of Heaven, I curse and deprive you of your office, joy and place, and bind you in the depths of the bottomless pit there to remain unto the day of the last judgement, and I bind you into Eternal fire and into the lake of fire and Brimstone unless you come quickly and appear here before this circle to do my will, therefore come ye in the Holy names, Adonai Zebaoth, Amioram, come ye, Adonai commands you.

If he do not yet appear, you may be sure he is sent to some other place by his King and cannot come, and if it be so, invocate the King as follows to send him, but if he does not come, then you may be sure he is bound in chains in hell, and he is not in the custody of his King, if so you have a desire to call him from thence, you must rehearse the Spirits chain.

The Invocation of the King is as Follows

O thou great and powerful King Amaymon, who bears rule by the power of the supreme God El, over all Spirits both superior and inferior, and the infernal order in the Dominion of the East I invocate and command you by the especial and true name of God and by the God that you worship and by the Seal of your creation, and by the most mighty and powerful names of God Jehovah, Tetragrammaton who cast you out of Heaven with all the other infernal Spirits, and by all the most powerful and great names of God who created heaven and Earth and hell, and all things contained therein, and by their powers and virtues and by the name Primematum[69] who commanded the whole host of Heaven that you cause, inforce, and compel the Spirit N_ unto me here before this circle in a fair and comely shape, without doing any harm to me or any other creature, to answer truly and faithfully all my requests that I may accomplish my will and desires, in knowing or obtaining any matter or thing which by his office you know is proper for him to perform, or accomplish, by the power of God El, who creates and disposes of all things both celestial, aerial, Terrestrial and infernal.

After you have invocated the King in this manner two or three times, then conjure the Spirit you would call forth, by the aforesaid form of conjuration, rehearsing them several times, and it will come, if not at first or 2nd time of rehearsing it he do not come, add the Spirits Chain to the aforesaid conjuration, and it will be forced to come, if he be bound in Hell the chain must break from him and he will be at liberty.

---

69. Primeumaton in Sl. 3825

Ars Goetia

The Chain Curse
Called the Spirits Chain against All Spirits that Rebel

O thou wicked and Disobedient N_ because thou hast not obeyed nor regarded my words which I have rehearsed, they being all glorious and incomprehensible names of the true God, maker and creator of all things which are in the world, I, by the power of these names which no creature is able to resist do curse you into the depth of the bottomless pit, and there to remain unto the day of doom in Hell and fire and Brimstine unquenchable, unless you forthwith appear here before this circle in this triangle △ to do my will, therefore come ye quickly and peaceably, and by these names Adonai, Zebaoth, Adonai[70] Amioram come ye, come ye, the King of Kings or Adonai commands you.

When you have read so far and he do not come, then with his Seal on parchment, and put it into a black box, with brimstone, assafedia,[71] and other like things that bear a stinking smell then bind the box up with iron wire, and hang it on your sword's point and hold it over the fire of charcoal, and say to the fire first, it being placed towards that quarter the Spirit is to come from –

I conjure the fire by him that made thee, and all other great creatures in the world, that thou torment, burn, and consume this Spirit N_ Everlastingly.
Because thou art disobedient and obeyest not my commandments nor keepest the precepts of the Lord thy God, neither will thou obey me nor my invocation having thereby called you forth, I, who am the servant of the most High and Imperial Lord God of Hosts Jehovah, having his celestial power and permission, neither come thou, to answer these my proposals here made unto you, for which averness and contempt you are guilty of great disobedience and rebellion, and therefore I shall Excommunicate you, and destroy thy name and Seal, which I have in this box, and shall burn them with immortal fire and shall bury them in immortal oblivion, unless though immediately come, and appear visibly, affably, friendly and courteously here unto me before this circle in this triangle △, in a fair and comely form, and in [no] way terrible, hurtful or frightful to me, or any other creature upon the Earth whatsoever and make rational answers to my requests, and perform all my desires in all things that I may ask of you.

And if he comes not yet say as follows.

---

70. The last two instances of 'Adonai' in this conjuration are given as 'Adonay' in Sl. 3825
71. asafoetida

N_ Thou art still pernicious and Disobedient, and will not appear to me to answer to such things as I have desired to know, or I would have been satisfied, I do now in the name and by the power and dignity of the omnipotent and immortal Lord God of Hosts, Jehoval Tetragrammaton, the only creator of heaven, and Earth and Hell, and all that are in them, who is the marvellous disposer of all things, both visible and invisible, curse you and deprive you of all your office, power and place, and bind you in the depths of the bottomless pit, there to remain unto the day of Judgement, and into the Lake of fire and brimstone, which is prepared for the rebellious, disobedient, obstinate and pernicious Spirits; Let all the company of Heaven curse you, the Sun, the Moon and the Stars, the light of all the hosts of Heaven, into the fire unquenchable and torments unspeakable, and as thy name and Seal is contained in this box, chained and bound up, and shall be choked in sulphurious and stinking substances, and burn in this material fire, so in the name of Jehovah, and by the power and dignity of Anexhexeton,[72] Primematum,[73] cast thee, o thou disobedient Spirit N_ into the lake of fire which is prepared for the Damned and cursed Spirits, there to remain to the Day of Doom, and never more to be remembered of, before the face of God, who shall come to judge the quick and the dead and the world by fire.

The Exorcist must put the box, into the fire, and he will come, and as soon as he does come, quench the fire that the box is in, and make sweet perfumes, and give him a good entertainment, showing him the pentacle which is at the bottom of your vestment, covered with a linen cloth and saying:

Behold your confusion if you be disobedient, behold the pentacle of Solomon, which I have brought here before your presence; behold the person of the Exorcist who is called Octinimoes[74] in midst of the Exorcism, who is armed by God and without fear, who potently invocateth you and calleth you to appear, therefore make rational answers to my demands and be obedient to me your master in the Name of the Lord Bathal[75] Rushing upon Abbrac,[76] Abeor coming upon Beror.[77]

---

72. Anaphexeton in Sl. 3825
73. Primeumaton in Sl. 3825
74. Octinomos Sl. 3825
75. Bathat Sl. 3825
76. Abrac Sl. 3825
77. Aberer Sl. 3825

Then he will be obedient, and bid you to ask him what you will, for he is subjected by God to fulfil your demands and desires, and when he appears and shows himself humbly and meek, then you are to say:

Welcome Spirit! Or most noble King I say you are welcome unto me, for I called you through him who created Heaven and Earth and hell, and all that are contained in them, and you have obeyed also by the same power I called you forth by, I bind you to remain affably and visibly here before this circle in this triangle, so constant and so long as I have occasion for you, and not to depart without my license, until you have truly and faithfully fulfilled my will without any falsity.

The Licence to Depart

O thou Spirit N_ because thou hast diligently answered my demands, and was ready and willing to come at my first call, I do here license you to depart, without doing any injury or danger to man or beast, Depart I say and be very ready and willing to come being duly exorcised and conjured by the Sacred rites of Magic, I charge you to withdraw peaceably and quickly, and the peace of God be ever continued between me and thee, Amen.

After you have given the Spirit license to depart, you are not to go out of the circle till they be gone, and you have made prayers to God for a great blessing he has bestowed upon you in granting your desires and delivering you from the malice of the enemy, the Devil; And note, you may command these Spirits into a brazen vessel as you do into a triangle, saying, that they forthwith appear in this circle in this vessel of Brass, in a fair and comely shape, and as it is shown before in the foregoing conjurations.

And so Ends the First Book
Called The Art Goetia

Here beginneth the Second Part called
The Art Theurgia Goëtia
of Kinge Salomon

In this following Treatise you have 31 names of cheife spirits with severall of the ministering spirits which are under them with their seals and characters which are to be worne as a lamin on your breasts, for without that the Spirit that is appeared will not obey you, to doe your will etc.

The offices of these spirits is all one, for what one can doe the other can doe the same. They can shew and discover all things that is hidd and done in the world, and can fetch and carry or doe any thinge that is to be done or is contained in any of the four Elements Fier, ayre, Earth and water etc. allso the secrets of kings or any other person or persons let it be in what kinde it will.

These spirits are by nature good and evill That is, one part is good, and the other part Evill. They are governed by their princes, and each prince hath his place of abode in the points of the compass — as is shewed in the following figure. Therefore, when you have a desire to call any of the kings or any of their servants, you are to direct yourselfe to that point of the compass the Kinge hath his mansion or please of abode, and you cannot well erre in your operations.

Note — every prince is to observe his conjuration, yet all of one form, except the name and place of the spirit, for in that they must change and differ allso the seal of the spirits is to be changed accordingly.

As for the garments and other materiall things they are spoken of in the Booke Goetia.

The form of the figure which discovereth the order of the 31 Kings or princes with their servant ministers for when the King is found his subjects are Easy to be found out &c.

Ars Theurgia Goetia

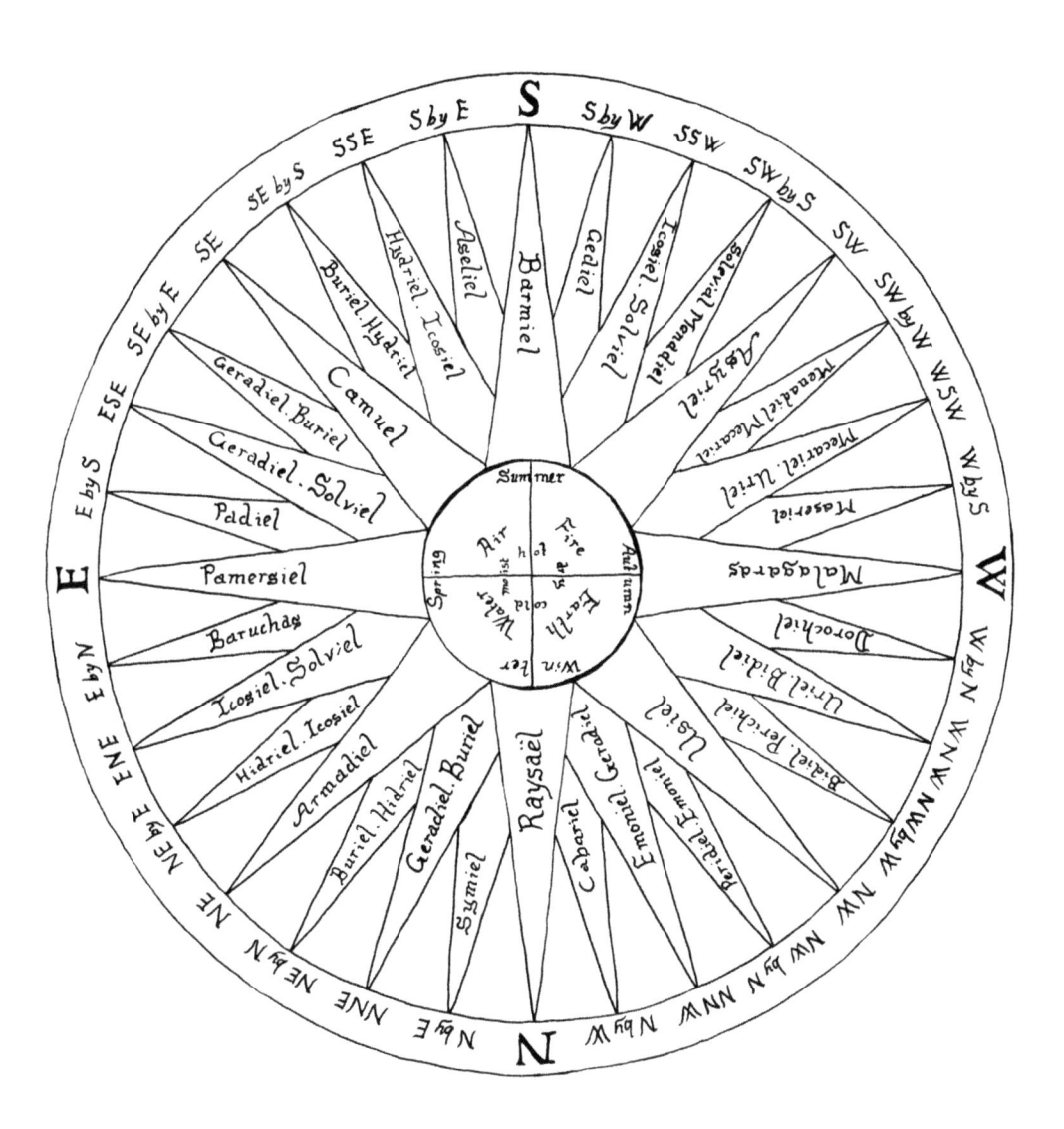

You may perceive by this figure that 20 of these kings have their first mantions and continue in one place and that the other 11 are moveable and are sometimes in one place sometime in another and in some other times together more or less – therefore its no matter which way you stand with your face, when you have a desire to call any of them forth or their servants.

Lemegeton Clavicula Salomonis

The Names, Seals, & Characters of the 31 Cheife Spirits & Their Ministering Spirits

Carnesiell is the most great and Cheefe Emporor ruling in the East who hath 1000 great Dukes and a 100 lesser Dukes under him, besides 50000000000000 of ministering spirits which is more inferiour than the Dukes, whereof we shall make no mention, but only 12 of the Cheefe Dukes and their seals because they are sufficient for practise.

Carnesiel his Seal

12 of his Dukes

Myrezyn	Benoham	Armany
Ornich	Arifiel	Capriel
Zabriel	Cumeriel	Bedary
Bucafas	Vadriel	Laphor

Note – Carnesiel, when he appears, day or night, attends him 60000000 000000 Dukes, but when you call any of these Dukes there never attend above 300 and sometimes not above 10 etc. The Conuration of Carnesiel as followeth: *We Conjure thee O thou mighty and potent Prince Carnesiel who is the Emperour & andcheife Comander, ruling as King in the dominion of the East who beares rule by the power of the supreame God El, over all Spirits etc.*

Ars Theurgia Goetia

Caspiel is the Great and Cheefe Emperor Ruling in the South who hath 200 great Dukes and 400 lesser Dukes under him, besides 1000200000000 ministering spirits, which are much Inferiour &c. whereof wee (Salomon saith) shall make noe mention, but only of 12 of the Cheefe Dukes and their seales, for they are sufficient for practise.

These 12 Dukes have 2660 under Dukes a peece to attend them, whereof some of them comes along with him when he is Invocated, but they are very Stuborne and Churlish etc.

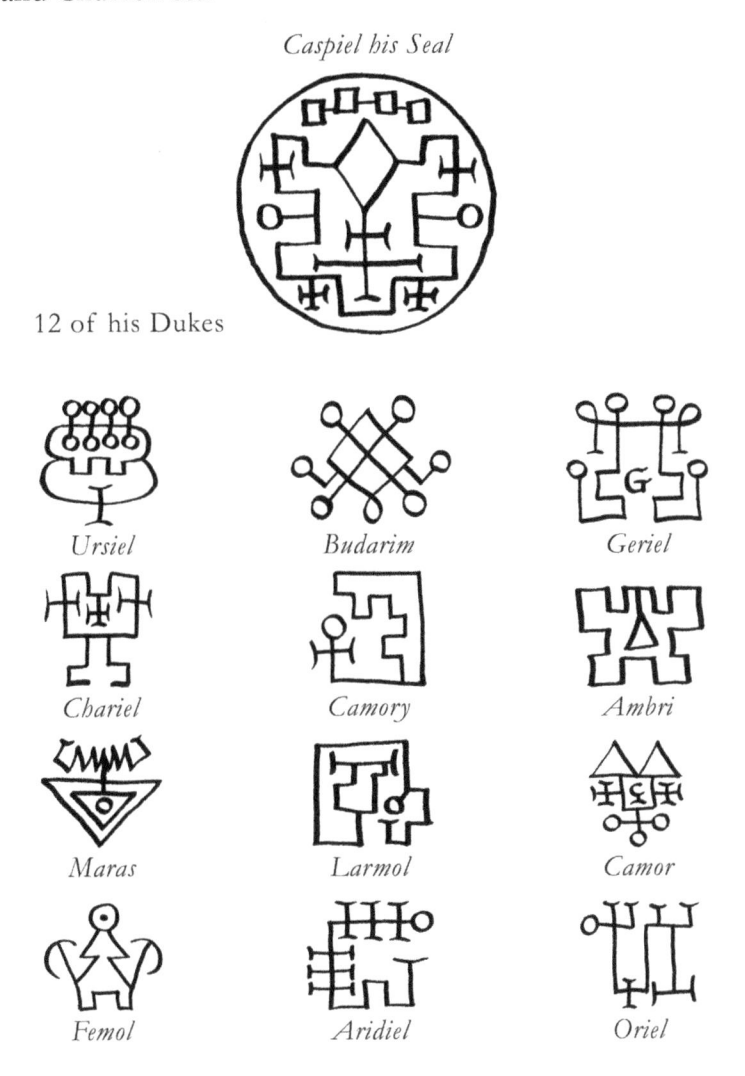

Caspiel his Seal

12 of his Dukes

Ursiel   *Budarim*   *Geriel*

Chariel   *Camory*   *Ambri*

Maras   *Larmol*   *Camor*

Femol   *Aridiel*   *Oriel*

The Conjuration of Caspiel: *Wee Conjure thee O thou Mighty and Potent Prince Caspiel etc.*

Lemegeton Clavicula Salomonis

Amenadiel is the Great Emperor of the west who hath 300 great Dukes and 500 lesser Dukes, besides 40000030000100000 other ministering spirits more Inferiour to attend him, wheof we shall not make any mention but only of 12 of the cheefe Dukes and their seales which is sufficient for practice.

Amenadiel his Seal

12 of his Dukes

Vadros   *Rapsiel*   *Almesiel*

Camiel   *Lamael*   *Codriel*

Luziel   *Zoeniel*   *Balsur*

Musiriel *Curifas*   *Nadroc*

Note – Amenadiel may be called at any hour of the day or night, but his dukes (who hath 3880 servants a peice to attend them) Are to be called in Certaine houres, as Vadros he may be called in the 2 first houres of the day, Camiel in the second 2 houres of the day and so successively till you come to Nadroc who is to be called in ye 2 last houres of the night and then begin againe at Vadros etc. The same Rule is to be observed in calling the Dukes belonging to Demoriel the Emperor of the North.

The Conjuration: *Wee Conjure the O thou mighty & potent Prince Amenadiel who is the Emperour & cheife King ruling in the dominion of the West etc.*

Ars Theurgia Goetia

Demoriel is the Great and Mighty Emperor of the North, who hath 400 great Dukes and 600 lesser Dukes with 70000080000900000 servants under his Command to attend him, whereof we shall make mention but of 12 of the cheefe Dukes and their seales, which will be sufficient for practice.

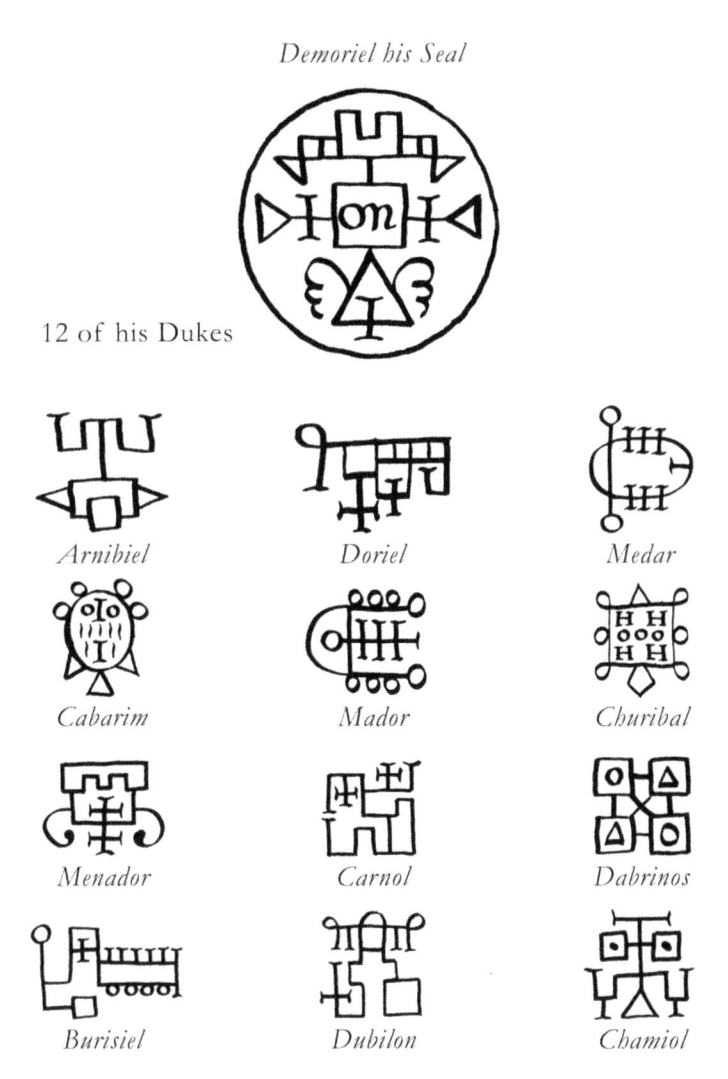

Demoriel his Seal

12 of his Dukes

Arnibiel   *Doriel*   *Medar*

Cabarim   *Mador*   *Churibal*

Menador   *Carnol*   *Dabrinos*

Burisiel   *Dubilon*   *Chamiol*

Note – Each of those Dukes hath 1140 Servants whoe attends them as need requireth for when that Duke yee call for have more to doe then ordenary, he hath the more servants to attend him.

The Conjuration of Demoriel: *Wee Conjure thee O thou &c.*

Lemegeton Clavicula Salomonis

Pamersiel is the First and Cheefe spirit in the East, under Carnesiel, who hath 1000 spirits under him which are to be called in the day time, but with great care for they are very lofty and stuborne whereof we shall make mention but of a 11 as followeth.

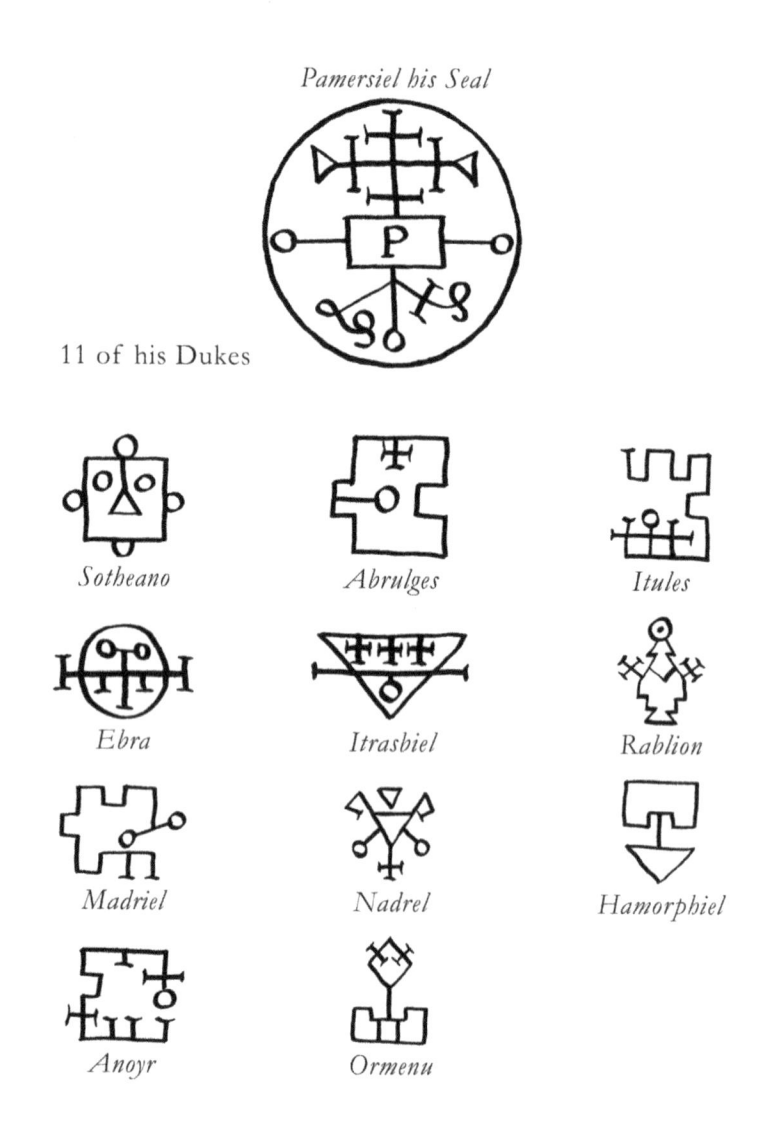

Pamersiel his Seal

11 of his Dukes

Sotheano

Abrulges

Itules

Ebra

Itrasbiel

Rablion

Madriel

Nadrel

Hamorphiel

Anoyr

Ormenu

Note – These Spirits are by Nature Evill, and verry false, not to be trusted in secrett things but is Excellent in driving away spirits of Darkness from any place, or house that is haunted &c.

Ars Theurgia Goetia

To call Forth Pamersiel, or any of these his servants, chuse the uppermost private or secrett and most tacit rome in the house, or in some certaine island wood or grove, or the most occult and hidden place from all commers and goers, that noe one chance by, may (if possible) happen that way (chamber or what soever place else, you act yr concerns in) observe that it be very Ayery because these spirits that is in this part are all of the Ayer.

You may call these spirits into a Crystall stone or Glass Receptacle, being an Ancient & usuall way of Receiveing & binding of spirits, This Cristall stone must be four Inches Diameter sett on a Table of Art made as followeth wch is truly called the secrett Table of Salomon, and having the seale of the spirit on your Breast, and the Girdle about your wasit and you cannot erre, the forme of the Table is thus, as this present figure doth here represent & shew, behold the[e] the figure:

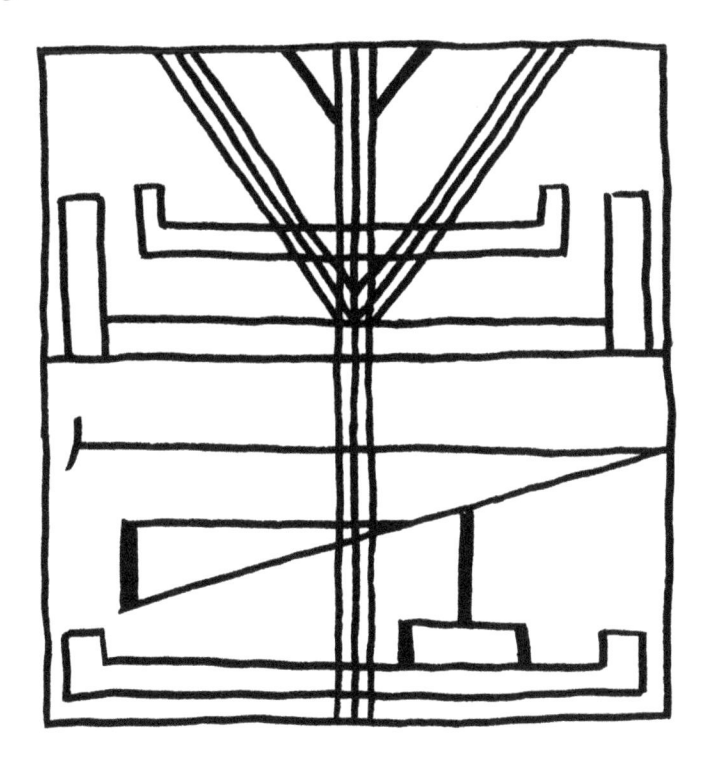

When you have thus prepared what is to be prepared, Rhearse the conjuration following severall times that is whilst the spirit come, for without dout he will come, note the same method is to be used in all the following part of this Booke as is here of Pamersiel and his servants. Also the same in calling the king and his servants &c.

The Conjuration of Pamersiel: *We Conjure thee O Pamersiel, a Cheefe Spirit. Ruling in the East, &c.*

Lemegeton Clavicula Salomonis

The Second Spiritt in order under the Emperor of the East is called Padiel, he Ruleth in the East and by South as King, and governeth 10000 spirits by day and 20000, by night, besides severall thousands under them, they are all good by nature and may be trusted. Salomon sayeth that these spirits have noe power of them selves but what is given unto them by their prince Padiel. Therefore he hath made noe mention of any of their names because if any of them is called they cannot appear without the leave of their prince as others can doe etc. You must use the same method in calling this prince Padiel, as is declared before of Pamersial the seale of Padiel, is this:

The Coniuration: *Wee Conjure thee o thou Mighty and Potent Prince Padiel, who rules as a cheife Prince or king in the dominion of the East & by South, We Invocate Camand & compell you, by the especiall name of yor God etc.*

The third Spirit placed and ranked in order under the Cheefe mighty great and potent King of the East is called Camuel who Regneth Ruleth and governeth as King in the South East part of the world and hath many and severall spirits under his Goverment and command whereof wee shall only make mention but of 10 that appertaineth and belongeth to the day and 10 to

Ars Theurgia Goetia

ye night. And Each of these have 10, servants to attend on each except Camyel, Sitgara, Asimel, Calym, Dobiel and Meras, for they have 100 a peice to attend them, but Tediel, Moriel and Tugaros, they have none at all, They appear all in A verry Beautifull forme and verry Courteously, and in ye night as well as in ye day etc. They are as followeth wth their Seales:

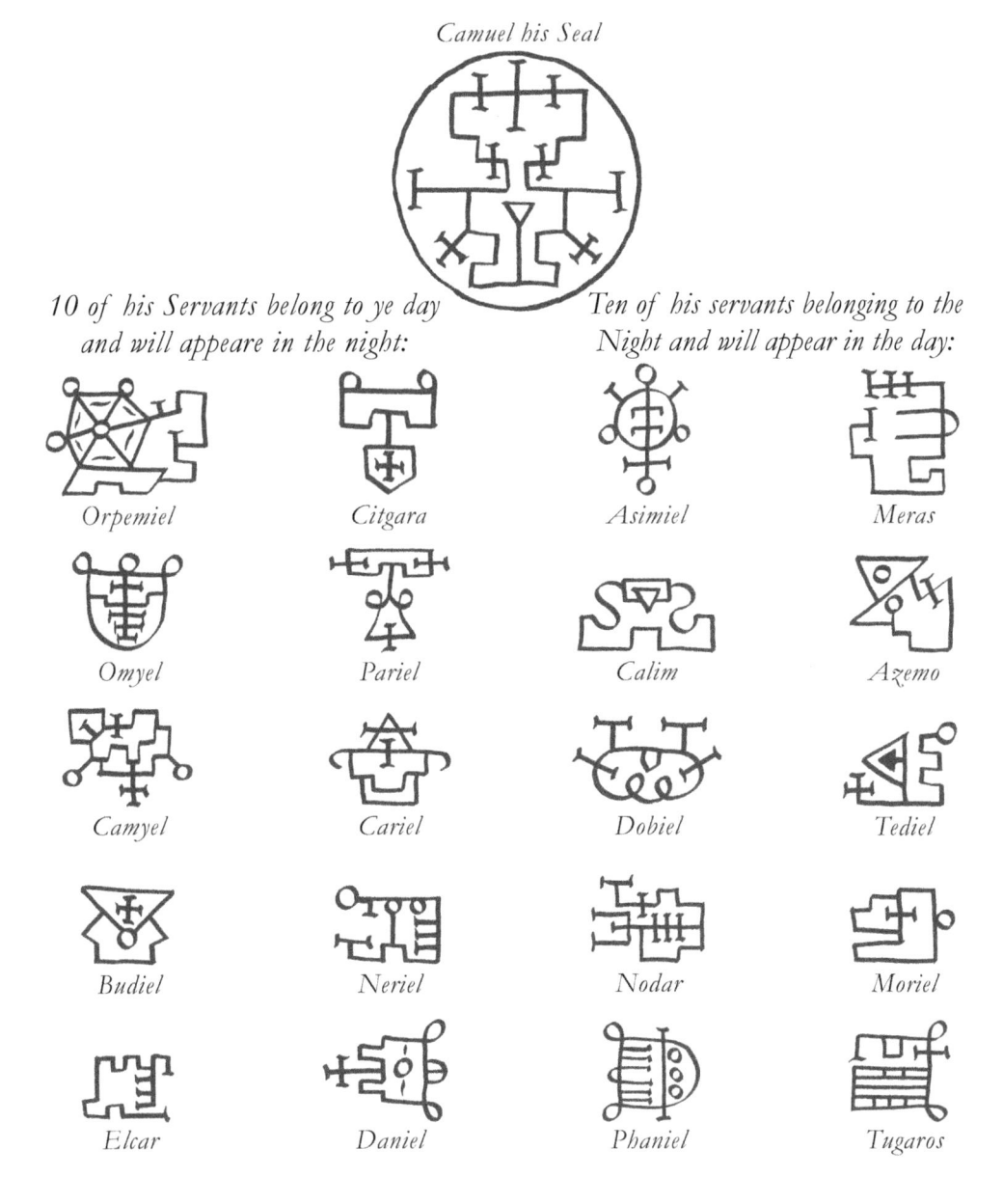

Camuel his Seal

10 of his Servants belong to ye day and will appeare in the night:

Ten of his servants belonging to the Night and will appear in the day:

Orpemiel   *Citgara*   *Asimiel*   *Meras*

Omyel   *Pariel*   *Calim*   *Azemo*

Camyel   *Cariel*   *Dobiel*   *Tediel*

Budiel   *Neriel*   *Nodar*   *Moriel*

Elcar   *Daniel*   *Phaniel*   *Tugaros*

The Conjuration of Camuel: *Wee Coniure the O thou etc: Camuel who rules etc. in the South East part of the World, We Invocate etc.*

Lemegeton Clavicula Salomonis

The fourth Spirit in order is called Aseliel he governeth as King under Carnesiel, in the South and by East he hath 10 cheefe spirits belonging to ye day, and 20 to the night, under whome are 30 principall spirits, and under those as many, whereof wee shall make mention but of 8 of ye cheefe presidents belonging to the day, and as many belonging to the night, and every one hath 20 servants at his command, they are all very courtious and Loving, and beautifull to behold etc. They are as followeth with their seales.

Aseliel his Seale

8 of his Servants belonging to the day:		8 of his Servants belonging to the Night:	
Sotheano	Abrulges	Itules	Itules
Ebra	Itrasbiel	Rablion	Rablion
Madriel	Nadrel	Hamorphiel	Hamorphiel
Anoyr	Ormenu	Ormenu	Ormenu

The Coniuration of Aseliel as followeth: *Wee Conjure thee O thou Mighty and potent prince Aseliel, who rules as a cheif prince or King under Carnesiel, in the South & by East,* etc.

Ars Theurgia Goetia

The fift spirit in order is called Barmiel; he is the first and cheefe spirit under Caspiel, The Emperour of the South as king under Caspiel, and hath 10 Dukes for the day, and 20 for the night to attend him to doe his will, the which is all very good, and willing to obey the Exorcist, whereof wee shall make mention but of 8 that belongs to the day, and as many for the night, with their seals for they are sufficient for practice. Note Every one of these Dukes hath 20 servants apiece to attend him when he is called, Excepting the 4 last that belongs to the night, for they have none, They are as followeth with their Seales.

Barmiel his Seale

8 of his servient dukes belonging to the day: *8 of his Servant dukes belonging to the Night:*

Sochas   Acteras   Barbis   Mareaiza

Tigara   Barbil   Marguns   Baaba

Chansi   Carpiel   Caniel   Gabio

Keriel   Mansi   Acreba   Astib

The Coniuration of Barmiel as followeth: *Wee Coniure thee O thou mighty & potent Prince Barmiel, who rules as a cheife Prince or King in the South under Caspiel,* etc.

Lemegeton Clavicula Salomonis

The six spirit in order, but the second under the Emperour of the south is called Gediel; who Ruleth as a kinge in the South and by West who hath 20 cheefe spirits to serve him in the day, and as many for the night, and they have many servants at their commands whereof wee shall make mention, but of 8 of the cheefe spirits that belonge to the day, And as many of those belonge to the night: who hath 20 servants apiece to attend them when they are called forth to appearance, they are very willing, loving and courteous to doe your will, etc. whose names and seals is as followeth:

Gediel his Seale

The 8 dukes belonging to the day that is under Gedial:

The 8 dukes belonging to the night:

Coliel	Sariel	Reciel	Aroan
Naras	Ranciel	Sadiel	Cirecas
Sabas	Mashel	Agra	Aglas
Assaba	Bariel	Anael	Vriel

The Coniuration of Gedial as followeth: *Wee I conjure thee O thou mighty and potent prince Gediel, who ruleth as King in the South and by West, We Invoke constraine comand etc.*

Ars Theurgia Goetia

The seventh spirit in order, but the third under the great Emperour of the South is called Asyriel, he is a mighty kinge, Ruling in the South West part of the world and hath 20 great Dukes to attend him, in the day time, and as many for the nights, who hath under them severall servants to attend them etc. Here wee shall make mention of 8 of the cheefe Dukes that belongs unto the day, and as many that belong to the night, because they are sufficient for practice: And the first 4 that belongs unto the day: And the first 4 that belongs to the night hath 40 servants apiece to attend them: And the last 4 of the day, 20, and the last 4 of ye Night 10 apiece: they are all good natured and willing to obey. Those that is of the day, is to be called then, And those of the night in the night: &c these be their names and Seales that followeth:

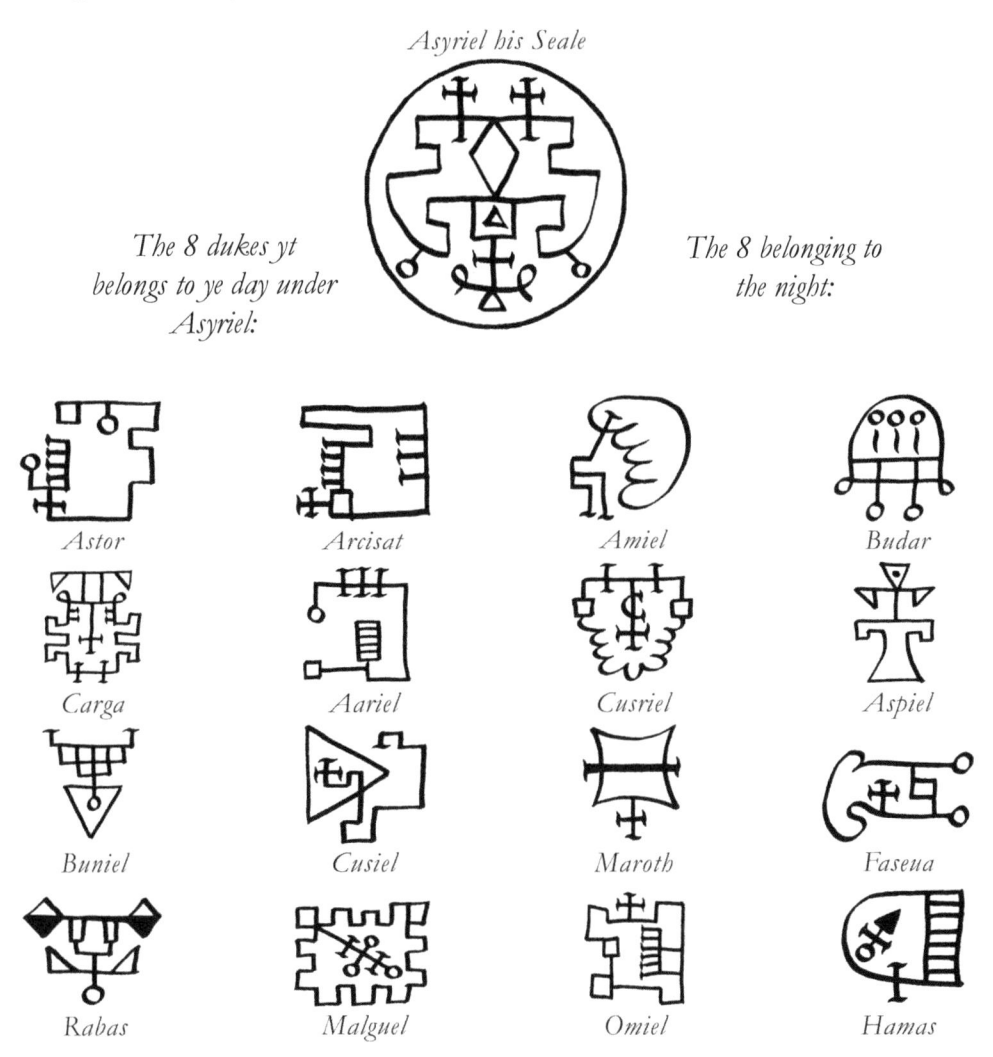

Asyriel his Seale

The 8 dukes yt belongs to ye day under Asyriel:

The 8 belonging to the night:

Astor *Arcisat* *Amiel* *Budar*

Carga *Aariel* *Cusriel* *Aspiel*

Buniel *Cusiel* *Maroth* *Faseua*

Rabas *Malguel* *Omiel* *Hamas*

The Conjuration: *Wee Conjure thee etc. who rules as a cheife king in the South West etc.*

Lemegeton Clavicula Salomonis

The eighth spirit in order but the fourth under the Emperour of the South is called Maseriel, Who Rulleth as king in the Dominion of ye West, and by South, and hath a great number of princes and servants under him, to attend him, whereof we shall make mention of 12 of the cheefe thatt attend him in the day time, and 12 that attend him to doe his will in the night time, which is sufficient for practice, they are all good by nature and willingly will doe your will in all things: those that is for the day, is to be called in the day, And those for the night in the night, they have every one 30 servants apiece to attend them and their names and seales is as followeth:

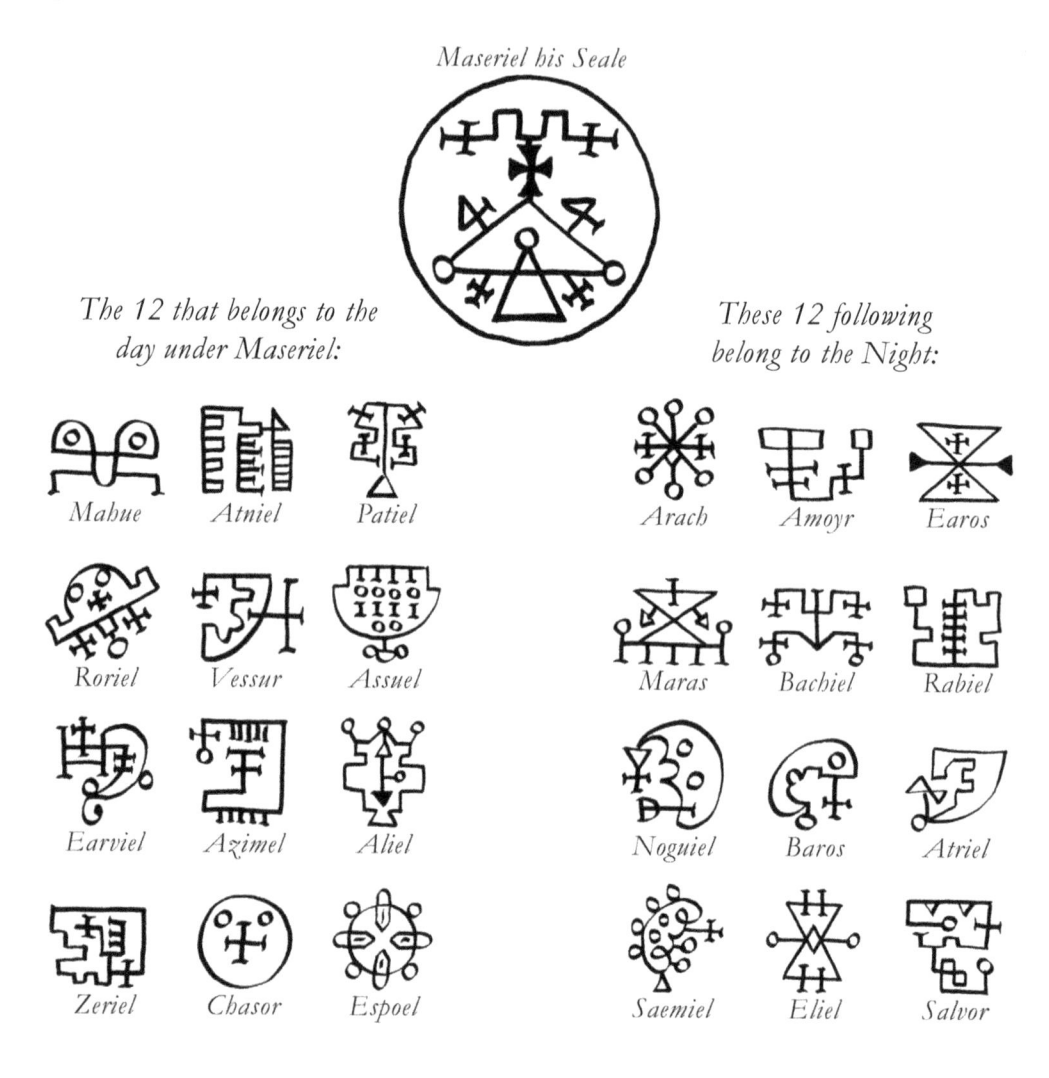

Maseriel his Seale

The 12 that belongs to the day under Maseriel:

Mahue   Atniel   Patiel

Roriel   Vessur   Assuel

Earviel   Azimel   Aliel

Zeriel   Chasor   Espoel

These 12 following belong to the Night:

Arach   Amoyr   Earos

Maras   Bachiel   Rabiel

Noguiel   Baros   Atriel

Saemiel   Eliel   Salvor

The Conjurat: *Wee Coniure thee* etc: *Maseriel who rules as cheife Prince or King in the dominion of West and by South* etc.

62

Ars Theurgia Goetia

The ninth spirit in order, but the first under the Emperour of the West is called Malgaras – he Rulleth as king in the Dominion of the West, and hath 30 Dukes under him to attend him, in the day, and as many for the night, and several under them againe; whereof wee shall make mention of 12 Dukes that belongs to the day, and as many as belongs to the night, And every one of them hath 30 servants to attend on them Excepting Misiel, Barfas, Aspar, and Deilas, for they have but 20 and Arois and Basiel, they have but 10. They are all very courteous and will appear willingly to due your will, they Appear 2 and 2 at a time wtih their servants. They that are for the day is to be called in the day and those for the night in the night. Their Names and seals is as followeth:

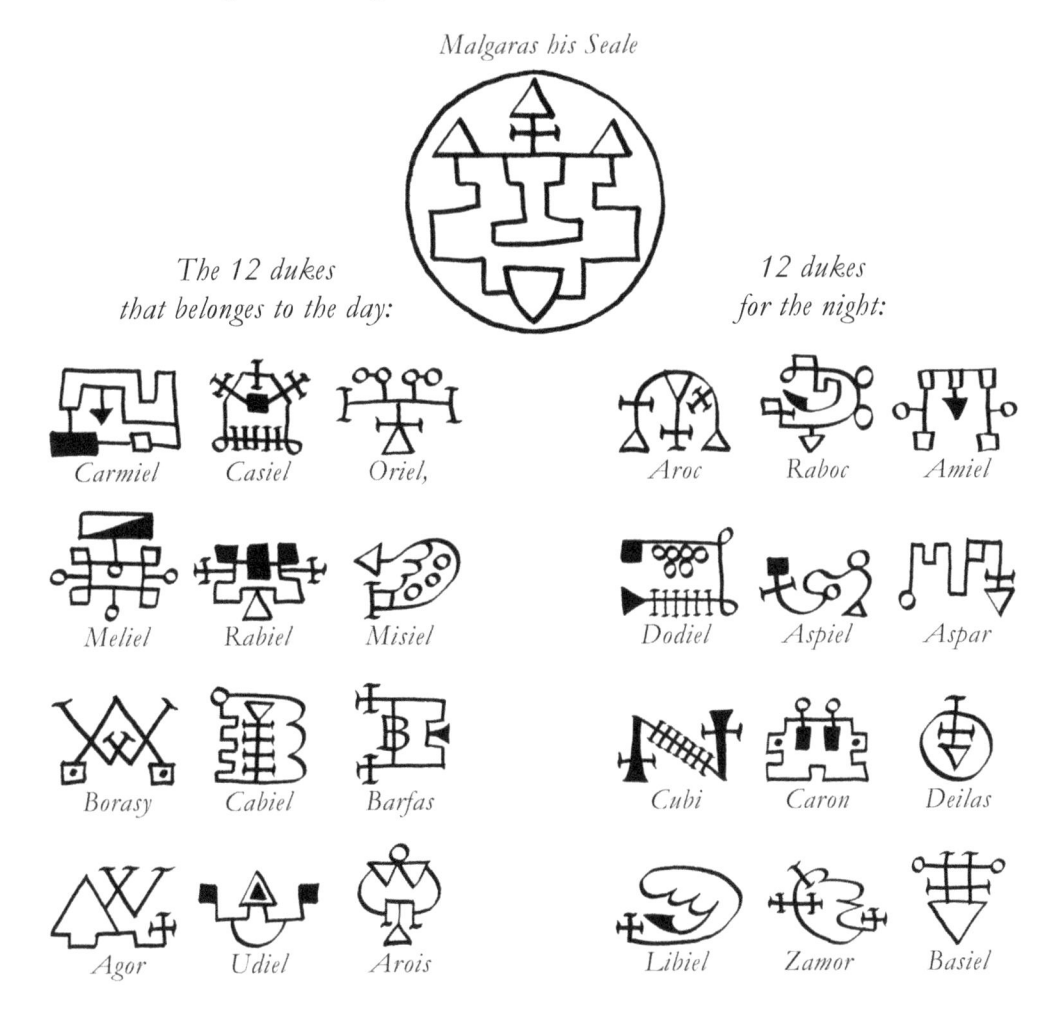

Malgaras his Seale

The 12 dukes that belonges to the day:

Carmiel *Casiel* *Oriel,*

Meliel *Rabiel* *Misiel*

Borasy *Cabiel* *Barfas*

Agor *Udiel* *Arois*

12 dukes for the night:

Aroc *Raboc* *Amiel*

Dodiel *Aspiel* *Aspar*

Cubi *Caron* *Deilas*

Libiel *Zamor* *Basiel*

The Coniuration: *Wee Coniure thee* etc: *Malgaras who ruleth* etc: *in ye West* etc.

Lemegeton Clavicula Salomonis

The tenth spirit in order, But the second under the Emperour of the West is called Dorochiel, who is a mighty prince bearing Rule in the West, and by North, and hath 40 Dukes to attend him in the day time, and as many for the night, with an innumerable company of servants spirits, whereof wee shall make mention of 24 Cheefe dukes that belongs to the day, and as many for the night, with their seales as followeth. Note the 12 first that belonge to the day, and ye 12 first that belongs to the night hath 40 servants apiece to attend on them: And the 12 last of both the day, and of the night hath 400 apiece to Attend on them when they appeare etc. Allso those of the day is to be called in the day and those of the night in the night: Observe the planetary motion in calling, for ye 2 first that belongs to the day are to be called in ye first planetary hour of ye day: and the 2 next in ye second planetary hour of the day, and soe successively on till you have gone quite threw ye day and night, till you come to the 2 first againe etc. They are all of a good nature and will willingly obey etc. Their names and seales is as followeth:

Dorochiel his Seale

The 24 dukes belongg to ye day, 12 before noone:

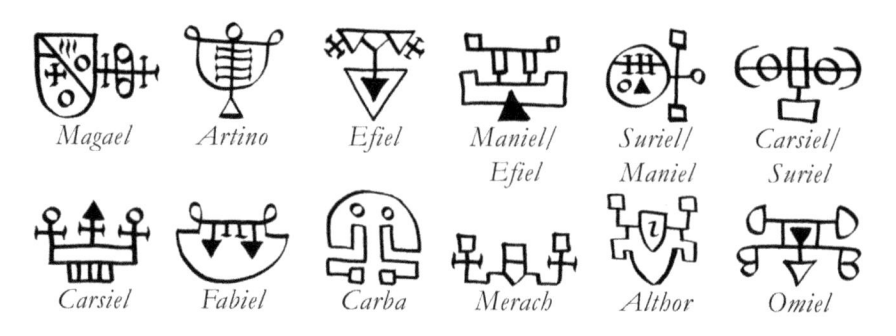

Magael   Artino   Efiel   Maniel/   Suriel/   Carsiel/
                              Efiel   Maniel   Suriel

Carsiel   Fabiel   Carba   Merach   Althor   Omiel

Ars Theurgia Goetia

Heere followeth the 12 dukes, afternoone:

Gudiel	Asphor	Emuel	Soriel	Cabron	Diviel

Abriel	Danael	Lomor	Casael	Busiel	Larfos

The 24 Dukes that belong to the night under Dorochiel etc. These 12 before Mightnight:

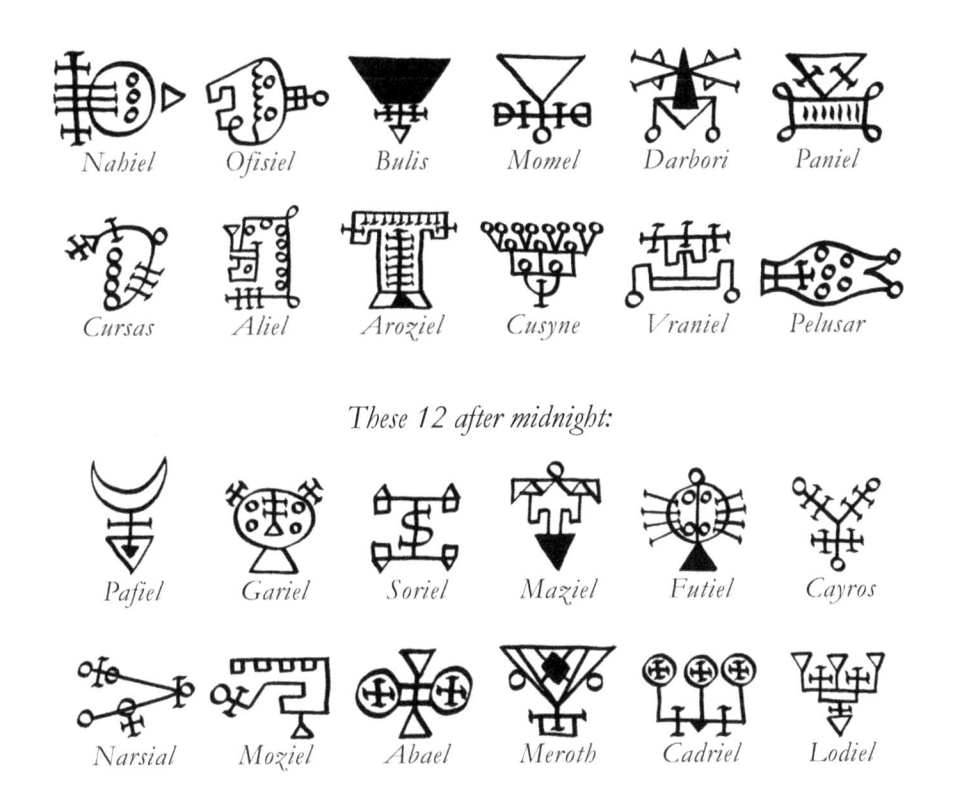

Nahiel	Ofisiel	Bulis	Momel	Darbori	Paniel

Cursas	Aliel	Aroziel	Cusyne	Vraniel	Pelusar

These 12 after midnight:

Pafiel	Gariel	Soriel	Maziel	Futiel	Cayros

Narsial	Moziel	Abael	Meroth	Cadriel	Lodiel

The Coniuration of Dorochiel as followeth: *Wee Coniure thee O thou mighty* etc: *Dorothiel, who ruleth as King in the West and by North, wee Invocate* etc:

65

Lemegeton Clavicula Salomonis

The eleventh spirit in order, but the third under the Emperour Amenadiel is called Usiel, who is a mighty prince Ruleing as king in the North West. he hath 40 dyurnall, and 40 nocturnall Dukes to attend on him in the day and the night, whereof wee shall make mention of 14 that belongs to ye day and as many for ye night which is sufficient for practice, the first 8 that belongs to the day hath 40 servants a piece and the other 6 hath 30. And the first 8 that belongs to ye night hath forty servants a piece to attend on them, and the next 4 Dukes 20 servants, and the last 2 hath 10 a piece, and they are very obedient and doth willingly appear when they are called, they have more power to hide or discover Treausures then any other spirits (saith Salomon) that is contained in this Booke, and when you hide, or would not have anything taken away that is hidden, make these four seals in virgins parchment and lay them with ye Treasury, where the Treasury lyeth and it will never be found nor taken away.

The names and seals of these spirits is as Followeth:

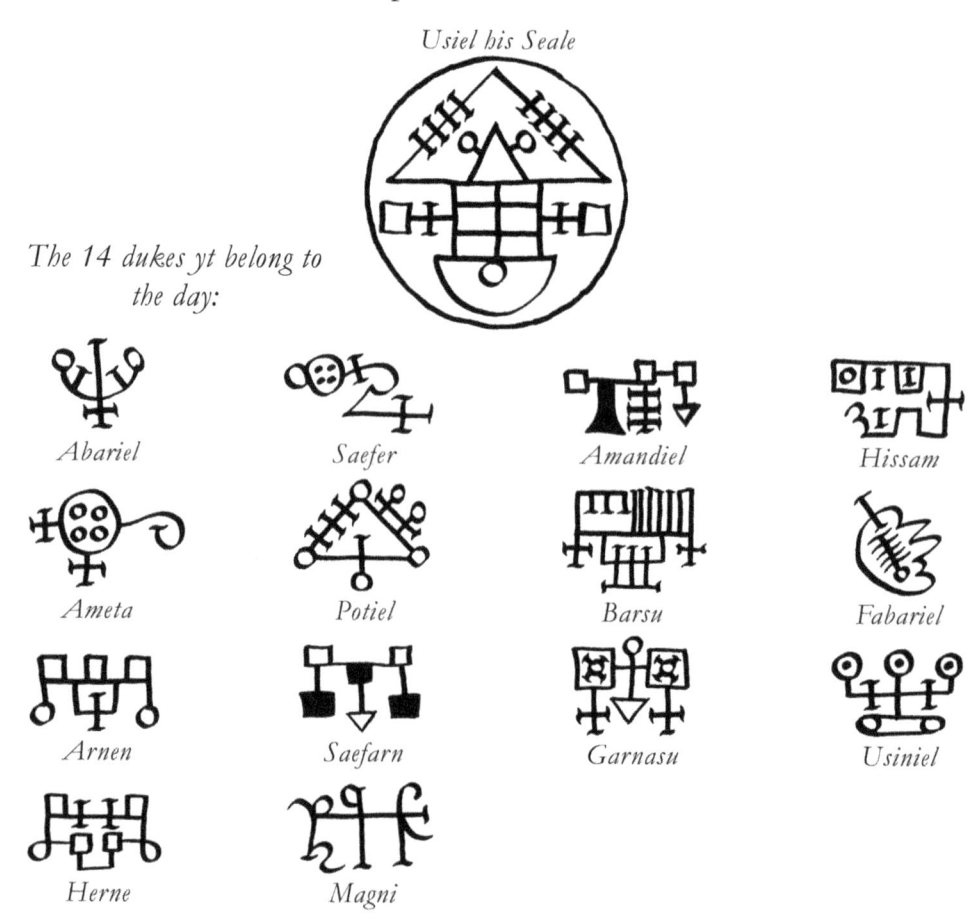

Usiel his Seale

The 14 dukes yt belong to the day:

Abariel

Saefer

Amandiel

Hissam

Ameta

Potiel

Barsu

Fabariel

Arnen

Saefarn

Garnasu

Usiniel

Herne

Magni

Ars Theurgia Goetia

The 14 dukes that belong to the Night:

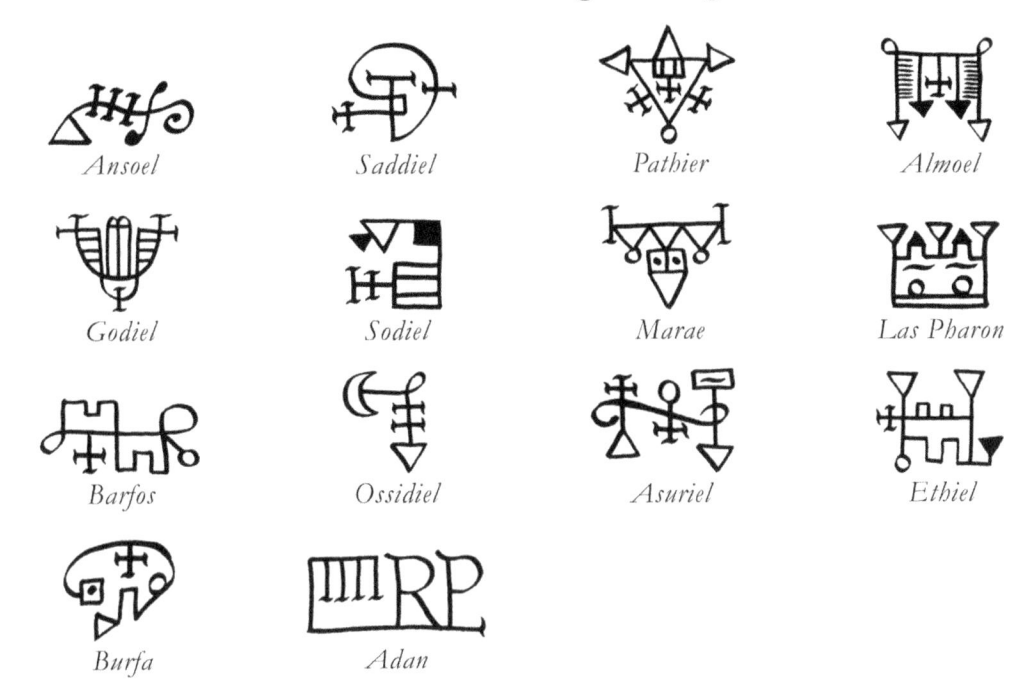

Ansoel   *Saddiel*   *Pathier*   *Almoel*

Godiel   *Sodiel*   *Marae*   *Las Pharon*

Barfos   *Ossidiel*   *Asuriel*   *Ethiel*

Burfa   *Adan*

The Conjuration of Usiel as fol: *Wee Conjure thee O thou mighty* etc: *Usiel who ruleth as cheif Prince or King under Amenadiel in the North West* etc.

The twelfth spirit in order, But the fourth under the Emperour of the West is called Cabariel, he hath 50 Dukes to attend on him in ye day and as many in the night, under whom are many servants to attend on them, whereof wee shall make mention but of 10 of the cheefe Dukes that belongs to the day, and as many for the night, and every of them hath 50 servants to give attendance when their masters is Invocated, etc. Note Those Dukes that belongs to the day is very good and willing to obey their Master, and are to be called in the day time, and they of the night are by nature Evill & Disobedient, and will deceive you if They can etc. They are to be called in the night: The names and seales of them all are as followeth:

Lemegeton Clavicula Salomonis

Cabariel his Seale

The 10 yt belongs to ye day: *The 10 dukes for the Night:*

Satifiel	Etimiel	Mador	Ladiel
Parius	Clyssan	Peniel	Morias
Godiel	Elitel	Cugiel	Pandor
Taros	Aniel	Thalbus	Cazul
Asoriel	Cuphal	Otim	Dubiel

The Coniuration of Cabariel as followeth: *We Conjure thee O thou mighty and potent Prince Cabariel* etc: *who ruleth as king in the North and by West* etc.

68

Ars Theurgia Goetia

The 13th Spirit in order But the first under Demoriel: the Emperour of the north is called Raysiel, he ruleth as King in the north, and hath fifty dukes for the day, and as many for the night to attend him, and they have many servants under them againe – for to doe there will etc. where of these we shall make mention of 16 cheife dukes that belong to the day, because they are by nature good and willing to obey, and but 14 that belong to the night, because they are by nature evil and stubborne and disobedient, and will not obey willingly – all those dukes that belong to the day have 50 servants a peece, exceping the 6th last, for they have but 30 a peece and the 8 first that belonge to the night have 40 sarvants a peece excepting the 4 next following for they have but 20 a peece, and the last 2 have but 10 a peece, there names and seales are as followeth vixt:

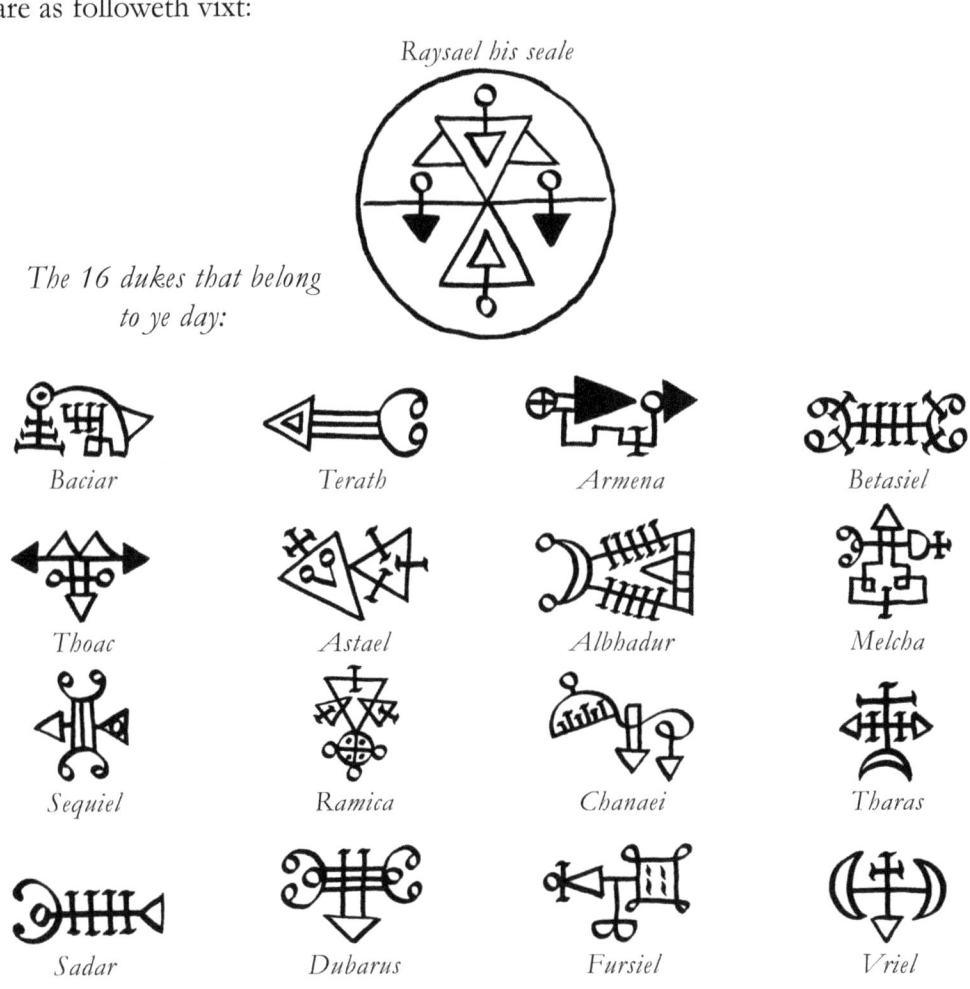

Raysael his seale

The 16 dukes that belong to ye day:

Baciar

Terath

Armena

Betasiel

Thoac

Astael

Albhadur

Melcha

Sequiel

Ramica

Chanaei

Tharas

Sadar

Dubarus

Fursiel

Vriel

Lemegeton Clavicula Salomonis

The 14 dukes that belong night:

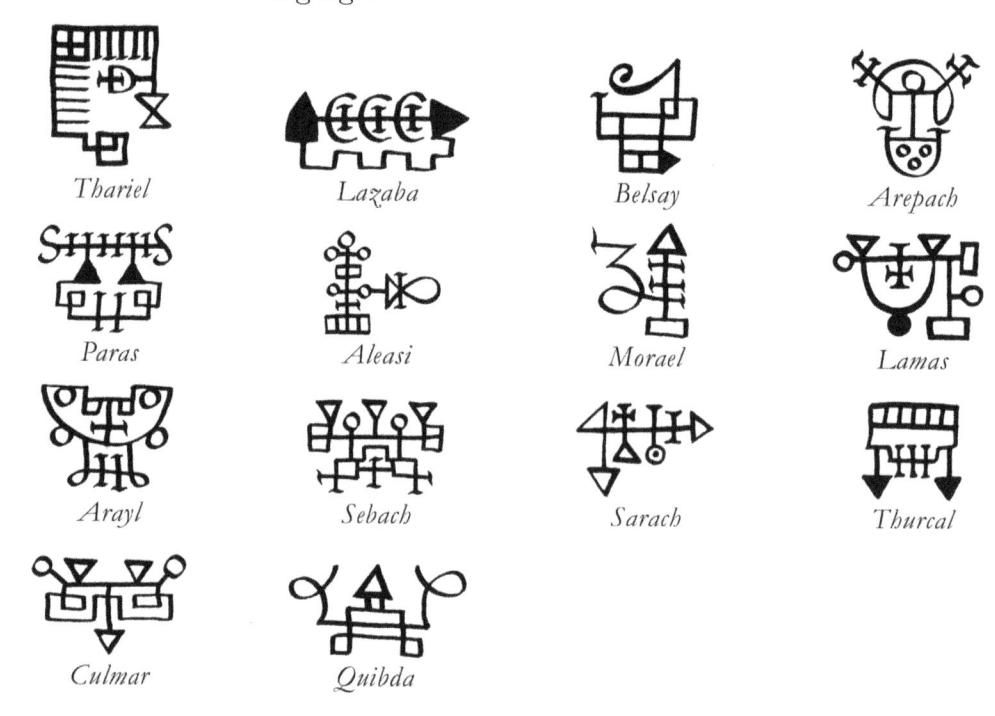

Thariel	Lazaba	Belsay	Arepach
Paras	Aleasi	Morael	Lamas
Arayl	Sebach	Sarach	Thurcal
Culmar	Quibda		

The Coniuration of Raysael as fol: *Wee Coniure thee* etc.

The 14th spirit in order, but the second under the Emperour of the North is called Symiel, who ruleth as King in the North and by Easte who hath 10 dukes to attend him in the day and 1000 for the night and every one of these have a certaine number of sarvants; whereof we shall make mention of the 10 that belong to the day, and 10 of those that belong to the night and those of the day are very good and not disobedient, as are those of the night for they are stubborne and will not appeare willingly etc. Allsoe those of the day have 720 sarvants amongst them to doe there will, and the rest of the night have 790 servants to attend on them as occasion sarveth, the names of these 20 are as followeth, with theire seales and number of sarvants.

Ars Theurgia Goetia

Symiel his Seale

The 10 dukes that belong to ye day:

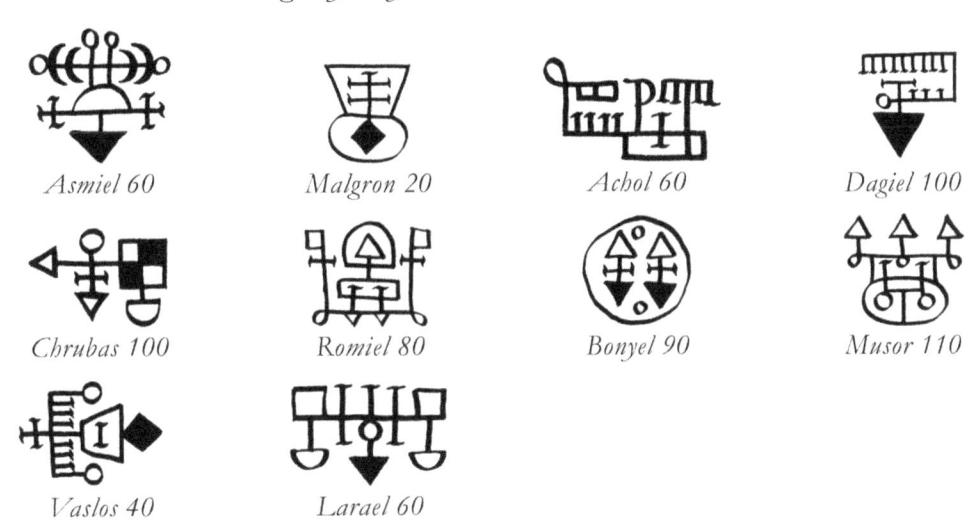

Asmiel 60 *Malgron 20* *Achol 60* *Dagiel 100*

Chrubas 100 *Romiel 80* *Bonyel 90* *Musor 110*

Vaslos 40 *Larael 60*

The 10 dukes that belong to the night:

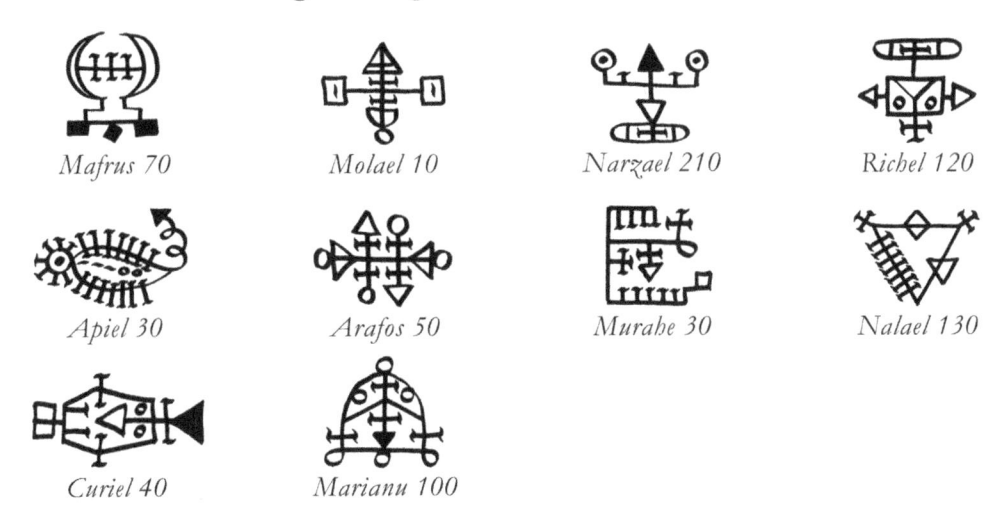

Mafrus 70 *Molael 10* *Narzael 210* *Richel 120*

Apiel 30 *Arafos 50* *Murahe 30* *Nalael 130*

Curiel 40 *Marianu 100*

Lemegeton Clavicula Salomonis

The fiveteenth spirit in order, but the third under the Emperour of the North is called Armadiel, who rulleth as king in the North East part, and have many dukes under him besides other servants, whereof we shall make mention of 15 of the cheefe Dukes who have 1260 servants to attend him. These dukes are to be called in ye day and night dividing ye same into 15 parts beginning at sun rising with ye first spirit and so on till you come to ye last spirit and last division of the night, these spirits are good by nature and willing to doe your will in all things. These be there names and seals etc.

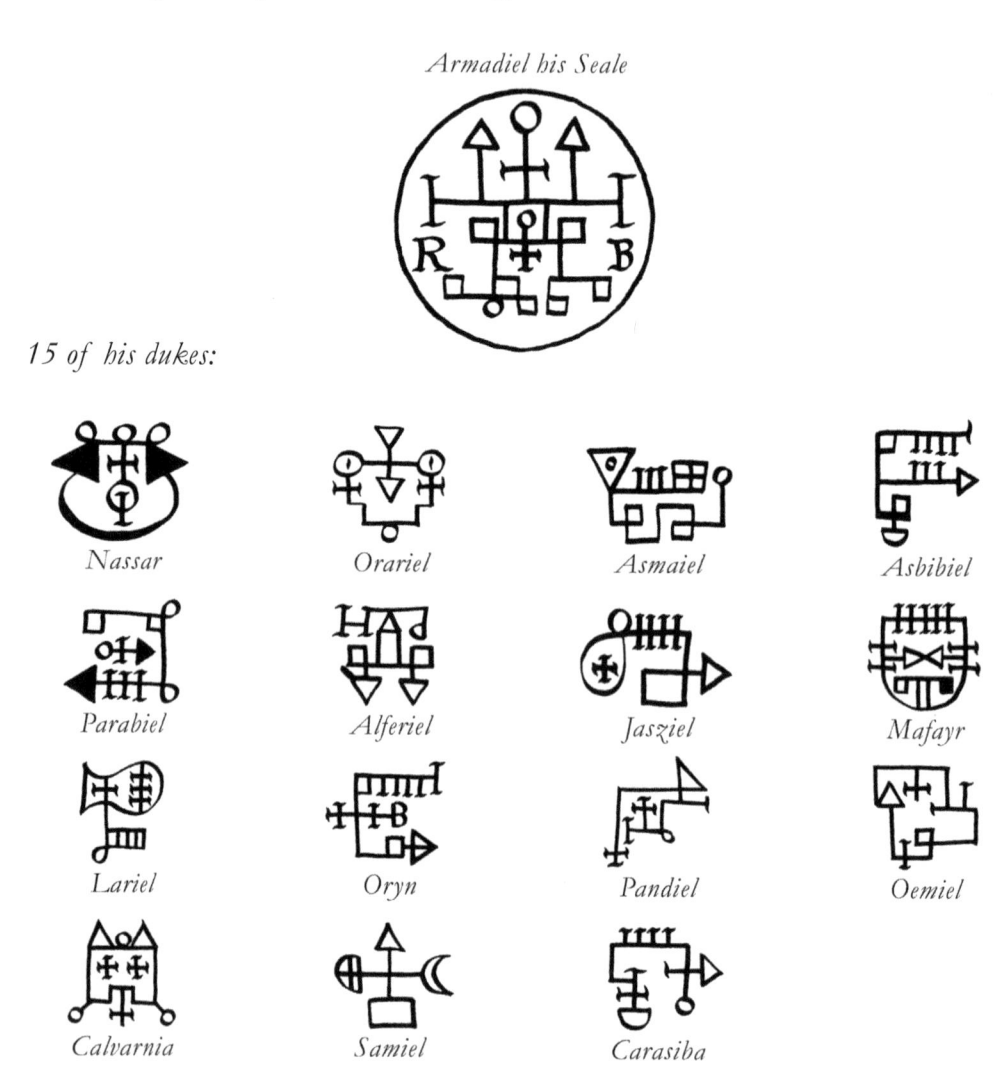

Armadiel his Seale

15 of his dukes:

Nassar	Orariel	Asmaiel	Asbibiel
Parabiel	Alferiel	Jasziel	Mafayr
Lariel	Oryn	Pandiel	Oemiel
Calvarnia	Samiel	Carasiba	

The Conjuration: *I conjure thee o thou mighty and potent prince Armadiel etc.*

Ars Theurgia Goetia

The 16th spirit in order, but the fourth under the Emperour of the North is called Baruchas – who rulleth as King in the East and by North and hath many Dukes and other several spirits to attend him whereof we shall make mention of 15 of the cheefe Dukes that belong to the day and night who have 7040 servants to attend on them: they are all by nature good and are willing to obey etc. You are to call these spirits in the same manner as I shewed in ye foregoing Experiment of Armadiel and his Dukes: vizt dividing ye day and night into 15 parts and etc. the names and seales of these as followeth:

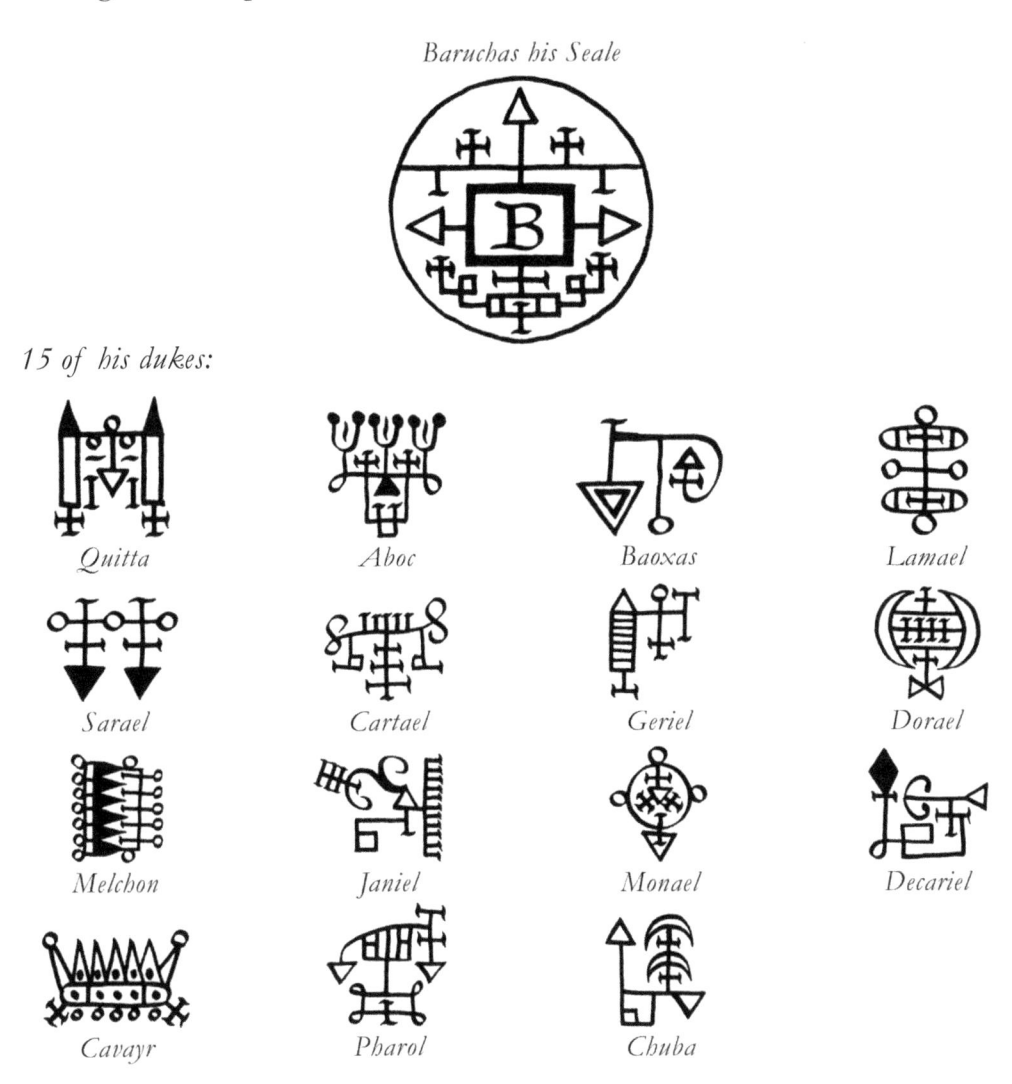

Baruchas his Seale

15 of his dukes:

Quitta

Aboc

Baoxas

Lamael

Sarael

Cartael

Geriel

Dorael

Melchon

Janiel

Monael

Decariel

Cavayr

Pharol

Chuba

The Conjuration of Barachus: *I conjure Thee o thou mighty and potent prince Barachus* etc.

Lemegeton Clavicula Salomonis

In this place we are to giue you the understanding of 11 of a mighty and potent princes with their servants wch wander up and down in ye Aire and never continue in one place, etc. whereof one of the Cheefe is called Geradiel, who hath 18150 servants to attend him, for he hath no Dukes nor princes. Therefore he is to be Invocated alone, but when he is called there cometh a great number of his servants with him, but more or less according to the howre of ye day and hour or night he is called in, for in 2 first hours of the day according to ye planatary motion, and the two second hour of the night there cometh 470 of his servants with him and in the 2 second hours of ye Day. and ye 2 third hours of ye night there cometh 590 of his servants with him and in ye 2 third hours of the day and ye 2 fourth hours of ye night there cometh 930 of his servants with him and in ye 2 fourth hours of ye day and ye 2 fifth hours of ye night there cometh 1560 of his servants &c and in ye 2 fifth hours of ye day and the 6th 2 hours of ye night there cometh 13710 of his servants and the 6th 2 or last 2 hours of ye day there cometh 930 and in the 2 first houres of ye night there cometh 1560 of his servants etc. They are all indifferent good by nature and will obey in all things willingly etc.

The Seal of Garadiel

The Conjuration of Garadiel: *I conjure thee o thou mighty and potent prince Garadiel who wandereth hear and there in the Aire with thy servants I conjure the Garadiel that thou forth with appeareth with thy attendance in this first hour of ye Day here before me in this Crystall stone or here before this Circle* etc.

Ars Theurgia Goetia

The next of these wandring princes is called Buriel, who hath many Dukes and other servants which doe attend on him to do his will they are all by nature evill and are hated by all other spirits. They appeare rugish and in the form of a serpent with a virgins head and speak with a mans voice. They are to be called in the night, because they hate the day and in the planetary houres, whereof wee shall mention 12 of the cheefe Dukes that answereth to the 12 planetary houres of the night who have 880 servants to attend on them in the night amongst them their names and seales are as followeth with the name of Buriel.

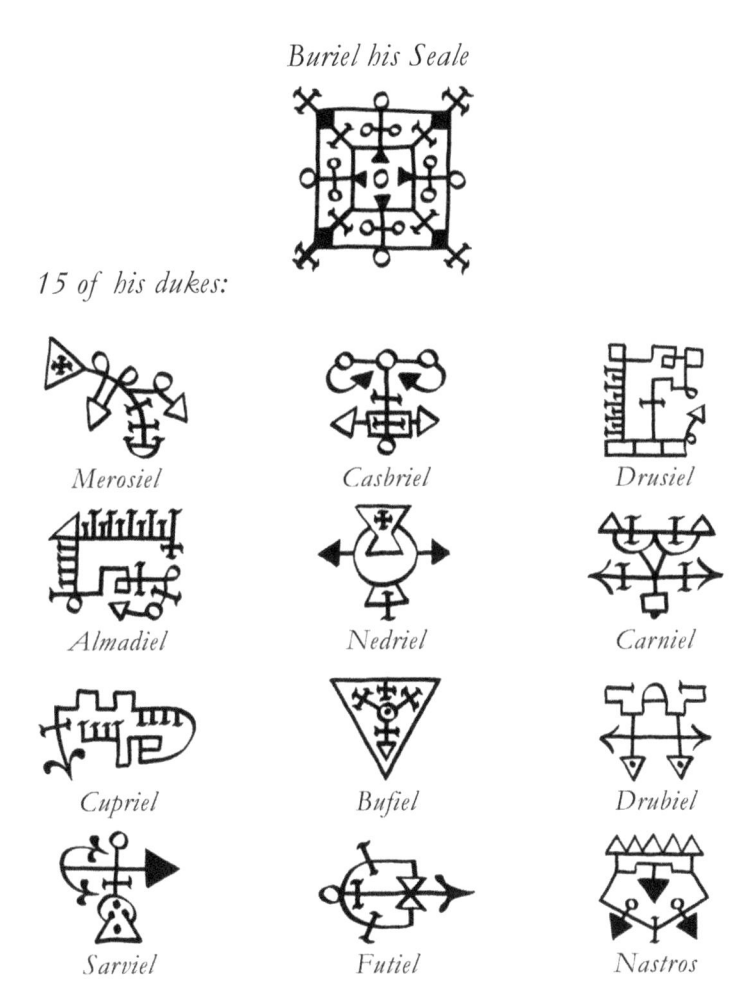

Buriel his Seale

15 of his dukes:

Merosiel   Casbriel   Drusiel

Almadiel   Nedriel   Carniel

Cupriel   Bufiel   Drubiel

Sarviel   Futiel   Nastros

The Conjuration: *I conjure Thee o thou mighty and potent prince Buriel who wandereth here and therre in the Aire with the Dukes and other thy Servient Spirits I conjure thee Buriel that thou fore with appeare with thy attendance in the first hour of ye night, here before me in this crystall stone (or here before this Circle) in a fair and comly shape to doe my will in all things that I shall desier of you* etc.

Lemegeton Clavicula Salomonis

The third of these wandering spirits or princes is called Hydriel, who hath 100 great Dukes besides 200 lesser Dukes and servants without number under him, whereof we shall mention 12 of the Cheefe Dukes which hath 1320 servants to attend them. They are to be called in ye Day as well as in ye night according to the planetary motion. The first beginneth with the first hour of ye day or night and so succesfully on till you come to the last, they appear in the forme of a serpent, with a virgins head and face: yet they are very courteous and willing to obey, they delight most in or about waters and all moist grounds. There names and Seales are as followeth:

Hydriel his Seale

The 12 dukes are as followeth:

Mortoliel	Musuziel	Samiel	Arbiel
Chamoriel	Lameniel	Dusiriel	Luciel
Pelariel	Barchiel	Camiel	Chariel

The conjuration: *I conjure thee O thou mighty and potent prince Hydriel etc.*

Ars Theurgia Goetia

The fourth of these wandering princes in order is called Pirichiel, He hath no princes nor Dukes under him But knights: whereof we shall mention 8 of them They being sufficient for practice who have 2000 servants under them, They are to be called according to ye planetary motion. They are all good by nature, and will doe your will willingly. Theire Names and Seales are as followeth:

Pirichiel his Seale

His eight Knights:

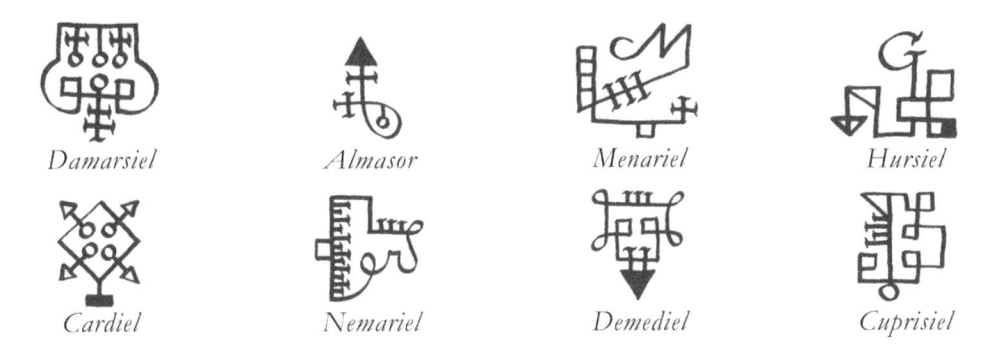

Damarsiel   *Almasor*   *Menariel*   *Hursiel*

Cardiel   *Nemariel*   *Demediel*   *Cuprisiel*

The Conjuration: *I conjure thee O thou mighty and potent prince Pirichiel; who wandreth* etc.

The 5th wandering prince is called Emoniel, who hath a hundred princes and cheef Dukes, besides 20 under Dukes and a multitude of servants to attend him whereof wee shall mention 12 of the cheef Princes or Dukes – who have 1320 Dukes and other Inferiour Servants to attend them They are all by nature good and willing to obey: it is said they Inhabit most in the woods: they are to be called in the day as well as in the Night, and according to ye Planetary order. Their names and seales are as followeth:

Lemegeton Clavicula Salomonis

Emoniel his Seale

His 12 dukes are as followeth:

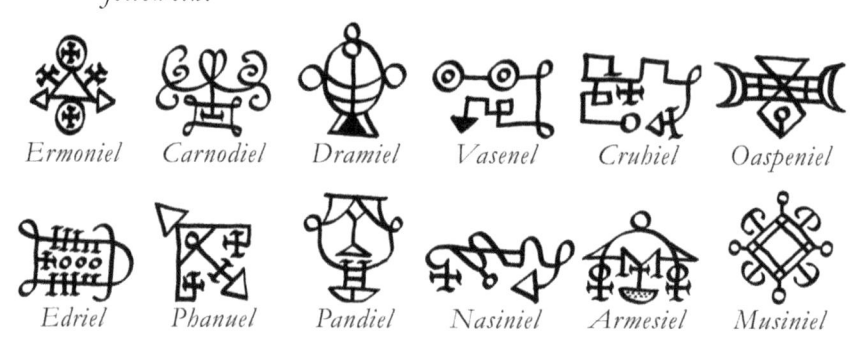

| Ermoniel | Carnodiel | Dramiel | Vasenel | Cruhiel | Oaspeniel |

| Edriel | Phanuel | Pandiel | Nasiniel | Armesiel | Musiniel |

The Conjuration: *I conjure thee o thou mighty and Potent Prince Emoniel: who wandereth* etc.

The sixth of these wandring princes is called Icosiel, Who hath a 100 Dukes and 300 companions besides other servants which are more Inferiour whereof we have taken 15 of ye Cheefe Dukes for Practice they being sufficient etc. they have 2200 servants to attend them. They are all of a good nature and will doe what they are commanded. They appear most commonly in houses because they delight most therein. They are to be called in the 24 hours of the day and night: That is to devide the 24 hours into fiveteen parts according to the number of the spirits, beginning with the first at Sunrise and with the last at Sun riseing next day etc. Their names and Seales are as followeth:

Ars Theurgia Goetia

Icosiel his Seale

The 15 dukes are as followeth:

Machariel	*Agapiel*	*Nathriel*	*Munefiel*
Pischiel	*Larphiel*	*Zachariel*	*Heresiel*
Thanatiel	*Amediel*	*Athesiel*	*Urbaniel*
Zosiel	*Cambriel*	*Cumariel*	

The Conjuration: *I conjure thee O thou mighty and Potent Prince Icosiel,* etc.

The 7th of these is called Soleviel, who hath under his command 200 Dukes, and 200 Companions who change every year their places, They have many servants to attend them They are all good and very obedient etc. Here we shall mention 12 of the Cheefe Dukes whereof the first 6 are Dukes one year, and the other 6 the next following and so rulling in order to

79

Lemegeton Clavicula Salomonis

serve there prince. They have under them 1840 servants to attend on them they are to be called in the day as well as in the night: according to the planetary hours or motion. Their names and seales are as followeth:

Soleviel his Seale

His 12 dukes:

Inachiel	Nadrusiel	Charoel
Praxeel	Cobusiel	Prasiel
Moracha	Amriel	Mursiel
Almodar	Axosiel	Penador

The Conjuration: *I conjure Thee O thou mighty and Potent Prince Soleviel who wandereth* etc.

Ars Theurgia Goetia

The eighth of those wandering princes is called Menadiel, who hath 20 Dukes and 100 companions and many other servants. They being all of a good nature and very obedient. Here wee have mentioned 6 of the cheefe Dukes and 6 of ye under Dukes or companions, they haue 390 servants to attend them: Note you must call these according to ye planetary motion a Duke in ye first hour and a companion in the next and so succesfully on through all the houres of ye day or night whose names and seales are as followeth:

Menadiel his seale

The 6 cheife dukes: *The 6 under dukes:*

Larmol   *Benodiel*   *Barchiel*   *Nedriel*

Drasiel   *Charsiel*   *Amasiel*   *Curasin*

Clamor   *Samyel*   *Baruch*   *Tharson*

The Conjuration: *I conjure thee O thou mighty and potent Prince Menadiel. who wandereth* etc.

Lemegeton Clavicula Salomonis

The 9th spirit in order that wandereth is called Macariel, who hath Dukes besides a very many other Inferiour Servants to attend on him, whereof wee shall mention 12 of the Cheefe Dukes who have 400 servants to attend them. They are all good by nature and obedient to doe ye will of ye Exorcist. They appear in divers formes but most commonly in ye forme of a dragon with virgins heads. These Dukes are to be called in the day as well as night according to ye planetary order. Their names and seales are as followeth:

Macariel his Seale

His 12 dukes:

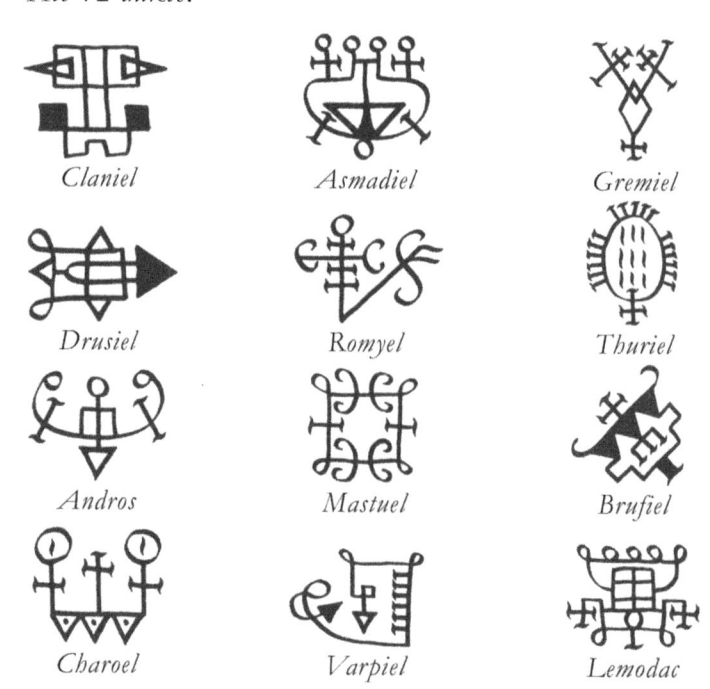

Claniel   *Asmadiel*   *Gremiel*

Drusiel   *Romyel*   *Thuriel*

Andros   *Mastuel*   *Brufiel*

Charoel   *Varpiel*   *Lemodac*

The Conjuration: *I conjure Thee O thou mighty and potent prince Macariel who wandereth* etc.

Ars Theurgia Goetia

The 10th spirit in order that wandereth or great prince is called Uriel, who hath 10 cheef Dukes and 100 under Dukes with many servants to attend him. They are by nature Evill and will not obey willingly and are very false in their doings. They appear in the form of a serpent with a virgins head and a face: whereof we shall mention but ye 10 cheefe Dukes who have 650 Companions and servants to attend them etc. There names and seales are as followeth:

Uriel his Seale

His 10 dukes:

Chabri

Frasmiel

Drapios

Drabros

Brymiel

Hermon

Narmiel

Dragon

Aldrusy

Curmas

The Conjuration: *I conjure thee O Thou mighty and potent prince Uriel. who wandereth* etc.

Lemegeton Clavicula Salomonis

The 11th and last prince of this wandering order is called Bidiel who hath under his command 20 Dukes and 200 other Dukes wch are more Inferiour, besides very many servants to attend him. These Dukes change every year their office and place. They are all good and willing to obey the Exorcist in all things etc. They appear very Beautifull and in a humane shape whereof wee shall mention 10 of ye Cheefe Dukes who have 2400 servants to attend them, their Names and Seales are:

Bidiel his Seale

His 10 great dukes:

Mudirel   *Armoniel*   *Charobiel*

Cruchan   *Lameniel*   *Parsifiel*

Bramsiel   *Andruchiel*   *Chremoas*

Merasiel

The Conjuration to the Wandring Princes: *I conjure Thee O Thou mighty and potent prince Bidiel, who wandereth hear and there in the aire with thy Dukes and other of thy Servants spirits, I conjure Thee Bidiel that thou forthwith come and appeare with attendance in this first hour of ye day here before me in this Cristall stone (or here before this Circle) in a fair and comly shape to do my will in all things that I shall desier of you* etc. ✱

Ars Theurgia Goetia

The Conjuration to the Princes that Govern the Points of the Compass

I conjure thee o thou mighty and potent prince N. *who ruleth as a cheefe prince or king in the dominion of the East* (or etc) *I conjure thee N that thou fortwith appeareth with Thy attendance in this first hour of ye day here before me in this cristall stone* (or *hear before this Circle*) *in a fair and comely shape to doe my will in all things that I shall desier of you* etc. ✱

To the Dukes that Wander

I conjure thee O thou mighty and potent duke N. *who wandereth hear and there with thy Prince N. and others of his etc. Thy servants in ye Aire. I conjure Thee N. that thou forwith appeareth* etc. △

To the Dukes that Governeth the Point of the Compasse with their Prince

I conjure Thee O thou mighty and Potent Duke N. *who ruleth under thy prince or king N. in the dominion of the East* (or etc) *I conjure thee N. that thou forthwith appeareth* △, *allone* (or *with servants*) *in this first* (or *second*) *houre of the day, here before me in this cristal stone* (or *here before this circle*) *in a fair and comely shape, to doe my will in all things that I shall desire or request of you* ✱. *I conjure and powerfully command of you N. By him who said the word and it was done: and by all the holy and powerfull names of god and by the name of the only creator of heaven, Earth, and hell and what is contained in them Adonay, El, Elohim, Elohe, Elion, Escerchie, Zebaoth, Jah, Tetragrammaton, Saday. The only lord god of the hosts, that you forthwith appearth unto me here in this Cristall stone* (or *here before this circle*) *in a fair and comely humane shape: without doeing any harme to me or any other creature that god Jehovah created or made; But come ye peacibly, vissibly and affably, now without delay manifesting what I desiere, being conjured by the name of ye Eternall Liveing and true god: Helioren, Tetragrammaton, Anephexeton. and fulfill my commands and persist unto the end; I conjure command and constraine you spirit N. by Alpha and Omega. By the name Primeumaton, which commandeth the whole host of heaven and by all those names which Moses named when he by the power of those names brought great plagues upon Pharao, and all the people of Ægypt. Zebaoth, Escerchie, Oriston, Elion, Adonay, Primeumaton and by the name of Schemes. Amathia. with Joshua called upon and the sun stayed his course, and by* the name of *Hagios*, and by the Seal of *Adonay* and by *Agla, On, Tetragrammaton. To whome all creatures are obedient and by the dreadfull Judgement of the high god and by the holly angells of heaven and by the mighty wisdome of the great god of hosts That you come from all Parts of ye world and make rational answers unto all things I shall aske of you, and come you peaceable vissible and affable speaking unto me with a voyce Intelligible and to my understanding Therefore come, come yee in the name of Adonay, Zebaoth, Adonay, Amioram, Come, why stay you, hasten. Adonay, Saday the king of kings commandeth you.*

When he is appeared shew him his seal, and the Pentacle of Salomon, saying: *Behold the Pentacle of Salomon which I have brought before your presence* etc. As is shewed in the first Booke Goëtia. at the latter end of the conjurations: allso when you haue had ye desier of the Spirits: licence them to depart as is shewed there etc.

And so Ends the Second Book Called Theurgia Goetia

Note: The above written conjurations doe onely differ in the first part as is shewed there untill you come to these markers △ and ✱ But from thence forward they are to be all one and ye same.

Here Beginneth the Third Part Called
The Art Pauline of King Salomon

This is divided into two parts, the first containing the Angells of the hours of the day and night: The second part the Angells of ye signs of the Zodiac as hereafter followeth etc.

The Nature of these 24 Angells of the day and night changeth every day and their offices is to doe all things that are attributed to the 7 planetts. But that changeth every day also: as for example you may see in the following Treatise That Samuel the Angell rulleth the first houre of the day beginning at Sunn Rising, supose it be on a munday in the first hour of ye (that houre is attributed to the ☽) That you call Samuel or any of his Dukes; There offices in that houre is to doe all things that are attributted to the ☽. But if you call him or any of his Servient Dukes on Tuesday Morning at Sunn Riseing: being the first hour of the day: Their offices are to doe all things that are attributed to ♂. And so the like is to be observed in the first houre of every day: and the like is to be observed of the Angells and their servants that Rule any of the other hours: either in the day or night: allso againe there is an observation to be observed in makeing the Seales of these 24 Angells according to the time of the years Day and hour that you call the Angells or his servants in to doe your will: But you cannot mise therein if you doe well observe the example that is laid down in the following worke: They being all fitted for the 10th day of March being on a wednesday in the year 1641 according to the old account etc and as for to know what is attributed to the planetts, I doe referr you to the books of Astrology whereof large volumes have been written. etc.

Of the first houre of any Day

The first houre of any Day is ruled by an angel called Samuel who hath under his command many Dukes and servants, wherof we shall mention 8 of the cheefe Dukes which is sufficient for practice: who have 444 servants to attend them. Theire Names are as Followeth: *Ameniel, Charpon, Darosiel, Monasiel, Brumiel, Nestoriel, Chremas, Meresyn*. Now for to fitt or make a seal for any of these 8 Dukes or the cheefe prince Samuel doe as followeth – first write the Character of ye lord of the ascendent secondly the

☽ afterwards the Rest of the planets, and after then the characters of ye signe that ascendeth on the 12 house in that hour that is shewed in this sigill which is fitted for the 10th Day of March in the year 1641 being on a wednesday in the first house etc:

This seal being thus made lay it on the Table of practice, Lay your hand on it and say The Conjuration that is written at the latter end of this first part for it serveth for all onely the names are to be changed according to the time you work in etc.

The Table of Practice

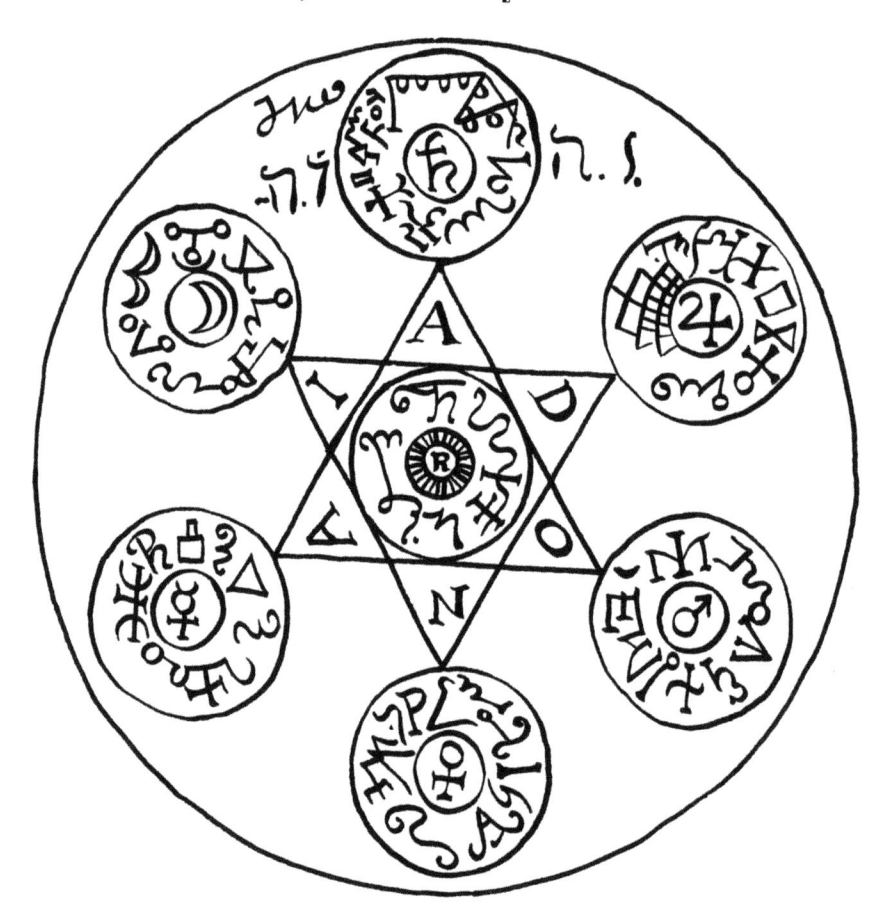

Ars Paulina

Nota: lay the seal on the Table or that of the table that is notted wth that charecter as lord of the ascendent is of, as ♂ is lord of the ascendent in the above said seal therefore it is to be laid upon the characters of ♂ in the table of practice: etc: doo the like with all other seales etc. The perfumes are to be made of such things as are attributed to the same planetts etc.

𝕿𝖍𝖊 𝖘𝖊𝖈𝖔𝖓𝖉 𝖍𝖔𝖚𝖗 𝖔𝖋 𝖙𝖍𝖊 𝖉𝖆𝖞 is called Cevorym, The Angell that governeth that hour is calld Anael, who hath 20 cheefe Dukes and 100 lesser Dukes to attend him whereof we shall mentione 9: But the thre first ar of ye cheefe, and the other 6 of the under Dukes. They have 330 Servants to attend them. Those 9 are as followeth vizt: *Menarchos, Archiel, Chardiel, Orphiel, Cursiel, Elmoym, Quosiel, Ermaziel, Granyel.* When you have a desier to worke in the second hour of wednesday on the 10th day of March make a seal as followeth on any clean paper or parchment writting first the characters of ye Lord of the ascendent – Then the Rest of the Planetts, and the signe of ye 12th house as yoiu may see in this following sigill and when it is made lay it upon the part of ye table as is noted with the same charrecter as the lord of the ascendent is. Observe this same rule in all the following part of this first part and you can not Eare etc. Then say the conjuration as is written at ye latter end etc.

𝕿𝖍𝖊 3𝖗𝖉 𝖍𝖔𝖚𝖗 𝖔𝖋 𝖆𝖓𝖞 𝖉𝖆𝖞 is called Dansor, and the Angell that rulleth that hour is called Vequaniel, who hath 20 cheefe Dukes and 200 lesser Dukes, and a great many other servants to attend him, whereof wee shall mention 4 of the cheefe Dukes and eight of the lesser who hath 1760 servants to attend them there names are as followeth vizt: *Asmiel, Persiel, Mursiel, Zoesiel;* and *Drelmech, Sadiniel, Parniel, Comadiel, Gemary, Xantiel, Serviel, Furiel.* These being sufficient for practice. Make a seal sutabble to the day hour and year as this is for the time before mentioned and you cannot Erre, then say the Conjuration.

The 4th hour of any day is called Elechym, and the Angell thereof is called Vathmiel, who hath 10 cheefe Dukes and 100 under Dukes, besides many servants whereof wee shall mention 5 of the cheefe and 10 of the under Dukes; who have 1550 servants to attend them. Their names are as followeth: viz *Armmyel, Larmich, Marfiel, Ormyel, Zardiel, Emarfiel, Permiel, Queriel, Strubiel, Diviel, Jermiel, Thuros, Vanesiel, Zasviel, Hermiel.* These being sufficient for practice, make a seal suitable to this hour as is before directed and you can not erre: the form it will be as this is heare for the time aforsaide etc when it is made: doe as before directed: and say The conjuration.

The 5th hour of every day is called Fealech, and the angel thereof is called Sasquiel. he hath 10 Dukes cheefe, and 100 lesser Dukes and very many servants whereof wee shall mention 5 of the cheefe Dukes and 10 of the lesser who have 5550 servants to attend them whose names are as followeth, vizt: *Damiel, Araniel, Maroch, Saraphiel, Putisiel; Jameriel, Futiniel, Rameriel, Amisiel, Uraniel, Omerach, Lameros, Zachiel, Fustiel, Camiel.* These being sufficient to practice: then make a seal suetable for the time as I here give you an Example of for the day before spoken of in the year 1641 and when you have made it lay it upon the Table as you was before shewed and say the conjuration.

Ars Paulina

The 6th houre of the day is called Genapherim, and the Angell rulling that houre is called Saniel, who hath 10 cheefe Dukes and 100 lesser Dukes besides many other Inferiour servants whereof wee shall mention 5 of the cheefe and 10 of the lesser who have 5550 servants to attend them: whose names are as followeth vizt: *Arnebiel, Charuch, Medusiel, Nathmiel, Pemiel, Gamyel, Jenotriel, Sameon, Trasiel, Xamyon, Nedabor, Permon, Brasiel, Camosiel, Evadar.* They being sufficient for practice in this houre of the day. Then make a seal sutable to the time of the day year and hour as here is made one for the time aforesaid Then lay it on the Table as you was before directed and you cannot erre. Then say the conjuration etc.

The 7th houre of the day is called Hamarym, and the Angell that governeth the same is called Barquiel, who hath 10 cheefe dukes and a 100 under Dukes besides servants which are very many whereof wee shall mention 5 of the cheefe Dukes and 10 of the lesser who have 600 servants which attend them in this hour whose names are as followeth viz: *Abrasiel, Farmos, Nestorii, Manuel, Sagiel, Harmiel, Nastrus, Varmay, Tulmas, Crosiel, Pasriel, Venesiel, Evarym, Drufiel, Kathos.* They being sufficient for practice in this houre etc. Then make a seal here I give you an Example Then lay on the Table as you was directed before and haveing all things in readines say the conjuration etc.

Lemegeton Clavicula Salomonis

𝕿𝖍𝖊 8𝖙𝖍 𝖍𝖔𝖚𝖗 𝖔𝖋 𝖊𝖛𝖊𝖗𝖞 𝖉𝖆𝖞 is called Jafanym, and the angell governeth the same is called Osmadiel, who hath a 100 cheefe Dukes and 100 lesser Dukes besides very many other servants whereof wee shall mention 5 of the cheefe Dukes and 10 of the lesser who have 1100 servants to attend them – They being sufficient for Practice: There names are as followeth vizt: *Sarfiel, Amalym, Chroel, Mesial, Lantrhots, Demarot, Janofiel, Larfuty, Vemael, Thribiel, Mariel, Remasyn, Theoriel, Framion, Ermiel*. Then make a seal for this 8th houre as is shewed by this seal which is made for an example – then lay it on the table and say the conjuration following etc.

𝕿𝖍𝖊 9𝖙𝖍 𝖍𝖔𝖚𝖗 𝖔𝖋 𝖊𝖛𝖊𝖗𝖞 𝖉𝖆𝖞 is called Karron, and the Angell rulling it is called Quabriel who hath many Dukes, 66 of ye greater and lesser order: besides many other servants: which are more Inferiour whereof 10 of the greater and 100 of the lesser Dukes have 192980 servants in 10 orders to obey and serve them whereof we shall mention the names of five great Dukes and 10 lesser Dukes who have 650 cheefe servants to attend on them in this houre they being sufficient for practice: These be their names: vizt: *Astroniel, Charmy, Pamory, Damyel, Nadriel, Kranos, Menas, Brasiel, Nefarym, Zoymiel, Trubas, Xermiel, Lameson, Zasnor, Janediel*. And when you have a desier to make an experiment in this house make a seal as you was tought before the forme of this is for an example and when it is made lay it on the Table as you was directed before Then say the Conjuration etc.

𝕿𝖍𝖊 10𝖙𝖍 𝖍𝖔𝖚𝖗 𝖔𝖋 𝖊𝖛𝖊𝖗𝖞 𝕯𝖆𝖞 is called Lamarhon and the angell rulling it is called Oriel who hath many Dukes and servants divided into 10 orders which contain 5600 spirits whereof wee shall mention 5 of the cheef Dukes and 10 of the next lesser Dukes who hath 1100 servants to attend on them. They being sufficient for practice. Their names are as followeth vizt *Armosy, Drabiel, Penaly, Mesriel, Choreb, Lemur, Ormas, Charny, Zazyor, Naveron, Xantros, Basilon, Nameron, Kranoti, Alfrael.* and when you have a desier to practice in this houre make a seal sutable to the time: as this hear is made for the 10th hour on wednesday the 10th of march in the year 1641 it being for an exameble and when it is made lay it on the Table of practice: and say the conjuration etc.

𝕿𝖍𝖊 11𝖙𝖍 𝖍𝖔𝖚𝖗 𝖎𝖓 𝖊𝖛𝖊𝖗𝖞 𝖉𝖆𝖞 is called Maneloym, and the angel governing that hour is called Bariel, who hath many Dukes and servants which are divided into 10 parts which contain ye number of 5600 whereof wee shall mention 5 of the Dukes of the first order and 10 lesser Dukes of the second order, who have 1100 servants to attend them, They being sufficient for practice. Their names are as followeth vizt: *Almarizel, Prasiniel, Chadros, Turmiel, Lamiel, Menafiel, Demasor, Omary, Helmas, Zemoel, Almas, Perman, Comial, Temas, Lanifiel.* and when you would practice make a seal sutable to ye time of the day: as I shew you here by an Example. And when it is made lay it on the Table of practice: and say the Conjuration etc.

The 12 hour of every day is called Nahalon, and the Angell governing that hour is called Beratiel, who hath many Dukes and other servants which are divided into 12 degrees the which contain the number of 3700 spirits in all whereof wee shall mention 5 the cheefe Dukes and 10 of the lesser Dukes who have 1100 servants to attend them, they being sufficient for practice. Their names are as followeth: vizt: *Camaron, Astrofiel, Penatiel, Demarac, Famaras, Plamiel, Nerastiel, Fimarson, Quirix, Sameron, Edriel, Choriel, Romiel, Fenosiel, Harmary.* And when you have a desier to worke in this hour make a seal sutable to the time as I have here for the same hour But the 10th of march in ye year 1641. When you have thus made it lay it on the Table of practice and lay your hand on it. and say the conjuration etc.

The first hour of every night is called Omalharien, and the Angell ruling it is called Sabrathan who hath 1540 Dukes and other servants which are divided into 10 orders or parts, whereof wee shall mention 5 of the cheefe Dukes and 10 of the lesser Dukes which are next to the 5 first: They being sufficient for practice in this houre. Their names are as followeth viz: *Domaras, Amerany, Penoles, Mardiel, Nastul, Ramesiel, Omedriel, Franedac, Chrasiel, Dormason, Hayzoym, Emalon, Turtiel, Quenol, Rymaliel.* They have 2000 servants to attend them and when you would worke in this houre make a seal sutable to the time as this is for an Example Then lay the seal on the Table of practice and you cannot erre, saying the conjuration etc.

Ars Paulina

The 2d hour of every night is called Panezur, and the Angell rulling it is called Tartys who hath 101550 to attend him they being divided into 12 degrees or orders whereof wee shall mention 6 of the cheefe Dukes of the first order and 12 of the next: They being sufficient for practice: Their names are as followeth viz *Almodar, Famoriel, Nedroz, Ormezyn, Chabriz, Praxiel, Permaz, Vameroz, Emaryel, Fromezyn, Ramaziel, Granozyn, Gabrinoz, Mercoph, Tameriel, Venomiel, Jenaziel, Xemyzin*. These have 1320 servants to attend them in this hour to doe their will and when you will worke in this hour make a Seal sutable for the time as I have here given an Example for the time aboue mentioned then lay it on ye table and say the conjuration etc.

The 3d hour of the night is called Quabrion, and the angel governing it is called Serquanich who hath 101550 servient Dukes and servants to attend him: The which are divided into 12 Degrees of orders whereof wee shall mention 6 Dukes of the first order and 12 of the second: They being sufficient for practice whose names are as followeth viz *Menarym, Chrusiel, Penargos, Amriel, Demanoz, Nestoroz, Evanuel, Sarmozyn, Haylon, Quabriel, Thurmytz, Fronyzon, Vanosyr, Lemaron, Almonoyz, Janothyel, Melrotz, Xanthyozod*. These have 1320 servants to attend them and when you will make any experiment in this houre make a Seal sutable to the time as I have here exemplifyed for the time aforesaid Then lay it on the Table of practice and say the conjuration etc.

The 4th hour of the night is called Ramersy, and the angell that governs it is called Jefischa – who hath 101550 Dukes and other servants, which are divided into 12 orders or degrees to attend him, whereof we shall mention 6 of the cheefe Dukes and 12 of those that are of the second order, they being sufficient for Practice. Their names are as followeth: vizt *Armosiel, Nedruan, Maneyloz, Ormael, Phorsiel, Rimezyn, Rayziel, Gemezin, Fremiel, Hamayz, Japuriel, Jasphiel, Lamediel, Adroziel, Zodiel, Bramiel, Coreziel, Enatriel.* Those have 7260 servants to attend them and if you have a desier to operate in this houre: make a seal sutable for the time you have one here for this howre for the time abouesaid it being for an Example Then lay the seal upon the Table of Practice and say the conjuration, etc.

The 5th houre of the night is called Sanayfar, and this angel is called Abasdarhon. He hath 101550 Dukes and other servants at his command: They being divided into 12 degrees of orders whereof wee shall mention 12 of the Dukes belonging to the first order and as many of the second order, They being sufficient for practice for this hour: There names are as followeth vizt: *Meniel, Charaby, Appiniel, Deinatz, Nechorym, Hameriel, Vulcaniel, Samelon, Gemary, Vanescor, Samerym, Xantropy, Herphatz, Chrymas, Patrozyn, Nameton, Barmas, Platiel, Neszomy, Quesdor, Caremaz, Umariel, Kralym, Habalon.* Who have 3200 servants to attend them and if you make any Experiment in this hour, make a seal sutable to the time as this seal is suted for the time aforesaid being ye 10th of March 1641 it being for an example. Then lay it on the Table of practice and doe as you where directed before and say the conjuration, etc.

96

The 6th hour of every night is called Thaazaron, and the angell governing it is called Zaazenach, who hath 101550 Dukes and other servants at his command to attend him, they being divided in 12 parts and orders: whereof wee shall mention 12 of the cheefest Dukes in the first order and 6 of the second order they being sufficient for practice in this hour. Their names are as followeth: vizt: *Amonazy, Menoriel, Prenostix, Namedor, Cherasiel, Dramaz, Tuberiel, Humaziel, Lanoziel Lamerotzod, Xerphiel, Zeziel, Pammon, Dracon, Gematzod, Enariel, Rudefor, Sarmon*, who have 2400 servants to attend on them and if you make any experiment in this hour make a seal fitt for the time as this is for the time before spoken of Then lay it on the Table and say the conjuration, etc.

The 7th houre of every night is called Venaydor, and its angell is called Mendrion, who hath 101550 dukes and other servants to attend him. They being divided into 12 orders, whereof we shall mention 12 of the first cheefe dukes and 6 of ye next lesser sort They being sufficient for practice – Their names are as followeth: vizt: *Ammiel, Choriel, Genarytz, Pandroz, Menesiel, Sameriel, Ventariel, Zachariel, Dubraz, Marchiel, Jonadriel, Pemoniel, Rayziel, Tarmytz, Anapion, Jmonyel, Framoth, Machmag*, who have 1860 servants to attend them and when you make any Experiment make a seal sutable to the time as you have hear an Example. Then lay it on ye Table: and say the conjuration, etc.

Nota I supose this seal to be wrong and that it must be as the following seal of the 8th houre:

The 8th hour of every night is called Xymalim, and the angell rulling it is called Narcoriel, who hath 101550 Dukes and other servient spirits to attend him, they being divided into 12 degrees or orders, whereof we shall mention 12 of the first order and 6 of the next order, They being sufficient to practice in this hour. Their names are as followeth vizt *Cambiel, Nedarym, Astrocon, Marifiel, Dramozyn, Lustifion, Amelson, Lemozar, Xernifiel, Kanorsiel, Bufanotz, Jamedroz, Xanoriz, Jastrion, Themaz, Hobraiym, Zymeloz, Gamsiel*: who have 30200 servants to attend them and when you make any Experiment in this houre make a seal sutable to the time as you have here in Example for the time aforesaid. Then lay it on the Table and say the conjuration, etc.

The 9th hour of the night is called Zeschar and the angell rulling it is called Pamyel. He hath 101550 dukes and other servants to attend him who are divided into 12 parts or orders, whereof wee shall mention 18 of the cheefe Dukes whose names are as followeth: vizt *Demaor, Nameal, Adrapan, Chermel, Fenadros, Vemasiel, Comary, Matiel, Zenoroz, Brandiel, Evandiel, Tameriel, Befranzy, Jachoroz, Xanthir, Armapy, Druchas, Sardiel*. Who have 1320 servants to Attend them and when you make any Experiment in this hour make a seal sutable to the time as you have hear an example for the time aforesaid. Then lay it on the table and lay your hands on it: and say the conjuration, etc.

Ars Paulina

The 10th hour of the night is called Malcho, and the angell governing it is called Iassuarim, who hath a 100 cheefe dukes and a 100 lesser dukes besides many other servants, whereof wee shall mention 6 that is three of the first order and 3 of the second order who have 1620 servants. There names are as followeth: vizt *Lapheriel, Emarziel, Nameroyz, Chameray, Hazaniel, Uraniel*. And when you operate in this houre make a seal sutable to the time as this is for time in the month of March 1641. Then lay it on the Table and say the conjuration, etc.

The 11th hour of ye night is called Aalacho, and the angell governing it is called Dardariel, who hath many servants and dukes whereof we shall mention 14 of the cheefe dukes and 7 of ye lesser Dukes who have 420 servants to attend them. They are all good and obey gods lawes. Their names are as followeth: vizt: *Cardiel, Permon, Armiel, Nastoriel, Casmiroz, Dameriel, Furamiel, Mafriel, Hariaz, Damar, Alachuc, Emeriel, Naveroz, Alaphar, Nermas, Druchas, Carman, Elamyz, Jatroziel, Lamersy, Hamarytzod*. And when you have a desere to make an Experiment: make a Seal sutable for the time as this is for the time in the month of March 1641. Then lay it on the Table and say the conjuration, etc.

99

Lemegeton Clavicula Salomonis

The 12 hour of the night is called Xephan, and the angell governing it is called Sarandiel, who hath many dukes and servants whereof wee shall mention 14 of ye cheefe and good Dukes of the first order and 7 of those of ye second order: who have 420 servants to attend on them. Their names are as followeth: vizt *Adoniel, Damasiel, Ambriel, Meriel, Denaryz, Emarion, Kabriel, Marachy, Chabrion, Nestoriel, Zachriel, Naveriel, Damery, Namael, Hardiel, Nefrias, Irmanotzod, Gerthiel, Dromiel, Ladrotzod, Melanas.* and when you have a desier to make any Experiment in this hour make a sigill sutable to the time as this is hear for the same hour for the 10th of March in the year 1641 and when it is so made lay it on the Table of practice and lay your hand on it and say this conjuration following.

The Conjuration as Followeth

O thou mighty great and potent Angell Samael who ruleth in the first hour of ye day – I the servant of the most high god: doe conjure and entreat thee in the name of ye most omnipotent and Immortall Lord god of hosts: Jehovah ✶ Tetragrammaton, and by the name of that god that you are obedient to and by ye head of ye hierarchy and by the seal or marke that you are known in power by and by the 7 Angels that stand before the Throne of god and by the 7 planetts and their seals and characters and by the angel that rulleth The signe of ye 12 house wch now ascends in this first hour that you would be graciously pleased to gird up and gather your selfe together and by devine permission to move and come from all parts of the world, wheresoever you be and shew your selfe visibly and plainly in this Cristall stone to the sight of my Eyes speaking with a voice Intelligible and to my understanding and that you would be favorably pleased That I may have familliar frindship and constant socity both now and at all times when I shall call thee forth to visible appearance to Informe and direct me in all things that I shall seem good and lawful unto the Creator and Thee: O thou great and powerfull angele Samael. I invocate, adjure, command and most powerfully call you forth from your orders and place of Residence to visible appirition in and through these great and mighty Incomprehensible signall and divine names of the great god who was and is and ever shall be Adonay,

Zebaoth, Adonay Amioram, Hagios, Agla, On, Tetragrammaton and by and in the name *Primeumaton*, which commandeth the whole host of heaven whose power and vertue is most Effectual for the calling you forth and commandeth you to Transmitt your Rayes vissible and perfectly into my sight: and your voice to my Ears, in and threw this Cristall stone: That I may plainly see you and perfectly hear you speak unto me. Therefore move yee, O Thou mighty and blessed angell Samael: and in this potent name of the great god Jehovah: and by the Imperiall dignity Thereof descend and shew your self vissible and perfectly in a pleasant and comely form before me in this Cristall stone: to the sight of my Eyes speaking with a voyce Intelligible and to my apprehension: shewing, declaring and accomplishing all my desires that I shall aske or Request of you both herein and in whatsoever Truths or things else that is Just and lawfull before the presence of Almighty god: the giver of all good gifts: unto whome I begg that he would be graciously plased to bestow upon me: O thou servant of mercy Samael, be thou therefore unto me friendly: and doe for me as for the servant of the highest god: so farr as god shall given you power in office to performe: whereunto I move you in Power and presence to appear that I may sing with his holy angells Omappa-la-man, Hallelujah, Amen.*

But before you call any of the princes or the Dukes: you are to Invocate his cheefe governing Angell that governeth the hour of the day or of the night, as follows:

The Invocation as Followeth

O Thou mighty and potent angell Samael, who is by the decree of the most high king of glory Ruler and governour of the first hour of the day I the servant of the highest doe desier and entreat you by these 3 great and mighty names of god: Agla, Tetragrammaton and by the power and vertue Thereof to assist and help me in my affairs: and by your power and authority, to send and cause to come and appear to me all or any of these angells that I shall call by name: that are residing under your government, to Instruct, help, aid and assist me, in all such matters and Things according to their office, as I shall desier and request of them (or him) and that they may doe for me as for the servant of ye highest creator.

Then Beginn to Invocate Them as Followeth

O thou mighty and potent angel Ameniel, who rulleth by divine permission under The great and potent angell Samael, who is the great and potent angel rulling this first hour of the day: I the servant of the most high god doe conjure and entreat thee In the name of the most omnipotent and Immortall lord god of hosts Jehovah ✱.

Note: from this sign ✷: to continue the contents of ye above written conjuration, etc. And when any spirit is come bidd him wellcome: Then aske your desier, and when you have done, dismiss him according to your orders of dissmission. etc.

And So Endeth the First Part of the Art Pauline

The Second Part of the Art Pauline

Which containeth the Mysticall names of the Angells of ye signes in general, and allso the names of the Angells of every degree and ye signes in general who are called the angells of men: because in some one of those signs and degrees, every man is born under. Therefore he that knoweth the moment of his Birth he may know the angel that governeth him: and thereby he may obtain to all arts and sciences, yea to all ye wisdome and knowledge that any mortall man can desier in this world: But note this: Those angells that are attributed to the fire have more knowledge therin than any other: So those that belong to the Aire have more knowledge therin than any other: and those of ye water have more knowledge therin then any other: and allso those of the Earth have more knowledge therein then any other: and to know wch belong to the fire, ayre, Earth, or water: observe the nature of the signes and you cannot erre: for those that are attributed to ♈: are of the same nature, and so the like in the rest. But if any Planett is in that degree that ascends: Then that angell is of the nature of the signe and Planett both, etc. Observe this following method and you cannot but obtain your desiere etc.

The Planets											
♂	♀	☿	☽	☉	☿	♀	♂	♃	♄	♄	♃
The signes											
♈	♉	♊	♋	♌	♍	♎	♏	♐	♑	♒	♓
The Nature of the signes											
Fire	Earth	Ayer	Wayter	Fire	Earth	Ayer	Wayter	Fire	Earth	Ayer	Wayter
The Angels											
Aiel	Tual	Giel	Cael	Ol	Voil	Jael	Josel	Suiajasel	Casujojah	Ausiul	Pasil

Ars Paulina

These 12 names are attributed by 12 signes of the Zodiac: Because of these that doe not know the very decree of their nativity: so that they may make use of these if he know but the signe that ascends, etc. The names of the other angells which are attributed to Every degree are as followeth:

	♈♂	♉♀	♊☿	♋☽	♌☉	♍☿	♎♀	♏♂	♐♃	♑♄	♒♄	♓♃
1	Biael	Latiel	Latiel	Sachiel	Mechiel	Celiel	Ibajah	Teliel	Taliel	Chushel	Chamiel	Lachiel
2	Gesiel	Hujael	Nagael	Metiel	Satiel	Senael	Chaiel	Jeniel	Janiel	Temael	Tesael	Neliel
3	Hael	Sachiel	Sachael	Asel	Ajel	Nasael	Sahael	Cesiel	Casiel	Jaajah	Jaajeh	Sanael
4	Vaniel	Gneliel	Gnaliel	Sachiel	Mechiel	Sangiel	Naviel	Lengael	Langael	Cashiel	Camiel	Gnasiel
5	Zaciel	Panael	Paniel	Mihel	Sahel	Gnaphiel	Saziel	Naphael	Naphael	Lamajah	Lashiel	Pangael
6	Cegnel	Jezisiel	Tzisiel	Aniel	Aniel	Parziel	Gnachiel	Satziel	Satziel	Naajah	Naajah	Tzapheal
7	Japhael	Kingael	Kingael	Sasael	Masiel	Tzakiel	Patiel	Gnakiel	Gnakiel	Sasajah	Samiel	Kphiel
8	Itael	Raphiel	Raphiel	Magnael	Sengael	Kriel	Trajael	Periel	Periel	Gnamiel	Gnashiel	Ratziel
9	Cakiel	Tezael	Gnetiel	Aphiel	Aphiel	Rathiel	Kachiel	Tzethiel	Tzangiel	Paajah	Paajah	Tarajah
10	Lariel	Gnakiel	Bakiel	Sersael	Metziel	Tangiel	Baliel	Rengliel	Jebiel	Tzashiel	Tzamiel	Gnathiel
11	Natheel	Beriel	Geriel	Makael	Sekiel	Gnasiel	Tamael	Rebiel	Regael	Kmiel	Kshiel	Bengiel
12	Sagnel	Gethiel	Dathiel	Ariel	Ariel	Bagiel	Gnamiel	Tagiel	Tediel	Riajah	Raajah	Gebiel
13	Gabiel	Dagnel	Hegnel	Sethiel	Methiel	Gediel	Bangiel	Gnadiel	Gnaheel	Tashiel	Tamiel	Dagiel
14	Pegiel	Vabiel	Vabiel	Magnael	Sagiel	Dahiel	Gepheel	Bevael	Bevael	Gnamiel	Gnashiel	Hadiel
15	Gadiel	Zegiel	Zagiel	Abiel	Abiel	Hevael	Datziel	Geziel	Geziel	Baajah	Baajah	Vahajah
16	Kheel	Chadiel	Chadiel	Sagel	Magiel	Vaziel	Hekiel	Dachiel	Dachiel	Gashiel	Garniel	Zavael
17	Leviel	Tahiel	Tahiel	Madiel	Sadiel	Zachiel	Variel	Hephiel	Hephiel	Darniel	Dashiel	Chazael
18	Hezael	Javiel	Javiel	Athiel	Ahiel	Chetiel	Zethiel	Vagael	Vagael	Haajah	Haajah	Tachael
19	Geciel	Chazael	Chazael	Savael	Muviel	Tiiel	Chengiel	Zackiel	Zackiel	Vashiel	Vamiel	Jatael
20	Betiel	Bachiel	Bachiel	Maziel	Saviel	Jechiel	Tibiel	Chabiel	Chabiel	Zamiel	Zashiel	Cajaiel
21	Giel	Getiel	Getiel	Achiel	Achiel	Cabiel	Jagiel	Tagiel	Tagiel	Chael	Chael	Bachiel
22	Dachael	Dajiel	Dajiel	Setiel	Metiel	Bagiel	Cediel	Jadiel	Jadiel	Tashiel	Tamiel	Gabiel
23	Habiel	Hachael	Hachael	Maiel	Siel	Gediel	Behel	Cahael	Cahael	Jmojah	Jashiel	Dagiel
24	Vagel	Vabiel	Vabiel	Achael	Achael	Dahiel	Gevael	Baviel	Baviel	Ciajah	Ciajah	Hediel
25	Zadiel	Zagiel	Zagiel	Sabiel	Mabiel	Hoviel	Daziel	Gezael	Gezael	Beshael	Bemiel	Vahejah
26	Chahel	Chadiel	Chadiel	Magiel	Sagiel	Vaziel	Heckiel	Dachael	Dachael	Gamael	Gashiel	Zavael
27	Tavael	Tahiel	Tahiel	Adiel	Adiel	Zachiel	Vatiel	Hatiel	Hatiel	Daael	Daael	Chazael
28	Jezel	Javael	Daviel	Sahiel	Mahiel	Chetivel	Zajel	Vajael	Vajael	Heshael	Hemiel	Tachiel
29	Cechiel	Chaziel	Hoziel	Meviel	Savael	Tajael	Chechiel	Zachiel	Zachiel	Vamiel	Vashiel	Jatael
30	Hetiel	Sachael	Vachael	Aziel	Aziel	Jachiel	Tehiel	Chasiel	Chasiel	Zaajah	Zaajah	Cajael

103

These are the 12 Seales
Which are attributed to the Signes & Angells aforegoeing

♈

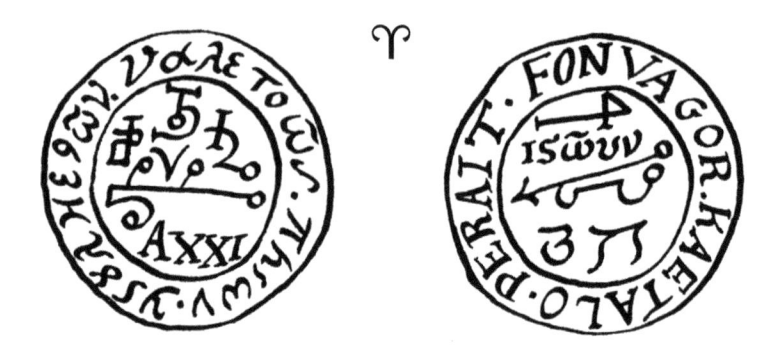

Make this seal of ♂ ℥ss ☉ ʒii ♀ ʒss and melt them together when the ☉ entereth the first Degree of ♈. Then on ♂ [*the day of mars – tuesday*], the ☽ being in 9 or 10 degrees of ♈, and make it and finish it etc.

♉

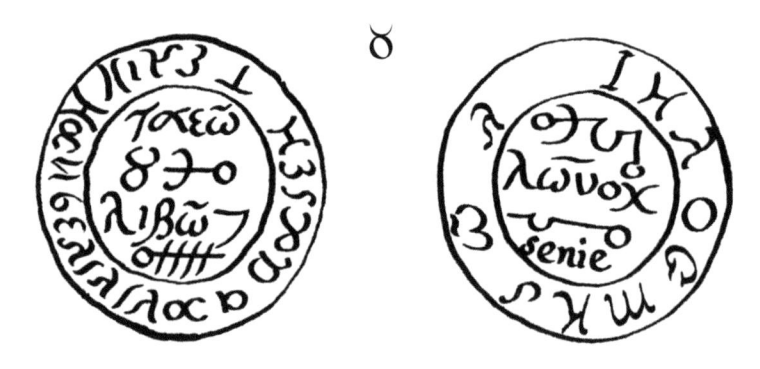

Make this seal of ♀ ʒi ♃ ʒi ♂ ℥ss ☉ ʒii and melt them together in the very point the ☉ entereth ♉, and so finish it etc.

♊

Make this seal of ☉ ʒi ☽ ʒi and melt them together when the ☉ entereth ♊, and make a lamin thereof when ☽ is in ♌ or ♓ etc.

Ars Paulina

♋

Make this seal of ☽ when the sun entereth ♋ in the hour of ☽ she ☽ encreasing and in a good aspect etc.

♌

Make this seal of ☉ when he entereth ♌, then after when ♃ is in ♓ engrave the first figure, and the other side, when the ☽ is in ♓, it must not come into the fire any more, but once, that is, when it is melted etc.

♍

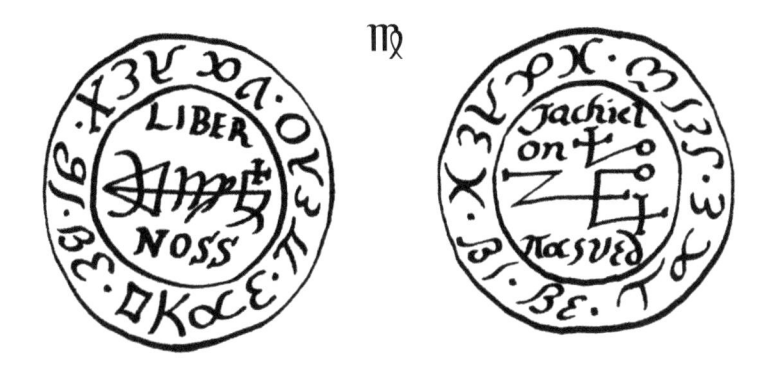

Make this seal of ♀ ʒi ☉ ʒss ☽ ʒii ♃ ʒss and melt them on ☉ day when the ☉ entereth ♍, then afterwards, when ☿ is well aspected, on his day engrave the words and Characters as you see in the figure etc.

105

Lemegeton Clavicula Salomonis

♎

Make this seal of ♀ melted powered & made when ☉ entreth ♎.

♏

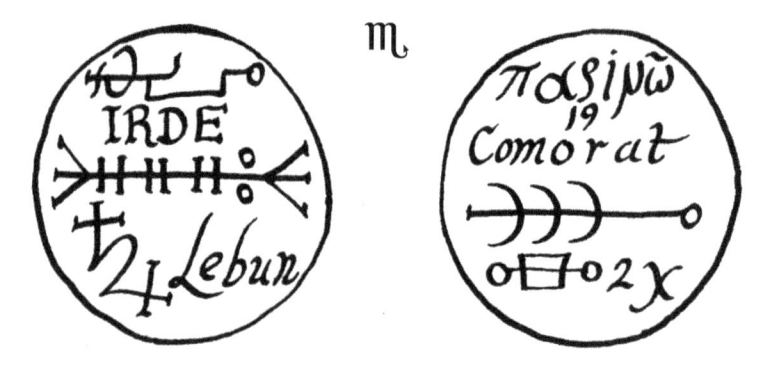

Make this seal of ♂ and in this day and hour when ☉ entereth ♏, and in that hour engrave the forepart of it, and afterwards, when ☉ entereth ♈, engrave the other.

♐

Make this seal of pure ♃ in the hour that ☉ entereth ♐, and engrave it in the hour of ♃. This seal is to be hung in a silver Ring.

Ars Paulina

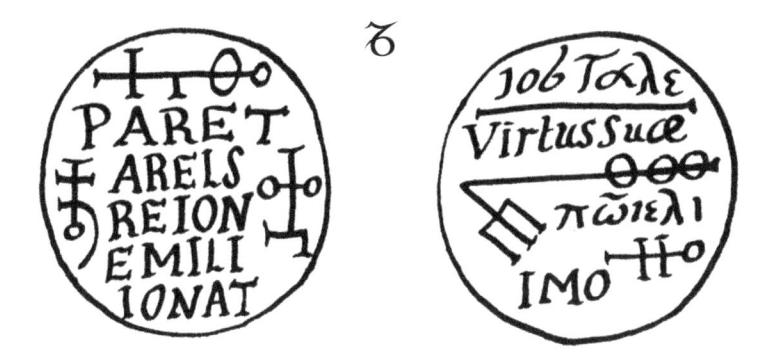

Make this seal of ☉, and a Ring of ♀ to hang it in, and when ☉ entereth ♑, and engrave it when ♄ is well aspected and in his day and houre.

Make this seal of ☉ ℥ss ♄ ʒii ♂ ʒi and melt them when ☉ entereth ♒, and engrave them as you see in the figure when ♄ is in ye 9th house etc.

Make this seal when ☉ entereth ♓, of ☉ ♂ ♀ ☽ of each ʒii, of ♃ ʒss, and let them be melted and engraven both in that hour of his increase, etc.

107

So when you know the Angell that governeth the sign, and degree of your nativity, and haveing the seal redy prepared that is suetable to the sign and dgree as is shewed before, then you are next to understand what order he is of and under what prince as is shewed hereafter in the following part.

First those genii that are attibruted to ♈, ♌, and ♐ are of the Fiery region, and are governed by Michael, The great Angell who is one of the great messengers of god, which is towards the South; therefore those geniis are to be observed in the first hour on a Sunday and at the eighth, allso at three and ten at night directing yourselfe towards that quarter. They appear in Royal Robes holding scepters in their hands, oft Ryding on a Lion or a Cock. Their robes are of a red and saffron collor and most commonly they assume the sheap of a crowned queen, very beautifull to behold etc.

Secondly those geniis that are attributed to ♉, ♍, & ♑, are of the Earthy Region and governed by Uriel, who hath three princes to attend him viz, Cassiel, Sachiel, & Assaiel. Therefore the geniis that are attributed to him and those signs are to be observed in the West, They appear like Kings having green and silver Robes, or like little children or women delighting in hunting etc. Saturdays. at the first and eighth hours of the day and at night at the third and tenth hours, You are with privacy to obtaine your desiers, directing yourselfe towards the West etc.

Thirdly those geniis that are attributed to ♊, ♎, & ♒, are of the aeiry region, whose sovereign prince is called Raphael; who hath under him 2 princes, wch are called Miel and Seraphiel. Therefore those genii wch are attributed to him and those signs are to be observed towards the east, on a wednesday, the first and eighth hours of the day and at night the third and tenth houre. They appear like kings or beautiful young men cloathed in Robes of divers collours, But most commonly like women Transcendently handsome; by reason of their admirable whiteness and Beauty etc.

Fourthly and lastly Those genii that are attributed to ♋, ♏, & ♓ are of the watry region, and are governed by Gabriel, who hath under him 3 mighty princes, vizt Samael, Madiel, and Mael. Therefore those genii which are attributed to these signes that are governed by gabriel, and are to be observed on a munday towards the north at the first and 8th houres of the day, and at night at the 3rd and 10th houres, they appear like kings haveing green and silver Robes or like little Children or women delighting in hunting etc.

So in the next place wee are to observe the season of the year according to the constellations of the celestial Bodies, otherwise wee shall lose all our labour, for if the genius be of Jyneal Hierarchy, its in vaine to observe him in any other season but when the sun entereth those signs which are of his nature, that is ♈, ♌, and ♐ :

So if it be a geniis of the Earth he is to be observed when ☉ entereth ♉, ♍, and ♑, and so the like in the rest.

Or otherwise thus: those geniis that are of the order of the fire, are to be observed in ye summer quarter and those of the earthy in Autume, and those of the ayr in the spring, and those of ye water in the winter quarter etc.

Their offices are to all things that are Just and not against the laws of the great god Jehovah But what is for our good and what shall concerne the protection of our life, our beinge and well being and doeing good to and oblidging our neighbours, etc.

Now he that desireth to see his genius, ought to prepare himselfe accordingly. Now if his genius be of the fire his demands must be the conservation of his Body or person that he receives no hurt ffrom or by any fire armes guns or the like and haveing a seal sutable, ready prepared, he is to weare it when he hath a desier to see his genius, That he may conferme it to him and for the time to come he may not fail of his assistance and protection at any time or occasion etc.

But if his genius be ayeriall he reconcileth mens natures Increaseth love and affection between them causeth the deserved favour of kings and princes and secretly promoteth marriages: and Therefore he that hath such a genius before he observeth him should prepare a seal suitable to his order that he may have it confermed by him in the day and hour of observation, where of he shall see wonderfull and strange Effects and so the like of ye other 2 hierarchies.

And when the time is come that you would see yr genius Turne yr face towards that quarter the signe is, and that with prayers to god: they being composed to your fancy, but sutable to ye matter in hand and there thou shalt find him; and haveing found him and sincerely acknowledged him doe your duty. Then will he, as being Benigne and sociable Illuminate your minde, takeing away all that is obscure and darke in the memory and make thee knowing in all sciences sacred and divine in an instant etc.

A form of prayer wch ought to be said upon that coast or quarter where the genius is several times, it being an Exorcisme to call the genius into the christall stone that is to stand upon the Table of practice before shewed, it being covered with a white linnen cloth. Note this prayer may be altered to the mind of the worker, for it is here set for an Example etc.

O thou great and blessed N. my angell guardian vouchsafe to descend from thy holy mansion which is Celestial, with thy holy Influence and presence, into this cristall stone, that I may behold thy glory; and enjoy thy society, aide and assistance, both now and for ever hereafter. O thou who art higer than the fortly heaven, and knoweth the secrets of Elanel. Thou that rideth upon the wings of ye winds and art mighty and potent in thy Celestial and superlunary motion, do thou descend and be present I pray thee; and I humbly desiere and entreat thee. That if ever I have merited Thy socity or if any of my actions and Intentions be real and pure and sanctified before thee bring thy external presence hither, and converse with me one of thy submissive pupils, By and in ye name of great god Jehovah, whereunto the whole quire of heaven singeth continualy: O Mappa la man Hallelujah. Amen.

When you have said this over several times you will at last see strange sights and pasages in the stone and at last you will see your genius: Then give him a kind entertainement as you was before directed declaring to him your minde and what you would have him doe, etc.

So Endeth the second Part of the Art Pauline

Here Beginneth

The Art Almadel

By this Art Solomon obtained great wisdom from the chief Angels that govern the 4 altitudes of the world, for you must observe that there are 4 altitudes which represent the 4 corners of the world, E. W. N. S. the which is divided into twelve parts, and the Angels of these have particular influence and power as will be shown in the following remarks.

Make 6 Almadels of pure white wax, but the others must be coloured suitable to the four altitudes which are to be 4" square and 6" over the other way, and in every corner a hole and write between every hole with a new pen these words or names of God following but it is to be done in the day and hour of the Sun. Upon the first part towards the East Adonai, Helomi, Pine, and upon the second towards the South write Helion, Heloi, Heli; and on the West side write Jah,[78] Hod, Agla, and on the N. write Tetragrammaton, Jah Sadai,[79] according to the following figure, and of the same wax, there must be made four candles, of the same color as the Almadel is, divide your wax into three parts, one to make the Almadel, and the other two parts to make the candles, and let there come forth of every one of them a foot made of the same wax to support the same, this being done you are to make a seal of pure Gold or Silver, Gold is best, whereon must be engraved these three names: Helion, Helinon, Adonay,[80] and note the 1st altitude is called chora Orientis, or the Eastern Altitude, and to make an experiment in this chora, is to [be] done in the day and hour of the Sun, and the power and office of those Spirits is to make all things fruitful, and increase both animals and vegetables, in Creation and Generation, and advancing the birth of children and making barren women fruitful, and their names are these: Almiel, Gabriel, Barachiel, Lebos, and Helison,[81] but note you must not pray to Angels, but to those who belong to the chora or altitude you desire to call, and when you operate set

---

78. *Jod* in Sl. 3825.
79. *Tetragrammaton, Shadai, Jah* in Sl. 3825.
80. *Helion, Hellujon, Adonai* in Sl. 3825.
81. Given as *Alimiel, Gabriel, Borachiel, Lebes & Hellison* in Sl. 3825

111

The Almadel

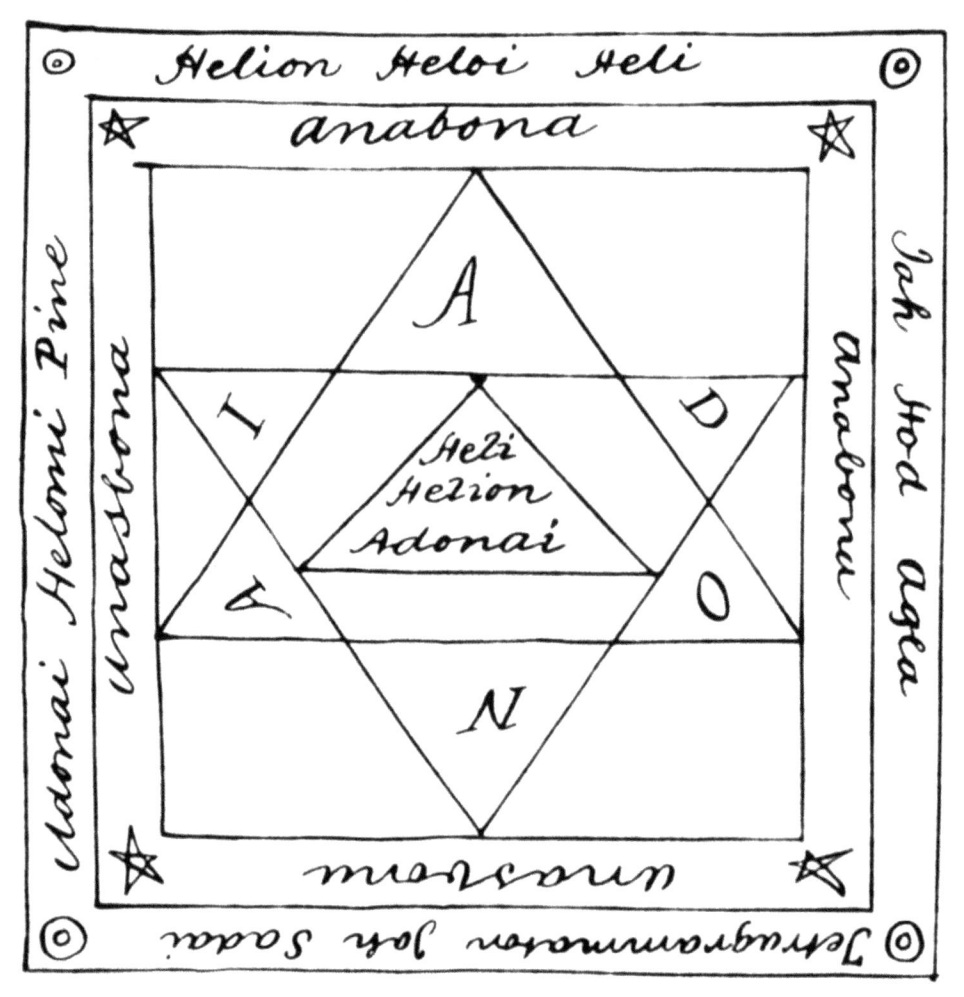

the four candles upon four candlesticks, but be careful you do not light them before you begin to operate, then lay the Almadel between the four candles upon waken feet that come from the candles, and lay the golden seal upon the Almadel, and having the invocation ready written on virgin parchment light the candles and read the invocation, and when he appears he comes in the form of an Angel carrying in his hand a fan or flag having the picture of a white cross upon it, his body being wrapped round by a fair cloud, and his face very fair and bright, and a crown of rose flowers upon his head, he descends first upon the Super-Scription of the Almadel in as it were a mist or fog, then must the exorcist have in readiness a vessel of Earth of the same colour as the Almadel and the other of his furniture, it being of the form of a bsasin and put therein a few hot ashes or coals, but not too much lest it should melt the wax of the Almadel, and put thereon 3 little grains of mastic in a powder so that it may

Ars Almadel

fume and the smell goes upwards through the holes of the Almadel when it is under it, and as soon as the Angel smells it he begins to speak with a low voice, asking what your desire is, and what you have called the King and the princes of this altitude for, then you must answer him, saying I desire that all my requests may be granted and what I pray for may be accomplished, for your office maketh it appear and declareth, that such is to be fulfilled by you if it please God, adding further the particulars of your requests, praying with great humility for what is lawful and just and that you shall obtain from him; but if he does not appear presently you must then take the golden Seal, and make with it three or four marks upon the candle, by which means the Angel will presently appear as aforesaid, and when the Angel departs he will fill the place with a sweet and pleasant smell, which wil be smelt a long time; and note the golden Seal will serve and is used in all the operations of the four Altitudes; the colour of the Almadel used for the first altitude or Chora is lilly white; the 2nd chora is perfect red rose colour; the Third is a green mixed with a white silver colour; the 4th is black with a little green or sad colour.

Of the 2nd Chora

NOTE: All the other three altitudes with their Kings and Princes have power over goods and riches and can make any man rich or poor, and as the 1st Chora gives increase, and maketh fruitful, so these give decrease and barrenness, and if any have a desire to operate in any of the 3 following Choras, they must do it in the day of the Sun, as is shown above, but do not pray for anything that is contrary to their nature or office, or that is against God and his laws, but what God giveth according to the custom or course of nature that you may desire to obtain. All the furniture to be used is to be of the same colour as the Almadel, and the Princes of this second Chora are named Aphiriza,[82] Genon, Geron, Armon, Gerdimon,[83] and when you operate kneel before the Almadel with clothes on of the same colour, and when he appears, put an earthen vessel with coals and hot ashes under the Almadel, and 3 grains of mastic to perfume as aforesaid, and when the Angels smell it, he turns his face towards you, asking the Exorcist in a low voice why he has called the Princes of this Chora, then you must answer as before, I desire that my requests may be granted and the contents thereof satisfied, for your office

---

82. *Alphariza* in Sl. 3825.
83. *Gereinon* in Sl. 3825.

maketh it appear and declareth that such is done by you, if it please God, and you must not be fearful, but speak humbly, saying, I recommend myself wholly to your office, and I pray unto you Princes of this altitude, that I may enjoy and obtain all things according to my wish and desires; and you may further express your mind in all particulars in your prayer and do the like in the other two Choras following.

The angels of the second Chora appear in the form of a young child with clothes of a satin or red rose colour, having a crown of red gilly flowers on his head, his face looks upwards towards heaven, and is of a red colour and is compassed about with a bright splendour, as of the beams of the Sun, and before he departs he speaks unto the Exorcist saying, I am your friend and brother, and illuminates the air round about with his splendour, and leaves a pleasant smell which lasts a long time.

The 3rd Chora

In this Chora you must do the same as you were before directed in the other two; The Angels of this altitude are named Eliphaniasia,[84] Geloniros,[85] Gedomiros,[86] Saranava,[87] and Elomina,[88] they appear in the form of little children dressed in green and divers colours very beautiful to behold, and the Crown of the boys beset with white and green colours upon their head and they seem to look a little downwards with their face, and they speak as the others do, and leave a most sweet perfume behind them.

---

84. *Eliphamasai* in Sl. 3825.
85. *Gelomiros* in Sl. 3825.
86. *Gedobonai* in Sl. 3825.
87. *Saranana* in Sl. 3825.
88. *Elomnia* in Sl. 3825.

Ars Almadel

The 4th Chora

In this Chora you must do as before in the other, and the Angels of this Chora are called, Barachiel,[89] Gediel, Deliel and Captiel,[90] they come in the form of little men or boys with clothes of a black colour mixed with dark green, and in their hands they hold a bird, and their heads compassed round with bright shining and divers colours, they leave a sweet smell behind them, but differing from the others.

Invocation

O thou blessed Glorious Angel of God N_ who rulest and is the chief governing Angel in this Chora, I, the servant of he highest, the same your God, Adonai, Elohim,[91] Pine and I command you by him ye do obey, and who is the distributor and disposer of all things, both in Heaven, Earth and Hell, and do invocate, conjure and instruct you, that you forthwith appear in the virtue and power of the same God, Adonai Helomi Pine, and I do command you by him, ye do obey and is set over you as King, by the dreadful power of God, that you forthwith descend from your orders or place of abode, and come unto me, and show me thyself, plainly and visibly before me here on this Almadel, in thy own proper shape and glory, speaking with a voice intelligible and to my understanding, Oh thou great and powerful Angel N_ who art by the power of God destined to govern all animals, regions and places, and cause them and all creatures of God to increase and bring forth according to their signs and natures, I, the servant of the most High God whom ye obey do entreat and humbly beseech thee to come from your celestial mansion, and show unto me all things that I shall desire to know, so far as in your office you may or can, or are capable to perform if God permit.

Or Say:

O thou servant of mercy, I do humbly beseech and entreat thee in and by those Holy and blessed names of God, Adonai, Elohim, Pine, and I do also constrain you in and by this powerful name Anasbona[92] that you forthwith appear plainly or visibly in your own proper shape and form on this Almadel, that I may visibly see you and audibly hear you speak, that I may have your blessed and glorious Angelical assistance,

89. *Barchiel* in Sl. 3825.
90. Absent here, yet found in Sl. 3825, is *Gabiel*.
91. *Helomi* in Sl. 3825.
92. *Anabona* in Sl. 3825.

familiar friendship, constant society, community and instruction, both now and at all other times, to inform and rightly instruct me in my depraved and ignorant intellect, judgement and understanding and to assist both therein, and in all other truths, also the Almighty Adonay, the King of Kings, and giver of all good gifts, that his bountiful and fatherly mercy may be graciously pleased to bestow upon me, therefore Blessed Angel be friendly unto me, so far as God shall give you power and presence to appear, that I may sing with his holy Angels, A mappa la man, Hallelujah, Amen.

When he appears give him or them a kind entertainment, then ask what is just and lawful, and that which is proper and suitable to his office and thou shalt obtain it.

So Endeth the Art Almadel

ARS NOTORIA

The Notory Art of Solomon

Shewing the
CABALISTICAL KEY

Of:
Magical Operations
The Liberal Sciences
Divine Revelation
&
The Art of Memory

Written originally in Latine,
and now Englished by Robert Turner

1657

Ars Notoria

The Epistle Dedicatory

*To his Ingenious and respected friend Mr. William Ryves,
of St. Saviours Southwark, Student in Physick and Astrology*

SIR.

The deep inspection and dove-like piercing Eye of your apprehension into the deepest Cabinets of Natures Arcana's, allures me (if I had no other attractive Magnetick engagements,) to set this Optick before your sight: not that it will make any addition to your knowledge; but by the fortitude of your judgment, be walled against the art-condemning and virtue-despising Calumniators. I know the candor of your Ingenuity will plead my excuse, and save me from that labour; resting to be

your real affectionate Friend,

ROBERT TURNER.

Little Brittain, die ♀. ☉ in ♎. 6.49.1656.

Lemegeton Clavicula Salomonis

To the Ingenious Readers

*A*mongst the rest of the labours of my long Winter hours, be pleased to accept of this as a flower of the Sun; which I have transplanted from the copious Roman banks into the English soyle; where I hope it will fruitfully spread its branches, and prove not a perishing gourd, but a continual green Laurel, which Authors say is the plant of the good Angel, and defends all persons neer its shade from the Penetrating blasts of Thunder and Lightening; so will this be a flower fit for every man's Garden; its virtues will soon be known, if practised, and the blasts of vice dispersed: its subject is too sublime to be exprest. Let not the carping Momi, nor envious black-jaw'd Zoili rayl; let not the ignorant bark at that which they know not; here they learn no such lesson: and against their Calumnies, the book I thus vindicate: quod potest per fidem intelligi, & non aliter, & per fidem in eo operare potes. Διὰ πίστεως κατήγω. ἴσαντο βασιλείας, εἰργάσαντο δικαιοσύνην, ἐπέτυχον ἐπαγγελιῶν, ἔφραξαν στόματα λεόντων. Ἔσβεσαν δύναμιν πυρός, &c. &c. Heb. 11. &c. *and my own intention I thus demonstrate;* Dico coram omnipotenti Deo, & coram *Jesu Christo* unigento Filio ejus, qui judicaturus est vivos & mortuous; quod omnia & singula quæ in hoc opere dixi, omnesque hujus Scientiæ vel artis proprietates, & universa quæ ad ejus speculationem pertinent, vel in hoc Volumine continenter, veris & naturalibus principiis innituntur, fuintque cum Deo & bona Conscientia, sine injuria Christianæ fidei, cum integritate; sine superstitione vel Idololatria quacunque, & non dedeceant virum sapientem Christianum bonum atque fidelem; Nam & *ego Christianus* sum, baptizatus in nomine Patris, &c. quam fidem cum Dei auxilio quam diu vixero firmiter inviolatam tenebo; Procul ergo absit a me, discere aut scribere aliquid Christianæ fidei & puritati contrarium, sanctis moribus noxium, aut quomodolibet adversum. Deum timeo & in ejus cultum Juravi, a quo nec vivus nec (ut confido) mortuus separabor: *This small treatise I therefore commend to all the lovers of art and learning, in which I hope they will attain their desires, quantum a Deo concessi erit; so that I hope I have not cast a Pearle before the swine, but set a glasse before the grateful doves.*

12 March 1656.

ROBERT TURNER.

Ars Notoria

The Notory Art of Solomon

*The Notory Art
revealed by the Most High Creator to Solomon*

In the Name of the holy and undivided Trinity, beginneth this most holy Art of Knowledge, Revealed to SOLOMON, which the Most High Creator by his holy Angel ministred to SOLOMON upon the Altar of the Temple; that thereby in a short time he knew all Arts and Sciences, both Liberal and Mechanick, with all the Faculties and Properties thereof: He had suddenly infused into him, and also was filled with all wisdom, to utter the sacred mysteries of most holy words.

Alpha and Omega! Oh Almighty God, the beginning of all things, without beginning, and without end: Graciously this day hear my prayers; neither do thou render unto me according to my sins, nor after mine iniquities, O Lord my God, but according to thy mercy, which is greater then all things visible and invisible. Have mercy upon me, O Christ, the Wisdom of the Father, the Light of Angels, the Glory of Saints, the Hope, Refuge, and Support of Sinners, the Creator of all things, the Redeemer of all humane Frailties, who holdest the Heaven, Earth, and Sea, and all the whole World, in the palm of thy Hand: I humbly implore and beseech, That thow wilt mercifully with the Father, illustrate my Minde with the beams of thy holy Spirit, that I may be able to come and attain to the perfection of this most holy Art, and that I may be able to gain the knowledge of every Science, Art, and Wisdom; and of every Faculty of Memory, Intelligences, Understanding, and Intellect, by the Vertue and Power of thy most holy Spirit, and in thy Name. And thou, O God my God, who in the beginning hast created the Heaven and the Earth, and all things out of nothing; who reformest, and makest all things by thy own Spirit; compleat, fulfil, restore, and implant a sound Understanding in me, that I may glorifie thee and all thy Works, in all my Thoughts, Words, and Deeds. O God the Father, confirm and grant this my Prayer, and increase my Understanding and Memory, and strengthen the same, to know and receive the Science, Memory, Eloquence, and Perseverance in all manner of Learning, who livest and reignest World without end. *Amen.*

Here beginneth the first Treatise of this Art
~ which Master Apollonius calleth, The golden Flowers, being the generall Introduction to all Natural Sciences; and this is Confirmed, Composed, and Approved by the Authority of Solomon, Manichæus, and Euduchæus

I *Apollonius* Master of Arts, duly called, to whom the Nature of Liberal Arts hath been granted, am intended to treat of the Knowledge of Liberal Arts, and of the Knowledge of Astronomy; and with what Experiments and Documents, a Compendious and Competent Knowledge of Arts may be attained unto; and how the highest and lowest Mysteries of Nature may be competently divided, and fitted and applied to the Natures of Times; and what proper dayes and hours are to be elected for the Deeds and Actions of men, to be begun and ended; what Qualifications a man ought to have, to attain the Efficacy of this Art; and how he ought to dispose of the actions of his life, and to behold and study the Course of the Moon. In the first place therefore, we shall declare certain precepts of the Spiritual Sciences; that all things which we intend to speak of, may be attained to in order. Wonder not therefore, at what you shall hear and see in this subsequent Treatise, and that you shall finde an Example of such inestimable Learning.

Some things which follow, which we will deliver to thee as Essayes of wonderful Effects, and have extracted them out of the most ancient Books of the Hebrews; which, where thou seest them, (although they are forgotten, and worn out of any humane Language) nevertheless esteem them as Miracles: For I do truly admire the great Power and Efficacy of Words in the Works of Nature.

Of what Efficacy Words are

There is so great Vertue, Power and Efficacy in certain Names and Words of God, that when you reade those very Words, it shall immediately increase and help your Eloquence, so that you shall be made eloquent of speech by them, and at length attain to the Effects of the powerful Sacred Names of God: but from whence the power hereof doth proceed, shall be fully demonstrated to you in the following Chapters of Prayers: and those which follow next to our hand, we shall lay open.

An Explanation of the Notary Art

This art is divided into two parts: The first containeth general Rules, the second special Rules. We come first to the special Rules; that is, First, to a threefold, and then to a fourfold Division: And in the third place we come to speak of Theology; which Sciences thou shalt attain to, by the Operation of these Orations, if thou pronounce them as it is written: Therefore there are certain Notes of the Notary Art, which are manifest to us; the Vertue whereof Human Reason cannot comprehend. The first Note hath his signification taken from the Hebrew; which though the expression thereof be comprehended in a very few words; nevertheless, in the expression of the Mystery, they do not lose their Vertue: That may be called their Vertue, which doth happen and proceed from their pronunciation, which ought to be greatly admired at.

The First Precept

Hely Scemath, Amazaz, Hemel; Sathusteon, hheli Tamazam, etc. which *Solomon* entituled, *His first Revelation*; and that to be without any Interpretation: It being a Science of so Transcendent a purity, that it hath its Original out of the depth and profundity of the *Chaldee, Hebrew*, and *Grecian* Languages; and therefore cannot possible by any means be explicated fully in the poor Thread-bare Scheme of our Language. And of what nature the Efficacy of the aforesaid words are, *Solomon* himself doth describe in his Eleventh Book, *Helisoe*, of the Mighty Glory of the Creator: but the Friend and Successor of *Solomon*, that is, *Apollonius*, with some few others, to whom that Science hath been manifested, have explained the same, and defined it to be most Holy, Divine, Deep, and Profound Mysteries; and not to be disclosed nor pronounced, without great Faith and Reverence.

A Spiritual Mandate of the Precedent Oration

Before any one begin to reade or pronounce any Orations of this Art, to bring them to effect, let them always first reverently and devoutly rehearse this Prayer in the beginning.

If any one will search the Scriptures, or would understand, or eloquently pronounce any part of Scripture, let him pronounce the words of the following Figure, to wit, *Hely scemath*, in the morning betimes of that day, wherein thou wilt begin any work. And in the Name of the Lord our God, let him diligently pronounce the Scripture proposed, with this Prayer which follows, which is, *Theos Megale*; And is mystically distorted, and miraculously and properly framed out of the *Hebrew, Greek*, and *Chaldean* Tongues: and it extendeth itself briefly into every Language, in what beginning soever they are declared. The second part of the Oration of the second Chapter, is taken out of the *Hebrew, Greek*, and *Chaldee*; and the following Exposition thereof, ought to be pronounced first, which is a Latine Oration: The third Oration of the three Chapters, always in the beginning of every Faculty, is first to be rehearsed.

The Oration is, *Theos Megale, in tu ymas Eurel,* etc.

This sheweth, how the foregoing Prayer is expounded: But although this is a particular and brief Exposition of this Oration; yet do not think, that all words are thus expounded.

The Exposition of this Oration

Oh God, the Light of the World, Father of Immense Eternity, Giver of all Wisdom and Knowledge, and of all Spiritual Grace; most Holy and Inestimable Dispenser, knowing all things before they are made; who makest Light and Darkness: Stretch forth thy Hand, and touch my Mouth, and make my Tongue as a sharp sword; to shew forth these words with Eloquence; Make my Tongue as an Arrow elected to declare thy Wonders, and to pronounce them memorably: Send forth thy holy Spirit, O Lord, into my Heart and Soul, to understand and retain them, and to meditate on them in my Conscience: By the Oath of thy Heart, that is, By the Right-hand of thy holy Knowledge, and mercifully inspire thy Grace into me; Teach and instruct me; Establish the coming in and going out of my Senses, and let thy Precepts teach and correct me until the end; and let the Councel of the most High assist me, through thy infinite Wisdom and Mercy. Amen.

The Words of these Orations Cannot be Wholly Expounded

Neither think, that all words of the preceding Oration can be translated into the Latin Tongue: For some words of that Oration contain in themselves a greater Sense of Mystical Profundity, of the Authority of *Solomon*; and having reference to his Writings, we acknowledge, That these Orations cannot be expounded nor understood by humane sense: For it is necessary, That all Orations, and distinct particulars of Astronomy, Astrology, and the Notary Art, be spoken and pronounced in their due time and season; and the Operations of them to be made according to the disposition of the Times.

Of the Triumphal Figures

How sparingly they are to be pronounced, and honestly and devoutly spoken

There are also certain Figures or Orations, which *Solomon* in *Chaldeack*, calleth *Hely*; that is, Triumphal Orations of the Liberal Arts, and sudden excellent Efficacies of Vertues; and they are the Introduction to the Notary Art. Wherefore *Solomon* made a special beginning of them, that they are to be pronounced at certain determinate times of the Moon; and not to be undertaken, without consideration of the end. Which also *Magister Apollonius* hath fully and perfectly taught, saying, Whosoever will pronounce these words let him do it in a determinate appointed time, and set aside all other occasions, and he shall profit in all Sciences in one Moneth, and attain to them in an extraordinary wonderful manner.

The Expositions of the Lunations of the Notary Art

These are the Expositions of the Lunation, and Introduction of the Notary Art, to wit, in the fourth and the eighth day of the Moon; and in the twelfth, sixteenth, four and twentieth, eight and twentieth, and thirtieth they ought to be put in operation. From whence *Solomon* saith, That to those times, we give the expositive times of the Moon; of the fourth day of the Moon which are written by the four Angels; and in the fourth day of the Moon is manifested to us; and are four times repeated and explained by the Angel, the Messenger of these Orations; and are also revealed and delivered to us that require them from the Angel, four times of the year, to shew the Eloquence and Fulness of the four Languages, *Greek*, *Hebrew*, *Chaldee* and *Latine*; and God hath determined the Power of the Faculties of Humane Understanding, to the four Parts of the Earth; and also the four Vertues of Humanities, Understanding, Memory, Eloquence, and the Faculty of Ruling those three. And these things are to be used as we have before spoken.

He Sheweth how the Precedent Oration
~ is the Beginning and Foundation of the whole Art

That is the first Figure of the Notary Art, which is manifestly sited upon a Quadrangle Note: And this is Angelical Wisdom, understood of few in Astronomy; but in the Glass of Astrology, it is called, The Ring of Philosophy; and in the Notary Art it is written, To be the Foundation of the whole Science. But it is to be rehearsed four times a day, beginning in the morning once, about the third hour once, once in the ninth hour, and once in the evening.

The precedent Oration ought to be spoken secretly; and let him that speaks it be alone, and pronounce it with a low voyce, so that he scarcely hear himself. And this is the condition hereof, that if necessity urge one to do any great works, he shall say it twice in the morning, and about the ninth hour twice; and let him fast the first day wherein he rehearseth it, and let him live chastly and devoutly. And this is the oration which he shall say:

This is the Oration of the four Tongues, *Chaldee*, *Greek*, *Hebrew* and *Latine*, evidently expounded, which is called, "the Splendor or *Speculum* of Wisdom." In all holy Lunations, these Orations ought to be read, once in the morning, once about the third hour, once about the ninth hour, and once in the evening.

Lemegeton Clavicula Salomonis

The Oration

Assaylemath, Assay, Lemeth, Azzabue.

The second part of the precedent Orations
~ which is to be said onely once

AZzaylemath, Lemath, Azacgessenio.

The third part of the precedent Oration
~ which is to be spoken together with the other

Lemath, Sebanche, Ellithy, Aygezo.

This Oration hath no Exposition in the Latine

This is a holy Prayer, without danger of any sin, which *Solomon* saith, is inexplicable be humane sense. And he addeth, and saith, That the Explication thereof is more prolixious, than can be considered of or apprehended by man; excepting also those secrets, which is not lawful, neither is it given to man to utter: Therefore he leaveth this Oration without any Exposition, because no man could attain to the perfection thereof: and it was left so Spiritual, because the Angel that declared it to *Solomon*, laid an inexcusable prohibition upon it, saying, See that thou do not presume to give to any other, nor to expound any thing out of this Oration, neither thou thy self, nor any one by thee, nor any one after thee: For it is a holy and Sacramental Mystery, that by expressing the words thereof, God heareth thy Prayer, and increaseth thy Memory, Understanding, Eloquence, and establisheth them all in thee. Let it be read in appointed times of the Lunation; as, in the fourth day of the Moon, the eighth and twelfth, as it is written and commanded: say that Oration very diligently four times in those dayes; verily believing, That thereby thy study shall suddenly be increased, and made clear, without any ambiguity, beyond the apprehension of humane Reason.

Of the Efficacy of that Oration
~ which is inexplicable to humane sense

This is that onely which *Solomon* calls The happiness of Wit, and M. *Apollonius* termeth it, The Light of the Soul, and the *Speculum* of Wisdom: And, I suppose, the said Oration may be called, The Image of Eternal Life: the Vertue and Efficacy whereof is so great, that it is understood or apprehended of very few or none.

Therefore having essayed some Petitions, Signs and Precepts, we give them as an entrance to those things whereof we intend to speak; of which they are part, that we have spoken of before. Nevertheless, before we come to speak of them, some things are necessary to be declared, whereby we may more clearly and plainly set forth our intended History: For, as we have said before, there are certain Exceptions of the Notary Art; some whereof are dark and obscure, and others plain and manifest.

For the Notary Art hath a Book in Astronomy, whereof it is the Beginning and mistris; and the Vertue thereof is such, that all Arts are taught and derived from her. And we are further to know, That the Notary Art doth in a wonderful manner contain and comprehend within it self, all Arts, and the Knowledge of all Learning, as *Solomon* witnesseth: Therefore it is called, *The Notary Art*, because in certain brief Notes, it teacheth and comprehendeth the knowledge of all Arts: for so *Solomon* also saith in his Treatise *Lemegeton*, that is, in his Treatise of Spiritual and Secret Experiments.

Here he sheweth, in what manner those Notes differ in Art
*~ and the reason thereof; for a Note is a certain knowledge
by the Oration and Figure before set down*

But of the Orations and Figures, mention shall be made in their due place, and how the Notes are called in the Notary Art. Now he maketh mention of that Oration, which is called, The Queen of Tongues: for amongst these Orations, there is one more excellent than the rest, which King *Solomon* would therefore have be called, The Queen of Tongues, because it takes away, as it were, with a certain Secret covering the Impediments of the Tongue, and giveth it a marvellous Faculty of Eloquence. Wherefore before we proceed further, take a little Essay of that Oration: For this is an Oration which in the Scriptures we are taught to have alwayes in our mouthes; but it is taken out of the *Chaldean* Language: which, although it be short, is of a wonderful Vertue; that when you reade that Scripture, with the Oration before-mentioned, you cannot keep silent those things, which the Tongue and Understanding suggest, and administer to thee.

The Oration which follows, is a certain Invocation of the Angels of God, and it provoketh Eloquence, and ought to be said in the beginning of the Scripture, and in the beginning of the Moneth.

The Oration

Lameth, Leynach, Semach, Belmay, (these Orations have not proper Lunations, as the Commentator saith upon the Gloss, *Azzailement, Gesegon, Lothamasim, Ozetogomaglial, Zeziphier, Josanum, Solatar, Bozefama, Defarciamar, Zemait, Lemaio, Pheralon, Anuc, Philosophi, Gregoon, Letos, Anum, Anum, Anum.*)

How this Oration is to be Said
~ in the beginning of every Moneth, chastly, and with a pure minde

In the beginning of the Scriptures, are to be taught, how the precedent Oration ought to be spoken most secretly, and nothing ought to be retained, which thy Minde and Understanding suggests and prompts to thee in the reading thereof: Then also follow certain words, which are Precepts thereof, which ought alwayes to be begun in the beginning of the Moneth, and also in other dayes. I would also note this, That it is to be pronounced wisely, and with the greatest reverence; and that fasting, before you have taken either Meat or Drink.

Here followeth the Prayer we Spake of Before
~ to Obtain a Good Memory

O Most Mighty God, Invisible God, *Theos Patir Heminas;* by thy Archangels, *Eliphamasay, Gelonuoa, Gebeche Banai, Gerabcai, Elomnit;* and by thy glorious Angels, whose Names are so Consecrated, that they cannot be uttered by us; which are these, *Do. Hel. X. P. A. Li. O. F.* etc. which cannot be Comprehended by Humane Sense.

Here following is the Prologue of the precedent Oration
~ Which provoketh and procureth Memory & is continued with the precedent Note

This Oration ought to be said next to the precedent Oration; to wit, *Lameth*: and with this, I beseech thee to day, *O Theos*, to be said always as one continued Oration. If it be for the Memory, let it be said in the morning; if for any other effect, in the evening. And thus let it be said in the hour of the evening, and in the morning: And being thus pronounced, with the precedent Oration, it increaseth the Memory, and helpeth the Imperfections of the Tongue.

Here beginneth the Prologue of this Oration

I Beseech thee, O my Lord, to illuminate the Light of my Conscience with the Splendor of thy Light: Illustrate and confirm my Understanding, with the sweet odour of thy Spirit. Adorn my Soul, that hearing I may hear and what I hear, I may retain in my Memory. O Lord, reform my heart, restore my senses, and strengthen them; qualifie my Memory with thy Gifts: Mercifully open the dulness of my Soul. O most merciful God, temper the frame of my Tongue, by thy most glorious and unspeakable Name: Thou who are the Fountain of all Goodness; the Original and Spring of Piety, have patience with me, give a good Memory unto me, and bestow upon me what I pray of thee in this holy Oration. O thou who dost not forthwith Judge a sinner, but mercifully waitest, expecting his Repentance; I (though unworthy) beseech thee to take away the guilt of my sins, and wash away my wickedness and offences, and grant me these my Petitions, by the verture of thy holy Angels, thou who art one God in Trinity. Amen.

Here he sheweth some other Vertue of the precedent Oration

If thou doubt of any great Vsion, what it may foreshew; or if thou wouldst see any great Vsion, of any danger present or to come; or if thou wouldst be certified of any one that is absent, say this Oration three times in the evening with great reverence and devotion, and thou shalt have and see that which thou desirest.

Here followeth an Oration of great Vertue
~ to attain the knowledge of the Physical Art
having also many other Vertues and Efficacy

If you would have the perfect knowledge of any Disease, whether the same tend to death or life: if the sick party lie languishing, stand before him, and say this Oration three times with great reverence.

The Oration of the Physical Art

IHesus fili Dominus Incomprehensibilis: Ancor, Anacor, Anylos, Zohorna, Theodonos, hely otes Phagor, Norizane, Corichito, Anosae, Helse Tonope, Phagora.

Another part of the same Oration

Elleminator, Candones helosi, Tephagain, Tecendum, Thaones, Behelos, Belhoros, Hocho Phagan, Corphandonos, Humanæ natus and vos Eloytus Phugora: Be present ye holy Angels, advertise and teach me, whether such a one shall recover, or dye of this Infirmity.

This being done, then ask the sick person, Friend, how dost thou feel thy self? And if he answer thee. I feel my self at good ease, I begin to mend, or the like; then judge without doubt, The sick person shall recover: but if he answer, I am very grievously ill, or worse and worse; then doubtless conclude, He will dye on the morrow: But if he answer, I know not how my state and condition is, whether better or worse; then you may know likewise, That he will either dye, or his disease will change and alter for the worse. If it be a Childe, that is not of years capable to make an answer; or that the sick languish so grievously, that he knoweth not how, or will not answer, say this Oration three times; and what you finde first revealed in your minde, that judge to come to pass of him.

Furthermore if any one dissemble and seek to hide or cover his infirmity; say the same Oration, and the Angelical Vertue shall suggest the truth to thee. If the diseased person be farre off; when you hear his Name, say likewise this Oration for him, and your minde shall reveal to you whether he shall live or dye.

If you touch the Pulse of any one that is sick, saying this Oration, the effect of his Infirmity shall be revealed to you.

Or if you touch the Pulse of any Woman with Childe, saying the same Oration, it shall be revealed, whether she shall bring forth a Male or Female. But know, that this Miracle proceeds not from your own Nature, but from the Nature and Vertue of the holy Angels; it being a part of their Office, wonderfully to reveal these things to you. If you doubt of the Virginity of any one, say this Oration in your minde, and it shall be revealed to you, whether she be a Virgin, or Corrupt.

Here follows an efficacious Preface of an Oration
~ shewing what Verture and Efficacy you may thereby prove every day

Of this Oration *Solomon* saith, That by it a new knowledge of Physick is to be received from God: Upon which, he hath laid this command, and calleth it, The Miraculous and Efficacious Foundation of the Physical Science; and that it containeth in it the quantity and quality of the whole Physical Art and Science: wherein there is contained, rather a miraculous and specious, then fearful or terrible Miracle, which as often-soever as thou readest the same, regard not the paucity of words, but praise the Vertue of so great a Mystery: For, *Solomon* himself speaking of the subtility of the Notory Art, wonderfully extolls the Divine Help; to wit, Because we have proposed a great thing, that is to say so many and so great Mysteries of Nature, contained under so specious brevity, that I suppose them to be as a general Problem to be proposed in the ordination of so subtile and excellent a work; that the minde of the Reader or Hearer may be the more confirmed and fixed hereupon.

Here he sheweth how every Note of every Art
~ ought to exercise his own office; and that the Notes of one Art profit not to the knowledge of another Art; and we are to know, that all Figures have their proper Orations

We come now, according to our strength, to divide the families of the Notory Art; and leaving that part which is natural, we come to the greater parts of the Art: for *Solomon*, a great Composer, and the greatest Master of the Notory Art, comprehendeth divers Arts under the Notion thereof. Therefore he calleth this a Notory Art, because it should be the Art of Arts, and Science of Sciences; which comprehendeth in it self all Arts and Sciences, Liberal and Mechanick: And those things which in other Arts are full of long and tedious locutions, filling up great prolixious Volumes of Books, wearying out the Student, through the length of time to attain to them: In this Art are comprehended very briefly in a few words or writings, so that it discovereth those things which are hard and difficult, making the ingenious learned in a very short time, by the wonderful and unheard-of Vertue of the words.

Therefore we, to whom such a faculty of the knowledge of the Scripture of Sciences is granted, have wholly received this great gift, and inestimable benefit, from the overflowing grace of the most high Creator. And whereas all Arts have their several Notes properly disposed to them, and signified by their Figures; and the Note of every Art, hath not any office of transcending to another Art, neither do the Notes of one Art profit or assist to the knowledge of another Art: Therefore this may seem a little difficult, as this small Treatise, which may be called a *Preludium* to the Body of the Art: we will explain the Notes severally; and that which is more necessary, we shall by the Divine Providence diligently search out the several Sciences of the Scripture.

A Certain Special Precept

This is necessary for us, and necessarily we suppose will be profitable to posterity, that we know how to comprehend the great prolixious Volumes of writings, in brief and compendious Treatises; which, that it may easily be done, we are diligently to enquire out the way of attaining to it, out of the three most ancient Books which were composed by *Solomon*; the first and chiefest thing to be understood therein, is, That the Oration before the second Chapter, is to be used long before every speech, the beginning whereof is *Assay*: and the words of the Oration are to be said in a competent space of time; but the subsequent part of the Oration is then chiefly to be said, when you desire the knowledge of the Volumes of writings, and looking into the Notes thereof. The same Oration is also to be said, when you would clearly and plainly understand and expound any Science or great Mystery, that is on a sudden proposed to you, which you never heard of before: say also the same Oration at such time, when any thing of great consequence is importuned of you, which at present you have not the faculty of expounding. This is a wonderful Oration, whereof we have spoken; the first part whereof is expounded in the Volume of the Magnitude of the quality of Art.

The Oration

Amed, Rogum, Ragia, Ragium, Ragiomal, Agaled, Eradioch, Anchovionos, Lochen, Saza, Ya, Manichel, Mamacuo, Lephoa, Bozaco, Cogemal, Salayel, Ytsunanu, Azaroch, Beyestar, Amak.

To the operation of the Magnitude of Art, this Oration containeth in the second place, a general Treatise of the first Note of all Scripture, part of the Exposition whereof, we have fully explained in the Magnitude of the quality of the same Art. But the Reader hath hardly heard of the admirable Mystery of the Sacramental Intellect of the same: Let him know this for a certain, and doubt not of the Greek words of the Oration aforesaid, but that the beginning of them is expounded in Latine.

The Beginning of the Oration

Oh Eternal and Unreprehensible Memory! Oh Uncontradictible Wisdom! Oh Unchangeable Power! Let thy right-hand encompass my heart, and the holy Angels of thy Eternal Counsel; compleat and fill up my Conscience with thy Memory, and the odour of thy Ointments; and let the sweetness of thy Grace strengthen and fortifie my Understanding, through the pure splendor and brightness of thy holy Spirit; by vertue whereof, the holy Angels always behold and admire the brightness of thy face, and all thy holy and heavenly Vertues; Wisdom, wherewith thou hast made all things; Understanding, by which thou hast reformed all things; Perseverance unto blessedness, whereby thou hast restored and confirmed the Angels; Love, whereby thou hast restored lost Mankinde, and raised him after his Fall to Heaven; Learning, whereby thou wer't pleased to teach Adam the knowledge of every Science: Inform, repleat, instruct, restore, correct, and refine me, that I may be made new in the understanding thy Precepts, and in receiving the Sciences which are profitable for my Soul and Body, and for all faithful believers in thy Name which is blessed for ever, world without end.

Here is also a particular Exposition of the fore-going Oration

~ which he hath left unexpounded, to be read by every one that is learned in this Art; and know, that no humane power nor faculty in man is sufficient to finde out the Exposition thereof

This Oration is also called by *Solomon*, The Gemme and Crown of the Lord: for he saith, It helpeth against danger of Fire, or of wilde Beasts of the Earth, being said with a believing faith: for it is affirmed to have been reported from one of the four Angels, to whom was given power to hurt the Earth, the Sea, and the Trees. There is an example of this Oration, in the Book called, *The Flower of heavenly Learning*; for herein *Solomon* glorifieth God, because by this he inspired into him the knowledge of Theologie, and dignified him with the Divine Mysteries of his Omnipotent Power and Greatness: which *Solomon* beholding in his night-Sacrifice, bestowed upon him by the Lord his God, he conveniently gathered the greater Mysteries together in this Notory Art, which were holy, and worthy, and reverend Mysteries. These things and Mysteries of Theologie the erring Gentiles have not all lost, which *Solomon* calleth, The Signe of the holy Mystery of God revealed by his Angel before; and that which is contained in them, is the fulness of our dignity and humane Salvation.

The first of these Orations which we call Spiritual
~ the vertue whereof teacheth Divinity, and preserveth the memory thereof

These are Orations also, which are of great virtue and efficacy to our Salvation: The first whereof is Spiritual, and teacheth Divinity; and also Perseverance in the Memory thereof: Therefore *Solomon* commandeth it to be called, The Signe of the Grace of God: for, as *Ecclesiastes* saith, *This is the Spiritual Grace of God, that hath given me knowledge to treat of all Plants, from the Cedar of Lebanon, to the Hyssop that groweth on the wall.*

The Election of Time
~ in what Lunation these Orations ought to be said

The first Oration ought to be said once in the first Lunation; in the third, three times; in the sixth, six times; in the ninth, nine times; in the twelfth. twelve times; in the seventeenth, seventeen times; and in the eighteenth, as many times; in the twenty sixth, as many; in the twenty ninth, as many; and so many in the thirty ninth: for this Oration is of so great vertue and efficacy, that in the very day thou shalt say the same, as if it were determined by the Father, it shall increase thy knowledge in the Science of Divinity.

But if otherwise that thou art ignorant, and it hath been seen by thy Companions, thy Superiours or Inferiours, though unto others thou shalt seem to have knowledge; enter into the study of Divinity, and hear the Lectures by the space of some moneths, casting off all doubt from thee, of them who shall see thee, to know such things: and in that day wherein thou wouldst say it, live chastly, and say it in the Morning.

Solomon testifieth, That an Angel delivered the following Oration in Thunder, who standeth always in the Presence of the Lord, to whom he is not dreadful. The Mystery hereof is holy, and of great efficacy: neither ought this Oration to be said above once, because it moveth the heavenly Spirits to perform any great work.

Of this Oration he saith, That so great is the Mystery thereof, that it moveth the Celestial Spirits to perform any great work which the Divine Power permitteth. It also giveth the vertue of its Mystery, that it exalteth the tongue and body of him that speaketh it, with so great inspiration, as if some new and great Mystery were suddenly revealed to his understanding.

Here followeth the beginning of this Oration
~ wherein is so great vertue and efficacy, as we have said
it being said with great devotion

Achacham, Yhel, Chelychem, Agzyraztor, Yegor, etc.

This is the beginning of the Oration, the parts whereof are four: But there is something to be said of the beginning by itself, and of the four parts severally; and then between the beginning and these Orations, which are four, we shall make this competent division.

For this is that which is to be spoken of the beginning severally: And this Oration is to be divided into four parts; and the first part thereof is to be said, that is, the beginning, before any other part of the Oration is to be compleated. These Greek Names following are to be pronounced. This is the division of these Orations, *Hielma, Helma, Hemna*, etc. Oh God the Father, God the Son, God the Holy Spirit, Confirm this Oration, and my Understanding and Memory, to receive, understand, and retain the knowledge of all good Scriptures; and give me perseverance of minde therein.

This is the beginning of that Oration, which, as we have said before, ought to be said according to the Prolations and Constitutions thereof; and ought to be repeated, because of the forgetfulness of our Memory, and according to the exercise of our wit, and according to the sanctity of our life; there being contained in it so great a Mystery, and such efficacious Vertue.

There followeth another subtile Oration, wherein is contained a Sacramental Mystery, and wherein every perfect Science is wonderfully compleated: For hereby God would have us to know, what things are Celestial, and what are Terrene; and what heavenly things the Celestial effecteth, and what earthly things things the Terrene: because the Lord hath said, My eyes have seen the imperfect, and in thy book every day shall be formed and written, and no man in them, *etc.* So it is in the Precepts of God: for we are not able to write all things, how the Sun hath the same course as at first, that our order may be confirmed: for all writing whatsoever, which is not from God, is not to be read; for God himself would have all things to be divided: and this is how these are to be used, before the second part, which containeth so glorious and excellent Consecrations of Orations, and defineth the Consecrated part to have power in the Heavens, and in no wise can be defined by humane tongues.

This is the Beginning of the second part of that Oration

~ spoken of before, which is of so great vertue
Aglaros, Theomiros, Thomitos, etc.

This is the second part of the precedent Oration, of which some singular thing is to be spoken. Wherefore if thou sayest this Oration, commemorating the first part thereof, say the Oration following, and thou shalt perceive the precepts which are therein.

Ars Notoria

Oh God of all things, who art my God, who in the beginning hast created all things out of nothing, and hast reformed all things by the Holy Spirit; compleat and restore my conscience, and heal my understanding, that I may glorify thee in all my works, thoughts and words.

And after thou hast said this Oration, make a little respite the space of half an hour, and then say the third part of the Oration, which follows: *Megal, Legal, Chariotos,* etc. having said this third part of the Oration, then meditate with thy self about the Scriptures thou desirest to know; and then say this Oration:

Oh thou that art the Truth, Light, and Way, of all Creatures: Oh just God, vivify me, and confirm my understanding, and restore my knowledge and conscience unto me, as thou didst unto King Solomon, Amen.

Commemorating the parts according to that which is laid down, add the Oration following: the other Orations being said, say the fourth part of the Oration, which is this: *Amasiel, Danyi, hayr,* etc.

Then the Parts being Commemorated as is Directed
~ add also the following Oration

I speak these things in thy presence, Oh Lord my God, before whose face all things are naked and open, that I being washed from the error of infidelity, thy all-quicking Spirit may assist me, and take away all incredulity from me.

How the Latine Orations
~ are not expounded by the words of the Orations

We are therefore to know, that the whole Oration remaineth unexpounded; because the words thereof are of so great subtilty, adorned with the Hebrew and Chaldean Tongue, with the subtile and wonderful elocution of God: that the office of the free exposition thereof, cannot possibly be transferred upon me. The Latine words which are subjoyned to the parts of the Oration aforesaid, are such words as have been translated out of the Chaldean Tongue: for they are not the whole Oration; but as certain heads of every Oration pertaining thereunto.

Here he speaketh of the efficacy of all these

For this Oration is such a mystery, as King *Solomon* himself witnesseth, that a Servant of his House having found this book by chance, and being too much overcome with Wine in the Company of a Woman, he presumptuously read it; but before he had finished a part thereof, he was stricken dumb, blind and lame, and his Memory taken from him; so he continued to the day of his death: and in the hour of his death, he spoke and said, that four Angels which he had offended in presumptuous reading so sacred a mystery, were the daily keepers and afflicters, one of his Memory, another of his speech, a third of his sight, and the fourth of his hearing.

By which Testimony this Oration is so much commended by the same King *Solomon*, and great is the mystery thereof: we do greatly require and charge every one, that will say or read it, that he do it not presumptuously; for in presumption is sin; wherefore let this Oration be said, according as is directed.

We therefore hold it convenient and necessary, to speak something of the general precepts of art, and of the knowledge of all arts; and of the several precepts of every singular art: but because we have touched somthing of the course of the Moon, it is necessary that we shew what her course signifies. The Moon passeth through 12 signs in one Moneth; and the Sun through 12 signs in a year; and in the same term and time, the Spirit inspireth, fructifieth and illustrateth them; whence it is said, that the Sun and the Moon run their course: it is understood the course which first they had. But because this is wanting in the Hebrew, we thought good to omit it in the Latine, having spoken sufficiently of the preceding Oration, and the three parts thereof.

In this Chapter he sheweth the efficacy of the subsequent Oration
~ it being special to obtain Eloquence

This Holy Oration which followeth, is a certain special Oration, to obtain eloquence; whereas all others have virtue and efficacy in other things, this containeth this certain special mystery in it self: And whereas one of the generals is shewing in it self, certain general precepts, common to all arts for so God instituted the soul in the body, saying, This I give unto you, that ye may keep and observe the Law of the Lord; And these are they that stand in the presence of God always, and see their Saviour face to face night and day. So of this Oration, I say, This is that most glorious, mystical and intelligible Oration, containing such mysteries in it, which the mind, conscience and tongue succeedeth. This is such a mystery, that a man shall keep it according to his will, who foreseeth all things in his sight that are made; for the mystery of this Oration is glorious and sacramental: let no man presume to say any of this Oration after too much drinking or Luxury; nor fasting, without great reverence and discretion. Whence *Solomon* saith, Let no man presume to treat any thing of this Oration, but in certain determinate and appointed times, unless he make mention of this Oration before some great President, for some weighty business; for which this Oration is of wonderful excellent virtue.

The goodness of this Oration, and the attaining to the effects thereof, it is read in that Psalm wherein it is said, Follow me, and I will make you fishers of men, as he said and did.

We know that it is not of our power, that this Oration is of so great Virtue, and such a mystery, as sometimes also the Lord said to his disciples, This we are not able to know: for this Oration is such a mystery, that it containeth in it the great Name of God; which many have lyed in saying they knew it; for *Jesus* himself performed many Miracles in the Temple by it: But many have lyed about what he did, and have hid and absconded the truth thereof; so that none have declared the same before it came to passe: but we suppose have spoken somthing about or concerning it.

In this Chapter He Setteth Down the Time and Manner
~ how this Oration is to be Pronounced

For this Oration is one of the generals, and the first of particulars, containing both in it self; having a special virtue and faculty, to gain Eloquence in it self: therefore it is necessary to be understood what time, ordination, and what dayes it is to be said and published.

It may always be rehearsed in every 14 Lunary as above said; but the ordination of the time for every day, wherein it is to be said, is especially in the morning betimes, before a man is defiled; and then all Orations are chiefly to be said. And this Oration must be then pronounced totally together, without any division. And although there are divisions therein, the Oration is not divided in it self; but only the Divine and Glorious Names are written severally, and are divided into parts, according to the terminations of every great and Glorious Name; and it is to be said together as a most excellent Name, but not as one Word, because of the fragility of our nature; Neither is it needful to know the Elements of sillables, posited in this Oration; they are not to be known; neither let any one presumptuously speak them; neither let him do any thing by way of temptation, concerning this Oration, which ought not to be done: *Elmot, Sehel, Hemech, Zaba*, etc.

No Man that is Impedited or Corrupted with any Crime
~ ought to Presume to Say this Oration

This is a thing agreed unto amongst the wise men of this World, that these things, as we have said before, be pronounced with great reverence and industry: it may be said every day, wherein thou art not hindred by some criminal sin; and in that day wherein thou art impedited by some criminal sin, thou maist remember it in thy heart; and if thou dost desire to be made Eloquent, repeat it three times. And if any evil thing trouble thee, or thou art ermerged and involved into any great business, repeat this Oration once, and Eloquence shall be added to thee, as much as is needful; and if thou repeat it over twice, great Eloquence shall be given to thee: so great a Sacrament is this Oration.

The third thing to be considered in this Oration, is; This Oration ought so to be pronounced, that confession of the Heart and Mouth ought to precede it: let it be pronounced in the morning early, and after that Oration say the Latine Oration following.

This is a Prologue or Exposition of the Precedent Oration
~ which Ought to be Said Together

Oh omnipotent and eternal God, and merciful Father, blessed before all Worlds; who art a God eternal, incomprehensible, and unchangeable, and hast granted this blessed gift of Salvation unto us; according to the omnipotency of thy Majesty, hast granted unto us the faculty of speaking and learning, which thou hast denied to all other animals; and hast disposed of all things by thy infallible providence: thou art God, whose nature is eternal and consubstantial, exalted above the Heavens; in whom the whole Deity corporally dwells: I implore thy Majesty, and Glorify thy omnipotency, with an intentive imploration, adoring the mighty Virtue, Power and Magnificence of thy eternity. I beseech thee, Oh my God, to grant me the inestimable Wisdome of the Life of thy holy Angels. Oh God the Holy Spirit, incomprehensible, in whose presence stand the Holy quires of Angels; I pray and beseech thee, by thy Holy and Glorious Name, and by the sight of thy Angels, and the Heavenly Principalities, to give thy GRACE unto me, to be present with mee:, and give unto me power to persevere in the Memory of thy Wisdome, who livest and reignest eternally one eternal God, through all worlds of worlds; in whose sight are all celestial virtues, now and alwayes, and everywhere, Amen.

This Oration being thus finished, there must of necessity some Mystery be added; so that you are to be silent a while after the Latine Oration is ended: and after a little taciturnity, that is, a little space of silence, begin to say this Oration following seriously: *Semet, Lamen,* &c.

This (saith *Solomon*) is the Oration of Orations, and a special experiments, whereby all things, whether generals or particulars, are known fully, efficaciously and perfectly, and are kept in the Memory. But when thou hast by this Oration attained the Eloquence thou desirest, be sparing thereof, and do not rashly declare those things which thy Tongue suggests and administers to thee; for this is the end of all general precepts, which are given to obtain Memory, Eloquence, and understanding. All those things which are before delivered, of general precepts, are given as signs how the faculty of attaining to the understanding of the general precepts may be had, which also *Solomon* calleth Spirituals; and those singular arts have singular virtues and powers.

Ars Notoria

Having now given a sufficient definition of general precepts; and the Orations are laid down, and the Authority of the Orations unto what they are designed; it is now necessary to set down what is to be done, concerning the singular Orations; because we are now to treat of the several and particular arts, that we may follow the example which our builder and Master hath laid before us; for *Solomon* saith, before we proceed to the singular notes and Orations of arts before noted, there ought to be said a *Præudium*, which is a beginning or Prologue.

How Every Several Art Hath its Proper Note

Before we proceed to the singular precepts of several Arts, it is necessary to discover how every several Art hath a several Note.

Of the Liberal Sciences
~ and other things, which may be had by that Art

The liberal Arts are seaven, and seaven exceptives, and seaven Mechanicks. The seaven exceptives are comprehended under the seaven liberal: It is manifest what the seaven liberal Arts are, of which we shall first treat. The Mechanicks are these, which are adulteratedly called *Hydromancy*, *Pyromancy*, *Nigromancy*, *Chiromancy*, *Geomancy*, *Geonegia*, which is comprehended under *Astronomy*, and *Neogia*.

Hydromancy, is a science of divining by the Water; whereby the Masters thereof judged by the standing or running of the Water. *Pyromancy*, is an experiment of divining by the flaming of the fire; which the ancient Philosophers esteemed of great efficacy. *Nigromancy*, is a Sacrifice of dead Animals, whereby the Ancients supposed to know many great Experiments without sin, and to attain to great knowledge: from whence *Solomon* commandeth that they might read seaven Books of that Art without sin; and that two he accompted Sacriledge, and that they could nor: read two Books of that Art without sin. But having spoken enough hereof, we proceed to the rest.

Of the Liberal Sciences
~ and other things which may be had thereby

There are seaven liberal Arts, which every one may learn and read without sin. For Philosophy is great, containing profound Mysteries in it self: These Arts are wonderfully known.

He declareth what notes the three first liberal Arts have

For *Grammar* hath three notes only, *Dialects* two, and *Rhetorick* four, and every one with open and distinct Orations. But wherefore *Grammar* hath three, *Dialects* two, and *Rhetorick* four; that we know King *Solomon* himself testifieth and affirmeth; for he saith, And as I was admiring and revolving in my heart and mind, which way, from whom and from whence was this science, An Angel brought one book, wherein was written the Figures and Orations, and delivered unto me the Notes and Orations of all Arts, plainly and openly, and told me of them all as much as was necessary: And he explained unto me, as to a Child are taught by certain Elements, some tedious Arts in a great space of time, how that I should have these Arts in a short space of time: Saying unto me, So shalt thou be promoted to every science by the increase of these virtues. And when I asked him, Lord, whence and how cometh this? The Angel answered, This is a great Sacrament of the Lord, and of his will: this writing is by the power of the Holy Ghost, which inspireth, fructifieth and increaseth all knowledge; And again the Angel said, Look upon these Notes and Orations, at the appointed and determinate times, and observe the times as appointed of God, and no otherwise. When he had thus said he shewed to King *Solomon* a book wherein was written, at what times all these things were to be pronounced and published, and plainly demonstrated it according to the Vision of God: Which things I having heard and seen, did operate in them all, according to the Word of the Lord by the Angel: And so *Solomon* declareth,it came to passe unto him: But we that come after him, ought to imitate his Authority, and as much as we are able observe those things he hath left unto us.

Here Solomon Sheweth, how the Angel Told him Distinctly
~ *wherefore the Grammar hath three Figures*

Behold wherefore the Grammatical Art hath only three Notes in the Book of *Solomon Gemeliath*, that is, in The Book of the Art of God, which we read is the Art of all other sciences, and of all other Arts; For *Solomon* saith, When I did inquire every thing singularly of the Angel of God, with fear, saying, Lord, from whence shall this come to passe to me, that I mayfully and perfectly know this Art? Why do so many Notes appertain to such an Art, and so many to such an Art, and are ascribed to several determinate Orations, to have the efficacy thereof? The Angel is thus said to answer: The Grammatical Art is called a liberal Art, And hath three things necessary thereunto: Ordination of words and times; and in them, of Adjuncts or Figures; Simple, compound and various; and a various declination of the parts to the parts, or a relation from the parts, and a Congruent and ordinate division. This is the reason, why there is three Notes in the Art of *Grammar*. And so it pleased the Divine Wisdome, that as there should be a full knowledge of declining by one; by another, there should be had a convenient Ordination of all the parts; by the third, there should be had a continual and convenient Division of all the parts, simple and compound.

The Reason why the Dialectical Art hath two Figures Onely

Dialect, which is called the form of Arts, and a Doctrinal speech, hath two things necessary thereunto, to wit, Eloquence of Arguing, and Prudence to answer; Therefore the greatness of the Divine Providence and Piety, hath appointed two Notes to it; that by the first, we may have Eloquence to Argue and Dispute; and by the second, industry to answer without ambiguity: Wherefore there are ascribed to *Grammar* three Notes, and to *Dialect* two Notes.

The Reason why Rhetorick hath four Figures

Let us see wherefore *Rhetorick* hath four Notes. For there are four things necessary therein; as the Angel of the Lord said unto *Solomon*; to wit, a continual and flourishing adornment of locution, an ordinate, competent and discreet judgement, a Testimony of Causes or Offices, of Chances & Losses, a composed disposition of buying and selling; An Eloquence of the matters of that Art, with a demonstrative understanding. Therefore the greatness of God hath appointed to the Art of *Rhetorick* four Notes, with their Holy and Glorious Orations; as they were reverently sent by the Hand of God; that every Note in this Art aforesaid, might have a several faculty, That the first Note in that Art, might give a continual locution, a competent and flourishing adornment thereof: The second, to discern Judgements, just and unjust, ordinate and inordinate, true and false: The third, competently to discover offices and causes: and the fourth giveth understanding and eloquence in all the operations of this Art, without prolixity. See therefore how in *Grammar*, *Logick*, and *Rhetorick*, the several Notes are disposed in the several Arts.

But of the other Arts and their Notes

~ we shall speak in their due place and time
as we find them disposed in the book of the same Solomon.
At what times and hours the Notes of these three liberal Arts are to be looked into ~

Now we proceed to shew at what time, and how the Notes of these Arts are to be looked into, and the Orations to be said, to attain to these Arts. If thou art altogether ignorant of the Grammatical Art, and wouldst have the knowledge thereof: if it be appointed thee of God to do this work of works, and have a firm understanding in this Art of Arts: Then know that thou maist not presume to do otherwise than this book commandeth thee; for this book of his shall be thy Master, And this Art of his thy Mistress.

How the Grammatical Notes are to be looked into in the first Moon

For in this manner, the Grammaticall Notes are to be looked into, and the Orations to be said.

In the dayes when the Moon is in her prime, the first Note is to be looked into 12 times, and the Orations thereof repeated 24 times with Holy reverence; making a little space between, let the Orations be twice repeated at the inspection of every Note, and chiefly abstain from sins: do this from the first day of the Moon to the 14, and from the 14 to the 17. The first and second Notes are to be looked into 20 times, and the Orations to be repeated 30 times, on the 15 and 17 dayes, using some interval between them, All the three Notes are then every day to be looked into 12 times, and the Orations to be repeated 20 times: and thus of the Notes of the Art of *Grammar*. But if thou hast read any books of this Art, and desirest perfection therein, do as is commanded; using the general Orations to increase Memory, Eloquence, understanding and perseverance therein, repeating these above in the due time and hours appointed; lest that going beyond thy precept, thou committest sin: but when thou dost this, see that it be secret to thy self, and that thou have no looker on but God. Now we come to the Notes.

Here followeth the knowledge of the Notes

In the beginning of the inspection of all Notes, fast the first day till the evening, if you can; if thou canst not, then take another hour. This is the Grammatical precept.

Of the Logical Notes

The Dialectical Notes may be used every day, except only in those dayes before told of: The Rhetorical every day, except only three dayes of the Moneth, to wit, ☽. 11, 17, and 19. And they are forbidden on these dayes, as *Solomon* testifyes, the Notes of all Arts, except the Notes of this Art are offered. These precepts are generally to be observed.

How the Logical Notes are to be Inspected
~ and the Orations thereof Said

Know, that the Dialectical Notes are four times to be looked into, and the Orations thereof in that day are 20 times to be repeated, making some respite, and having the books of that Art before your Eyes; and so likewise the books of Rhetorick, when the Notes thereof are inspected, as it is appointed. This sufficeth for the knowledge of the 3 Arts.

How we must Beware of Offences

Before we proceed to begin the first Note of the Art of *Grammar*, somthing is to be tryed before, that we may have the knowledge of the 1, 2, and 3 Notes. And you ought first to know, in what the Notes of the Grammatical,

Logical, or Rhetorical Art are to be inspected, it being necessary that your greatest intentions be to keep from all offences.

How the Notes ought to be Inspected, at Certain Elected Times

This is a special and manifest knowledge, wherewith the Notes of the Grammatical Art are known: how they are to be published, at what times, and with what distinction, is duly and competently manifest; it is spoken already of the publishing and inspection of the Notes and Orations: now we shall digresse a little to speak somthing of the times, it being in part done already.

How Divers Months are to be Sought Out
~ *in the inspection of the Notes*

We have spoken already of the tearms of this Art, wherein the Orations are to be read, and the Notes to be looked into: it remaineth to declare, how the Lunations of these Orations are to be inspected and found out. But see that you mistake not: yet I have already noted the Lunations, wherein the Notes ought to be looked into, and the Orations rehearsed: But there are some Months, wherein the Lunation is more profitable than others: if thou wouldst operate in Theology or Astronomy, do it in a fiery sign; if Grammar or Logick, in Gemini or Virgo; if Musick or Physick, in Taurus or Libra; if Rhetorick, Philosophy, Arithmetick or Geometry, in Gemini or Cancer; for Mathematicks, in Taurus or Gemini: so they are well placed, and free from evil; for all the Heavenly Potestates and Chorus of Angels, do rejoyce in their Lunations, and determinate dayes.

Here is made mention of the Notes of all Arts

I *Apollonius* following the power of *Solomon*, have disposed my self to keep his works and observations, as it is spoken of the three Notes of Grammar, so will I observe the times as they are to be observed: But the Orations thereof are not written, but are more fully demonstrated in the following work; for what is written of those three Notes, are not Orations, but Definitions of those Notes, written by the Greek, Hebrew, and Chaldean, and other things which are apprehended by us: For those writings which are not understood in Latine, ought not to be pronounced, but on those dayes which are appointed by King *Solomon*, and in those dayes wherein the Notes are inspected, but on those dayes those Holy writings are always to be repeated: and the Latine, on those dayes wherein the Notes are not inspected. The Notes of the Logical Art are two: and at what times they are to be published is already shewn in part: more shall hereafter be said of them: now we come to the rest. The Latine writings may be published, according to the Antiquity of the Hebrews, except on those dayes we have spoken of: for *Solomon* saith, See that thou perform all those precepts as they are given: But of the rest which follow, it is to be done otherwise: for when thou seest the first Note of Logick, repeat in thy heart the sign in the first Note, and so in the Notes of all Arts except those whereof a definition shall be given.

Definitions of several Arts, and the Notes thereof

We will give also Definitions of several Arts, as it is in the Book of *Solomon*; Geometry hath one Note, Arithmetick a Note and a half; Philosophy, with the Arts and Sciences contained therein, hath 7 Species; Theology and Astronomy, with the Sciences in them contained, hath 7 Notes, but they are great and dangerous; not great in the pronunciation, but have great efficacy: Musick hath one Note, and Physick one Note; but they are all to be published and rehearsed in their appointed dayes: But know, that in every day wherein you beholdest the Notes of Theology, Philosophy, or of any Arts contained in them, that thou neither laugh nor play, nor sport, because King *Solomon*, when he saw the forms of these Notes, having over-drunk himself, God was angry with him, and spoke unto him by his Angel, saying, Because thou hast despised my Sacrament, and Polluted and derided my Holy things; *I will take away part of thy Kingdome, and I will shorten the dayes of thy Children.* And the Angel added, *The Lord hath forbid thee to enter into the Temple 80 days, that thou maist repent of thy sin.* And when *Solomon* wept and besought mercy of the Lord, the Angel answered, *Thy dayes shall be prolonged; nevertheless many evills and iniquities shall come upon thy Children, and they shall be destroyed of the iniquities that shall come upon them.*

At the beginning of a Note, having seen the generals; let the specials be looked into. The word of *Solomon* is to seek unto God for his promises, before the Notes of the three Arts.

The first Oration at the beginning of the Note

The *Light, Truth, Life, Way, Judge, Mercy, Fortitude and Patience, preserve, help me, and have Mercy upon me, Amen.*

This Oration, with the preceding, ought to be said in the beginning of the first Note of Grammar.

Oh Lord, Holy Father, Almighty, eternal God, in whose sight are all the foundations of all Creatures, and invisible beings, whose Eyes behold my imperfections, of the sweetness of whose love the Earth and Heavens are filled; who sawest all things before they were made, in whose book every day is formed, and all mankind are written therein: behold me thy Servant this day prostrate before thee, with my whole Heart and Soul, by thy Holy Spirit confirm me, blesse me, protect all my Actions in this inspection or repetition, and illuminate me with the constancy of thy visitation.

The 3 Oration

This Oration ought to be said before the second Note of Grammar ~

Behold, O Lord, merciful Father of all things; eternal dispensor of all virtues, and consider my operations this day; Thou art the Beholder and Discerner of all the Actions of Men and Angels: Let the wonderful grace of thy promises condescend to fulfil this sudden virtue in me, and infuse such efficacy into me, operating in thy Holy and great Name, thou who infusest thy praise into the mouths of them that love thee, Amen.

The 4 Oration

Let this Oration be rehearsed before the third Grammatical Note ~

O Adonay, Creator of all visible Creatures! Oh most Holy Father, who dwellest incompassed about with eternal light, disposing and by thy power governing all things before all beginnings; I most humbly beseech thy eternity and thy incomprehensible goodness may come to perfection in me, by the operation of thy most Holy Angels; And be confirmed in my Memory, and establish these thy Holy works in me, Amen.

A little space after this Oration, say the following: the first Oration ought to be said before the first Note of Logick.

Oh Holy God, great good, and the eternal Maker of all things, thy Attributes not to be exprest, who hast Created the Heaven and the Earth, the Sea and all things in them, and the bottomless pit, according to thy pleasure; in whose sight are the Words and Actions of all men: Grant unto me, by these Sacramental Mysteries of thy Holy Angels, the precious knowledge of this art, which I desire by the Ministry of thy Holy Angels, it being without any Malignant or Malitious intent, Amen.

Pronounce this Oration in the beginning of the first Figure of the Logick art; and after this Oration rehearse incontinently with some interval, the Orations written between the first Figure. The 6 Oration ought to be said before the first Note of the Dialect.

Helay: Most Merciful Creator, Inspirer, Reformer, and Approver of all Divine wills, Ordeyner of all things, Mercifully give ear to my Prayer, gloriously intend unto the desires of my heart, that what I humbly desire, according to thy promises, thou wilt Mercifully grant, Amen.

This Oration following, ought to be pronounced before the first Note of the Rhetorical Art.

Omnipotent and merciful Father, Ordeyner and Creator of all Creatures: Oh most Holy Judge, eternal King of Kings, and Lord of Lords; who wonderfully condescendest to give wisdome and understanding to thy Saints, who judgest and discernest all things: I beseech thee to illuminate my heart this day with the Splendor of thy Beauty, that I may understand and know what I desire, and what things are considerable to be known in this Art, Amen.

This Oration with the following *Hanazay*, &c. ought to be pronounced before the first Figure of Rhetorick: and although the Oration is divided into two parts, yet it is one and the same: And they are divided only for this cause, that there might be some mean interval used in the pronouncing of them; and they ought to be pronounced before the other Orations written in the Figure.

Hanazay, Sazhaon, Hubi, Sene, Hay, Ginbar, Ronail, Selmora, Hyramay, Lohal, Yzazamael, Amathomatois, Yaboageyors, Sozomcrat, Ampho, Delmedos, Geroch, Agalos, Meihatagiel, Secamai, Saheleton, Mechogrisces, Lerirencrhon.

The 8 Oration, let it be pronounced before the second Note of the Rhetorical Art:

Oh great eternal and wonderful Lord God, who of thy eternal counsel hast disposed of all virtues, and art Ordeyner of all goodness; Adorn and Beautify my understanding, and give unto me Reason to know and learn the Mysteries of thy Holy Angels: And grant unto me all knowledge and learning thou hast promised to thy Servants by the vertue of thy holy Angels, Amen.

This Oration, with the other two following, ought to be pronounced, (viz. Vision, &c.) *Azelechias*, &c. in the beginning of the second Figure of Rhetorick, and before the other Orations; and there ought to be some interval between them. Let this Oration following be said, before the second Note of Rhetorick:

Vision; beholding with thy eternal conspiration all Powers, Kingdomes and Judges, Administring all manner of Languages to all, and of whose power there is no end; restore I beseech thee and increase my Memory, my heart and understanding, to know, understand, and judge all things which thy Divine authority commendeth necessary in this art, perfectly fulfill them in me, Amen.

Let this Oration following, with the Precedent, be rehearsed before the second Note of Rhetorick.

Azelechias, Velozeos, Inoanzama, Samelo, Hotens, Sagnath, Adonay, Soma, Jezochos, Hicon, Jezomethon, Sadaot. And thou Oh God propitiously confirm thy promises in me, as thou hast confirmed them by the same words to King Solomon; send unto me, Oh Lord, thy virtue from Heaven, that may illuminate my mind and understanding: strengthen, Oh God, my understanding, renew my Soul within me, and wash me with the Waters which are above the Heavens; pour out thy Spirit upon my flesh, and fill my bowels with thy Judgements, with humility and charity: thou who hast created the Heaven and the Earth, and made man according to thy own Image; pour out the light of thy love into my understanding, that being radicated and established in thy love and thy mercy, I may love thy Name, and know, and worship thee, and understand all thy Scriptures, And all the Mysteries which thou hast declared by thy Holy Angels, I may receive and understand in my heart, and use this Art to thy Honor and Glory, through thy mighty Counsel, Amen.

The 11 Oration ought to be said before the pronounciation of the third Note of Rhetorick.

I know, that I love thy Glory, and my delight is in thy wonderful works, and that thou wilt give unto me wisdome, according to thy goodness and thy power, which is incomprehensible: *Theon, Haltanagon, Haramalon, Zamoyma, Chamasal, Jeconamril, Harionatar, Jechomagol, Gela Magos, Kemolihot, Kamanatar, Hariomolatar, Hanaces, Velonionathar, Azoroy, Jezabali*; by these most Holy and Glorious profound Mysteries, precious Offices, virtue and knowledge of God, compleat and perfect my beginnings, and reform my beginnings, *Zembar, Henoranat, Grenatayl, Samzatam, Jecornazay*: Oh thou great Fountain of all goodness, knowledge and virtue, give unto thy Servant power to eschew all evill, and cleave unto goodness and knowledge, and to follow the same with an Holy intention, that with my whole heart I may understand & learn thy Laws and Decrees; especially these Holy Mysteries; wherein that I may profit, I beseech thee, Amen.

12. This Oration ought to be said before the ninth Rhetorical Note:

Oh most reverend Almighty Lord, ruling all Creatures both Angels and Arch-Angels, and all Celestial, terrestrial, and infernal Creatures; of whose greatness comes all plenty, who hast made man after thy own Image; Grant unto me the knowledge of this Art, and strengthen all Sciences in me, Amen.

13. Pronounce this before the first Figure of Arithmetick:

Oh God who numbrest, weighest, and measurest all things, given the day his order, and called the Sun by his Name; Grant the knowledge of this Art unto my understanding, that I may love thee, and acknowledge the gift of thy goodness, Amen.

Lemegeton Clavicula Salomonis

14. Say this before the semi-note of Arithmetick:

Oh God, the Operator of all things, from whom proceeds every good and perfect gift; sow the Seeds of thy Word in my Heart, that I may understand the excellent Mysteries of this Art, Amen.

15. Say this before the second Figure of Arithmetick:

Oh God the perfect Judge of all good works, who makest known thy saving goodness amongst all Nations; open my Eyes and my Heart, with the beams of thy mercy, that I may understand and persevere in these thy Heavenly Mysteries, Amen.

16. This Oration before the second Note of Geometry:

Oh God the giver of all wisdome and knowledge to them that are without sin, Instructor and Master of all Spiritual Learning, by thy Angels and Arch-Angels, by Thrones, Potestates, Principates and Powers, by Cherubim and Seraphim, and by the 24 Elders, by the 4 Animals, and all the host of Heaven, I adore, invocate, worship and glorify thy Name, and exalt thee: most terrible and most merciful, I do humbly beseech thee this day to illuminate and fill my Heart with the grace of thy Holy Spirit, thou who art three in one, Amen.

17. Say this Oration before the second Note of Theology.

I adore thee, Oh King of Kings, my light, my substance, my life, my King, and my God, my Memory, and my strength; who in a Moment gavest sundry Tongues, and threwest down a Mighty Tower, And gavest by thy Holy Spirit the knowledge of Tongues to thy Apostles, infusing thy knowledge into them in a Moment, giving them the understanding of all Languages: inspire my Heart, and pour the dew of thy grace and Holy Spirit into me, that I may understand the Exposition of Tongues and Languages, Amen.

Three Chapters to be published, before any of the Notes

What we have spoken of the three first Chap. are generally and specially to be pronounced, so that you say them, and the Orations on the dayes appointed, and work by the Notes as it is demonstrated to you. These Orations ought to be said always before noon, every day of the Moneth; and before the Notes say the proper Orations: and in all reading, observe the precepts commanded.

How the Proper Notes are to be inspected

If you would learn anything of any one Art, look into the proper Notes thereof in their due time. Enough is said already of the three liberal Arts.

What dayes are to be observed in the inspection
~ of the Notes of the four Arts

In the four other Arts, only the four first dayes are to be observed: The Philosophical Notes, with all Sciences contained therein, the 7 and 17 days of the Moon are to be inspected, 7 times a day, with their several Orations. The Note is to be looked into, with fear, silence and trembling.

Of the Notes of the liberal Arts, it is spoken already; but only know this, that when you would use them, live chaste and soberly; for the Note hath in it self 24 Angels, is fully and perfectly to be pronounced, as you have heard: but when you look into them, repeat all the Theological Orations, and the rest in their due time.

Of the inspection of general Notes

Say the general Notes 10 times a day, when you have occasion to use any common Arts, having the books of those Arts before you, using some interval or space of time between them, as you have been taught already.

How the three first Chapters are to be pronounced
~ before Orations

To have perfection herein, know, that in the general pronunciation of Orations, the Notes of the three heads are to be rehearsed; whether the Orations be pronounced or not.

How the fifth Oration of Theology ought to be rehearsed
~ upon these Orations

There is also somthing else to be said of the four other liberal Arts; if you would have the perfect knowledge of them, make the first Oration of Theology before you say the Orations of the other Notes. These are sufficiently declared, that you may understand and know them; And let the capitular Orations be pronounced before the several Notes of every Art, and kept as is determined, *etc*. These are the Augmentations of the Orations, which belong to all Arts liberal and exceptive, except *Mechanick*, and are especially ascribed to the Notes of Theology. And they are thus to be pronounced, that whensoever you would look into any one Note of any Art, and would profit therein, say these Orations following.

Lemegeton Clavicula Salomonis

1. *Ezomamos, Hazalat, Ezityne, Hezemechel, Czemomechel, Zamay, Zaton, Ziamy Nayzaton, Hyzemogoy, Jeccomantha, Jaraphy, Phalezeton, Sacramphal, Sagamazaim, Secranale, Sacramathan; Jezennalaton Hacheriatos, Jetelemathon, Zaymazay, Zamaihay, Gigutheio Geurlagon, Garyos, Megalon Hera Cruhic, Crarihuc, Amen.*

Let this Oration with the following be pronounced before the first Note of Philosophy:

Oh Lord God, holy Father, almighty and incomprehensible; hear my Prayers, thou that art invisible, immortal and intelligible, whose face the Angels and Arch-angels, and all the powers of Heaven, do so much desire to see; whose Majesty I desire eternally to adore, and honour the only one God for ever and ever, Amen.

2. Say this before the second Note of Philosophy:

Oh Lord God, Holy and Almighty Father, hear my Prayers this day, and incline thy ears to my Orations; Gezomelion Samach, Semath, Cemon, Gezagam, Gezatrhin, Zheamoth, Zeze Hator Sezeator Samay Sarnanda, Gezyel, Iezel, Gaziety, Hel, Gazayethyhel, Amen.

Say this following with the former:

Oh God eternal, the way, the truth, and the life; give thy light and the flower of thy Holy Spirit into my mind and understanding, and grant that the gift of thy grace may shine forth in my heart, and into my Soul, now and for ever, Amen.

Pronounce the Oration following before the third Note of Philosophy;

Lemogethom, Hegemochom, Hazachay Hazatha, Azamachar, Azacham, Cohathay. Geomothay Logomothay, Zathana, Lachanma, Legomezon, Legornozon, Lembdemachon, Zegomaday, Hathanayos, Hatamam, Helesymom, Vagedaren, Vadeyabar, Lamnanath, Lamadai, Gomongchor, Gemecher, Ellemay, Gecromal, Gecrohahi, Colomanos, Colomaythos, Amen.

Say this following with the precedent Oration:

Oh God the life of all visible Creatures, eternal brightness, and virtue of all things; who art the original of all piety, who knewest all things before the were; who judgest all things, and discernest all things by thy unspeakeable knowledge: glorify thy Holy and unspeakable Name this day in my heart, and strengthen my intellectual understanding;

increase my Memory, and confirm my eloquence; make my Tongue ready, quick, and perfect in thy Sciences and Scriptures, that by thy power given unto me, and thy wisdome taught in my heart, I may praise thee, and know and understand thy Holy Name for ever World without end, Amen.

Say this Oration following before the fourth Note of Philosophy.

Oh King of Kings, the Giver and Dispenser of infinite Majesty, and of infinite mercy, the founder of all foundations; lay the foundation of all thy virtues in me, remove all foolishness from my heart, that my senses may be established in the love of thy charity, and my Spirit informed by thee, according to the recreation and invocation of they will, who livest and reignest God throughout all Worlds of Worlds, Amen.

How these Orations are to be said every day
~ *once before the general Notes, and the Notes of the liberal Arts*

These 4 Orations are necessary for liberal Arts, but chiefly do appertain to Theology, which are to be said everyday before the general Notes, or the Notes of the liberal Arts; but to Theology say every one of these 7 times to every Note; but if you would learn or teach any thing of dictating, versifying, singing or Musick, or any of these Sciences, first teach him these Orations, that thou would'st teach, how he should read them: but if he be a Child of mean understanding, read them before him, and let him say after thee word for word; but if he be of a good understanding, let him read them 7 times a day for 7 dayes: or if it be a general Note, pronounce these Orations, and the Virtue thereof shall profit you much, and you shall therein find great virtue.

Solomon saith of these Orations, let no man presume to make use of them unless for the proper office they are instituted for.

Oh Father, incomprehensible, from whom proceedeth every thing that is good; whose greatness is incomprehensible: Hear this day my Prayers, which I make in thy sight, and grant to me the Joy of thy saving health, that I may teach unto the wicked the Wayes and Paths of thy Sciences, and convert the Rebellious and incredulous unto thee, that whatsoever I commemorate and repeat in my heart and mouth, may take root and foundation in me; that I may be made powerful and efficacious in thy works, Amen.

Say this Oration before the 6 Note of Philosophy:

Gezemothon, Oromathian, Hayatha, Aygyay, Lethasihel, Lechizliel, Gegohay, Gerhonay, Samasatel, Samasathel, Gessiomo, Hatel, Segomasay, Azomathon,

Helomathon, Gerochor, Hejazay, Samin, Heliel, Sanihelyel, Siloth, Silerech, Garamathal, Gesemathal, Gecoromay, Gecorenay, Samyel, Samihahel, Hesemyhel, Sedolamax, Secothamay, Samya, Rabiathos, Avinosch, Annas, Amen.

Then say this following:

Oh eternal King! O God, the Judge and discerner of all things, knower of all good Sciences; instruct me this day for thy Holy Names sake, and by these Holy Sacraments; and purify my understanding, that thy knowledge may enter into my inward parts, as water flowing from Heaven, and as Oil into my bones, by thee, Oh God Saviour of all things, who art the Fountain of goodness, and original of piety; instruct me this day in those Sciences which I desire, thou who art one God for ever, Amen.

Oh God Father, incomprehensible, from whom proceedeth all good, the greatness of whose mercy is fathomless, hear my Prayers, which I make this day before thee, and render unto me the joy of thy Salvation, that I may teach the unjust the knowledge of thy wayes, and convert the unbelieving and Rebellious unto thee; and may have power to perform thy works, Amen.

The 7 Oration
~ which is the end of the Orations, belonging to the ineffable Note, the last of Theology, having 24 Angels

Oh God of all piety, Author and Foundation of all things, the eternal Health and Redemption of thy people; Inspirer and great Giver of all graces, Sciences and Arts, from whose gift it cometh: Inspire into me thy servant, an increase of those Sciences: who hast granted life to me miserable sinner, defend my Soul, and deliver my Heart from the wicked cogitations of this World; extinguish and quench in me the flames of all lust and fornication, that I may the more attentively delight in thy Sciences and Arts; and give unto me the desire of my Heart, that I being confirmed and exalted in thy glory, may love thee: and increase in me the power of thy Holy Spirit, by thy Salvation and reward of the faithful, to the Salvation of my Soul and Body, Amen.

Then say this following:

Oh God most mighty Father, from whom proceedeth all good, the greatness of whose mercy is incomprehensible; hear my Prayers, which I make in thy sight.

Ars Notoria

Special precepts of the Notes of Theology
~ *chiefly of the 1. 2. and 3*

These 7 Orations are an augmentation of the rest, and ought to be said before all the Notes of Theology, but especially before the ineffable Note; these are the precepts to make thee sufficient, which we command thee to observe by the authority of *Solomon*: diligently inquire them out, and do as we have proposed, and perfectly pronounce the Orations, and look into the Notes of the other Arts.

How Solomon received that ineffable Note from the Angel

Because thou desirest the Mystery of the Notes, take this of the ineffable Note, the expression whereof is given in the Angels by the Figures of Swords, birds, trees, Flowers, Candles, and Serpents; For *Solomon* received this from the Lord in the night of Pacification, ingraven in a book of Gold; and heard this from the Lord: Doubt not, neither be affraid; for this Sacrament is greater than all the rest; And the Lord joyned it unto him, When thou look'st into this Note, and read'st the Orations thereof, observe the precepts before, and diligently look into them; And beware that thou prudently conceal and keep whatsoever thou read'st in this Note of God, and whatsoever shall be revealed to thee in the vision. And when the Angel of the Lord appeareth to thee, keep and conceal the words and writings he revealeth to thee; and observe them to practice and operate in them, observing all things with great reverence, and pronounce them at the appointed dayes and hours, as before is directed: and afterwards say: *Sapienter die illo; Age, & caste vivas*. But if thou dost anything uncertain, there is danger; as then wilt have experience from the other Notes and the Orations of them; but consider that which is most wonderful in those Orations; for these words are ineffable Names, and are spiritually to be pronounced before the ineffable Note, *Hosel, Jesel, Anchiator, Aratol, Hasiatol, Gemor, Gesameor*. Those are the Orations which ought to be pronounced after the inspection of all Arts, and after the Note of Theology.

This is the fulfilling of the whole work; but what is necessary for an experiment of the work, we will more plainly declare. In the beginning of the knowledge of all Art, there is given almost the perfect doctrine of operating: I say almost, because some flourishing institutions hereof remain, whereof this is the first beginning.

How the precepts are to be observed in the operation of all Arts

Observe the 4 ☽ in every operation of Theology. Exhibit that operation with efficacy every 4 ☽ *quartam lunam*; and diligently look into the books and writings of those Arts; if thou doubt of any of the Chapters, they are to be pronounced, as is taught of the superiour Chapters; but know this, that these Holy Words of Orations, we appoint to be said before the bed of the sick, for an experiment of life or death. And this thou maist do often, if thou wilt operate nothing else in the whole body of Art: And know this, that if thou hast not the books in thy hands, or the faculty of looking into them is not given to thee; the effect of this work will not be the lesse therefore: but the Orations are twice then to be pronounced, where they were to be but once: And as to the knowledge of a vision, and the other virtues which these holy Orations have; thou maist prove and try them, when and how thou wilt.

These precepts are specially to be observed

But when thou would'st operate in Theology, observe only those dayes which are appointed; but all times are convenient for those Notes and Operations, for which there is a competent time given; but in the pronounciation of the three liberal Arts, or in the inspection of their Notes, perhaps thou maist pretermit some day appointed, if thou observe the rest; or if thou transgress two dayes, leave not off the work, for it loseth not its effect for this, for the Moon is more to be observed in the greater numbers than the dayes or hours. For *Solomon* saith, if thou miss a day or two, fear not, but operate on the general Chapters. This is enough to say of them: but by no means forget any of the words which are to be said in the beginning of the reading to attain to Arts; for there is great virtue in them. And thou maist frequently use the Holy Words of the visions: but if thou wouldst operate in the whole body of the Physical Art, the first Chapters are first to be repeated as before are defined. And in Theology, thou must operate only by thy self: Often repeat the Orations, and look into the Notes of Theology: this produceth great effects. It is necessary that thou have the Note of the 24 Angels always in Memory; and faithfully keep those things, which the Angel reveales to thee in the vision.

The Experiment of the precedent work

~ is the beginning of the following Orations, which Solomon calleth Artem Novam

These Orations may be said before all Arts generally, and before all Notes specially; And they may be pronounced without any other Chapters, if thou wouldst operate in any of the aforesaid Arts, saying these Orations in due time and order; thou maist have great efficacy in any Art. And in saying these Orations, neither the time, day, nor ☽, are to be observed: but take heed, that on these dayes you abstain from all sin, as drunkenness, gluttony, especially swearing, before you proceed thereunto, that your knowledge therein may be the more cleer and perfect.

Ars Notoria

Wherefore *Solomon* saith, When I was to pronounce these Orations, I feared lest I should offend God; and I appointed unto my self a time wherein to begin them; that living chastly, I might appear the more innocent.

These are the Proaemiums of these Orations, that I might lay down in order every thing whereof thou maist doubt, without any other definition. And before thou begin to try any of these subtile works, it is good to fast two or three dayes; that it may be divinely revealed, whether thy desires be good or evil.

These are the precepts appointed before every operation; but if thou doubt of any beginning, either of the three first Chapters, or of the four subsequent Arts, that thou maist have the effect of perfect knowledge; if thou consider and pronounce the Orations, as they are above described, although thou overpass somthing ignorantly; thou maist be reconciled by the spiritual virtue of the subsequent Orations.

The Angel said of these Orations to *Solomon*: See the holiness of these Orations; and if thou hast transgrest any therein presumptuously or ignorantly, say reverently and wisely these Orations, of which the great Angel saith: This is a great sacrament of God, which the Lord sendeth to thee by my hand; at the veneration of which sacrament, when King *Solomon* offered with great patience before the Lord upon the Altar, he saw the book covered with fine linen, and in this book were written 10 Orations, and upon every Oration the sign of golden Seal: and he heard in his Spirit, These are they which the Lord hath figured, and are far excluded from the hearts of the unfaithful.

Therefore *Solomon* trembled lest he should offend the Lord, and kept them, saying it was wickedness to reveal them to unbelievers: but he that would learn any great or spiritual thing in any Art or necessary Science, if he cannot have a higher work, he may say these Orations at what time soever he will; the three first, for the three first liberal Arts; a several Oration for every several Art, or generally all the three for the three Arts are to be said; and in like manner the four subsequent Orations, for four other liberal Arts. And if thou wouldst have the whole body of Art, without any definition of time, thou maist pronounce these Orations before the several Arts, and before the Orations and Notes of these Arts, as often as thou wilt, fully, manifestly and secretly; but beware that thou live chastly and soberly in the pronounciation thereof.

This is the first Oration of the 10, which may be pronounced by its self, without any precedent work to acquire Memory, Eloquence and understanding, and stableness of these three and singularly to be rehearsed before the first figure of Theology:

Omnipotent, Incomprehensible, invisible and indissolvable Lord God; I adore this day thy Holy Name; I an unworthy and miserable sinner, do lift up my Prayer, *understanding and reason towards thy Holy and Heavenly Temple, declaring thee, Oh Lord God, to be my Creator and Saviour: and I a rational Creature do this day invocate thy most glorious clemency, that thy Holy Spirit may vivify my infirmity: And thou, Oh my God, who didst confer the Elements of letters, and efficacious Doctrine of thy Tongue to thy Servants Moses and Aaron, confer the same grace of thy sweetness upon me, which thou hast investigated into thy Servants and Prophets: as thou hast given them learning in a moment, confer the same learning upon me, and cleanse my Conscience from dead works; direct my Heart into the right way, and open the same to understand, and drop the truth into my understanding. And thou, Oh Lord God, who didst condescend to create me after thy own image, hear me in thy Justice, and teach me in thy truth, and fill up my soul with thy knowledge according to thy great mercy, that in the multitude of thy mercies, thou maist love me the more, and the greater in thy works, and that I may delight in the administration of thy Commandments; that I being helped and restored by the work of thy grace, and purified in Heart and Conscience to trust in thee, I may feast in thy sight, and exalt thy name, for it is good, before thy Saints, Sanctifie me this day, that I may live in faith, perfect in hope, and constant in charity, and may learn and obtain the knowledge I desire; and being illuminated, strengthened, and exalted by the Science obtained, I may know thee, and love thee, and love the knowledge and wisdom of thy Scriptures; and that I may understand and firmly retain, that which thou hast permitted man to know: Oh Lord Jesus Christ, eternal only begotten Son of God, into whose hands the Father gave all things before all Worlds, give unto me this day, for thy Holy and glorious Name, the unspeakable nutriment of Soul and Body, a fit, fluent, free and perfect Tongue; and that whatsoever I shall ask in thy mercy, will and truth, I may obtain; and confirm all my Prayers and actions, according to thy good pleasure. Oh Lord my God, the Father of Life, open the Fountain of Sciences, which I desire; open to me, Oh Lord, the Fountain which thou openedst to Adam, and to thy Servants Abraham, and Isaac, and Jacob, to understand, learn and judge; receive Oh Lord my Prayers, through all thy Heavenly virtues, Amen.*

The next Oration is the second of ten, and giveth Eloquence, which ought to be said after the other; a little interval between, and before the first Figure of Theology.

I adore thee, thou King of Kings, and Lords, eternal and unchangeable King: Hearken this day to the cry and sighing of my Heart and Spirit, that thou maist change my understanding, and give to me a heart of flesh, for my heart of stone, that I may breath before my Lord and Saviour; and wash Oh Lord with thy new Spirit the inward parts of my heart, and wash away the evil of my flesh: infuse into me a good understanding, that I may become a new man; reform me in thy love, and let thy salvation give me increase of knowledge: hear my Prayers, O Lord, wherewith I cry unto thee, and open the Eyes of my flesh, and understanding, to understand the wonderful things of thy Law; that being vivified by thy Justification, I may prevail against the Devil, the adversary of the faithful; hear me Oh Lord my God, and be merciful unto me, and shew me thy mercy; and reach to me the vessel of Salvation, that I may drink and be satisfied of the Fountain of thy grace, that I may obtain the knowledge and understanding; and let the grace of thy Holy Spirit come, and rest upon me, Amen.

For Eloquence and stability of mind

This is the third Oration of the ten, and is to be said before the first Figure of Astronomy.

I confesse my self guilty this day before thee Oh God, Father of Heaven and Earth, Maker of all things, visible and invisible, of all Creatures, Dispenser and Giver of all grace and virtue; who hidest wisdom and knowledge from the proud and wicked, and givest it to the faithful and humble; illuminate my Heart, and establish my Conscience and understanding: set the light of thy countenance upon me, that I may love thee, and be established in the knowledge of my understanding, that I being cleansed from evil works, may attain to the knowledge of those Sciences, which thou hast reserved for believers. Oh merciful and omnipotent God, cleanse my Heart and reins, strengthen my Soul and Senses with the grace of thy Holy Spirit, and establish me with the fire of the same grace: illuminate me; gird up my loyns, and give the staffe of thy Consolation into my right hand, direct me in thy Doctrine, root out of me all vices and sin, and comfort me in the love of thy mercies: Breath into me Oh Lord the breath of Life, and increase my reason and understanding; send thy Holy Spirit into me, that I may be perfect in all knowledge: behold Oh Lord, and consider the dolour of my mind, that my will may be comforted in thee; send into me from Heaven thy Holy Spirit, that I may understand those things I desire. Give unto me invention, Oh Lord, thou Fountain of perfect reason and riches of knowledge, that I may obtain wisdom by thy Divine assistance, Amen.

To Comfort the outward and inward Senses

Oh Holy God, merciful and omnipotent Father, Giver of all things; strengthen me by thy power, and help me by thy presence, as thou wert merciful to Adam, and suddenly gavest him the knowledge of all Arts through thy great mercy; grant unto me power to obtain the same knowledge by the same mercy: be present with me Oh Lord, and instruct me: Oh most merciful Lord Jesus Christ Son of God, breath thy Holy Spirit into me, proceeding from thee and the Father; strengthen my work this day, and teach me, that I may walk in thy knowledge, and glorify the abundance of thy grace: Let the flames of thy Holy Spirit rejoyce the City of my Heart, by breathing into me thy Divine Scriptures; replenish my Heart with all Eloquence, and vivify me with thy Holy visitation; blot out of me the spots of all vices, I beseech thee, Oh Lord God incomprehensible; let thy grace alwayes rest upon me, and be increased in me; heal my Soul by thy inestimable goodness, and comfort my heart all my life, that what I hear I may understand, and what I understand I may keep, and retain in my Memory; give me a teachable Heart and Tongue; through thy inexhaustible grace and goodness; and the grace of the Father, Son, and Holy Ghost, Amen.

This following is for the Memory

O Holy Father, merciful Son, and Holy Ghost, inestimable King; I adore, invocate, and beseech thy Holy Name, that of thy overflowing goodness, thou wilt forget all my sins: be mercyful to me a sinner, presuming to go about this office of knowledge, and occult learning; and grant, Oh Lord, it may be efficatious in me; open Oh Lord my ears, that I may hear; and take away the scales from my Eyes, that I may see: strengthen my hands, that I may work; open my face, that I may understand thy will; to the glory of thy Name, which is blessed for ever, Amen.

This following strengtheneth the interiour and exteriour Sences

Lift up the senses of my Heart and Soul unto thee, Oh Lord my God, and elevate my heart this day unto thee; that my words and works may please thee in the sight of all people; let thy mercy and omnipotency shine in my bowels; let my understanding be enlarged, and let thy Holy Eloquence be sweet in my mouth, that what I read or hear I may understand and repeat: as Adam understood, and as Abraham kept, so let me keep understanding; and as Jacob was founded and rooted in thy wisedome, so let me be: let the foundation of thy mercy be confirmed in me, that I may delight in the works of thy hands, and persevere in Justice, and peace of Soul and Body; the grace of thy Holy Spirit working in me, that I may rejoyce in the overthrow of all my adversaryes, Amen.

This following giveth Eloquence, Memory and Stability

Disposer of all Kingdomes, and of all visible and invisible gifts: Oh God, the Ordeyner and Ruler of all wills, by the Counsel of thy Spirit dispose and vivify the weakness of my understanding, that I may burn in the accesse of thy Holy will to good: do good to me in thy good pleasure, not looking upon my sins; grant me my desire, though unworthy; confirm my Memory and reason to know, understand, and retain, and give good effect to my senses through thy grace, and justify me with the justification of thy Holy Spirit, that what spots soever of sin are contracted in my flesh, thy Divine power may blot out; thou who hast been pleased in the beginning, to create the Heaven and Earth, of thy Mercy restore the same, who art pleased to restore lost man to thy most Holy Kingdome ; Oh Lord of wisdom , restore Eloquence into all my senses , that I, though an unworthy sinner, may be confirmed in thy knowledge, and in all thy works, by the grace of the Father, Son, and Holy Ghost, who livest and reignest three in one, Amen.

An Oration to recover lost wisdome

Oh God of living, Lord of all Creatures visible and invisible, Administrator and Dispenser of all things, enlighten my Heart this day by the grace of thy Holy Spirit, strengthen my inward man, and pour into me the dew of thy grace, whereby thou instructest the Angels; inform me with the plenty of thy knowledge, wherewith from the beginning thou hast taught thy faithful; let thy grace work in me, and the flouds of thy grace and Spirit, cleanse and correct the filth of my Conscience. Thou who comest from Heaven upon the Waters of thy Majesty, confirm this wonderful Sacrament in me.

To obtain the grace of the Holy Spirit

Oh Lord my God, Father of all things, who revealest thy celestial and terrestrial secrets to thy Servants, I humbly beseech and implore thy Majesty, as thou art the King and Prince of all knowledge, hear my Prayers; and direct my works, and let my Actions prevail in Heavenly virtues, by thy Holy Spirit: I cry unto thee, Oh God, hear my Clamor, I sigh to thee, hear the sighings of my heart, and always preserve my Spirit, Soul, and Body, under the Safeguard of thy Holy Spirit; O God thou Holy Spirit, perpetual and Heavenly charity, whereof the Heaven and Earth is full, breath upon my operation; and what I require to thy honour and praise, grant unto me; let thy Holy Spirit come upon me, rule and reign in me, Amen.

To recover intellectual wisdome

Oh Lord, I thy Servant confesse my self unto thee, before the Majesty of thy glory, in whose Spirit is all Magnificence and Sanctimony: I beseech thee according to thy unspeakeable Name, extend thy merciful Ears and Eyes to the office of my operation; and opening thy hand, I may be filled with the grace I desire, and satiated with charity and goodness; whereby thou hast founded Heaven and Earth, who livest, etc.

Say these Orations from the first day of the month, to the fourth day

~ in the fourth day Alpha and Omega, and that following it, viz. Helischemat azatan; As it is in the beginning: afterwards say ~

Theos Megale patyr, ymas heth heldya, hebeath heleotezygel, Salatyel, Salus, Telli, Samel, Zadaziel, Zadan, Sadiz Leogio, Yemegas, Mengas, Omchon Myeroym, Ezel, Ezely, Yegrogamal, Sameldach, Somelta, Sanay, Geltonama, Hanns, Simon Salte, Patyr, Osyon, Hate, Haylos, Amen.

Oh light of the World immense God, &c.

Hereby is increased so much Eloquence, that nothing is above it

Thezay lemach ossanlomach azabath azach azare gessemon relaame azathabelial biliarsonor tintingote amussiton sebamay halbuchyre gemaybe redayl hermayl textossepha pamphilos Cytrogoomon bapada lampdayochim yochyle tahencior yastamor

Lemegeton Clavicula Salomonis

Sadomegol gyeleiton zomagon Somasgei baltea achetom gegerametos halyphala semean utangelsemon barya therica getraman sechalmata balnat hariynos haylos halos genegat gemnegal saneyalaix samartaix camael satabmal simalena gaycyah salmancha sabanon salmalsay silimacroton zegasme bacherietas zemethim theameabal gezorabal craton henna glungh hariagil parimegos zamariel leozomach rex maleosia mission zebmay aliaox gemois sazayl neomagil Xe Xe Sepha caphamal azeton gezain holhanhihala semeanay gehosynon caryacta gemyazan zeamphalachin zegelaman hathanatos, semach gerorabat syrnosyel, halaboem hebalor halebech ruos sabor ydelmasan falior sabor megiozgoz neyather pharamshe forantes saza mogh schampeton sadomthe nepotz minaba zanon suafnezenon inhancon maninas gereuran gethamayh passamoth theon beth sathamac hamolnera galsemariach nechomnan regnali phaga messyym demogempta teremegarz salmachaon alpibanon balon septzurz sapremo sapiazte baryon aria usyon sameszion sepha athmiti sobonan Armissiton tintingit telo ylon usyon, Amen.

Azay lemach azae gessemon thelamech azabhaihal sezyon traheo emagal gyeotheon samegon pamphilos sitragramon limpda jachim alna hasios genonagal samalayp camiel secal hanagogan heselemach getal sam sademon sebmassan traphon oriaglpan thonagas tyngen amissus coysodaman assonnap senaly sodan alup theonantriatos copha anaphial Azathon azaza hamel hyala saraman gelyor synon banadacha gennam sassetal maga halgozaman setraphangon zegelune Athanathay senach zere zabal somayel leosamach githacal halebriatos Jaboy del masan negbare phacamech schon nehooz cherisemach gethazayhy amilya semem ames gemay passaynach tagayl agamal fragal mesi themegemach samalacha nabolem zopmon usyon felam semessi theon, Amen.

The third part, the sign Lemach

Lemach sabrice elchyan gezagan tomaspin hegety gemial exyophyam soratum salathahom bezapha saphatez Calmichan samolich lena zotha phete him hapnies sengengeon lethis, Amen.

For the memory

Oh great invisible God, Theos patyr behominas Cadagamias imas by thy Holy Angels, who are Michael the Medicine of God; Raphael the Fortitude of God, Gabriel ardens holy per Amassan, Cherubin, Gelommeios, Sezaphim gedabanan, tochrosi gade anathon, zatraman zamanary gebrienam: Oh fulness, Holy Cherubins, by all thy Angels, and by all thy glorious Arch-angels, whose Names are consecrated by God, which ought not to be spoken by us, which are these, dichal, dehel depymon exluse exmegon pharconas Nanagon hossyelozogon gathena ramon garbona vramani Mogon hamas; Which humane sence cannot apprehend: I beseech thee, Oh Lord illuminate my Conscience with the Splender of thy light, and illustrate and confirm my understanding with the sweet odor of thy Spirit; adorne my Soul, reform my heart, that hearing I may understand, and retain what I hear in my Memory. Oh mercyful God, appease *my bowels, strengthen my Memory, open my mouth mercifully; temperate my Tongue by thy glorious and unspeakable Name: thou who art the Fountain of all goodness, have patience with me, and give a good Memory unto me, etc.*

Say these Orations in the fourth ☽, viz. *Hely schemath*, Alpha and Omega, *Theos megale*. Oh light of the World *Azalemach*, great God I beseech thee: These ought to be said in the 8, 12, 10, 20, 24, 28, 30. and in all these Lunations rehearse 2 four times; in the morning once, the third hour once, the ninth once, and once in the evening; and in the other dayes rehearse none, but them of the first day, which are Alpha and Omega, *Helyschemat*, Almighty, incomprehensible, I adore thee; I confess my self guilty: *O Theos hazamagiel*: Oh mercyful Lord God, raise up the sences of my flesh: Oh God of all living, and of all Kingdomes, I confess Oh Lord this day, that I am thy servant. Rehearse these Orations also in the other dayes four times, once in the morning, once in the evening, once about the third hour, and once on the ninth; And thou shalt acquire Memory, Eloquence and stability fully, *Amen*.

The Conclusion of the whole work
~ and Confirmation of the Science obtained

Oh God, Maker of all things; who hast created all things out of nothing; who hast wonderfully created the Heaven and Earth, and all things by degrees in order, in the beginning, with thy Son, by whom all things are made, and into whom all things shall at last return: Who art *Alpha* and *Omega*: I beseech thee though a sinner, & unworthy, that I may attain to my desired end in this Holy Art, speedily, and not lose the same by my sins; but do good unto me, according to thy unspeakable mercy: who doth not to us after our sins, nor rewardeth us after our iniquities, Amen.

Say this in the end devoutly:

Oh wisdome of God the Father incomprehensible, Oh most mercyful Son, give unto me of thy ineffable mercy, great knowledge and wisdom, as thou didst wonderfully bestow all Science to King Solomon, not looking upon his sins or wickedness, but thy own mercies: wherefore I implore thy mercy, although I am a most vile and unworthy sinner, give such an end to my desires in this art, whereby the hands of thy bounty may be enlarged towards me, and that I may the more devoutly walk by thy light in thy wayes, and be a good example to others; by which all that see mee, and hear me, may restrain themselves from their vices, and praise thy holyness through all Worlds, *Amen*. Blessed be the Name of the Lord, etc.

Rehearse these two Orations alwayes in the end, to confirm thy knowledge gained.

Lemegeton Clavicula Salomonis

The Benediction of the place

Blesse Oh Lord this place, that there may be in it Holy Sanctity, chastity, meekness, victory, holiness, humility, goodness, plenty, obedience of the Law, to the Father, Son, and Holy Ghost; Hear Oh Lord, holy Father, Almighty eternal God; and send thy Holy Angel Michael, who may protect, keep, preserve and visit me, dwelling in this Tabernacle, by him who liveth, etc.

When you would operate, have respect to the Lunations: they are to be chosen in those moneths, when the ☉ Rules in ♊ and ♍ ♈ ♌ ♎ ♉, in these moneths you may begin.

In the Name of the Lord beginneth this most Holy Art, which the most high God Administered to *Solomon* by his Angel upon the Altar, that thereby suddenly in a short space of time, he was established in the knowledge of all Sciences; and know, that in these Orations are contained all Sciences, Lawful and unlawful; First, if you pronounce the Orations of Memory, Eloquence, and understanding, and the stability thereof; they will be mightily increased, insomuch that you will hardly keep silence; for by a word all things were Created, and by the virtue of that word all created beings stand, and every Sacrament, and that Word is God. Therefore let the Operator be constant in his faith, and confidently believe, that he shall obtain such knowledge and wisdome, in the pronouncing these Orations, for with God nothing is impossible: therefore let the Operator proceed in his work, with faith, hope, and a constant desire: firmly believing; because we can obtain nothing but by faith; Therfore have no doubt in this Operation, whereof there are three species whereby the Art may be obtained.

The first species is Oration, and reason of a Godly mind, not by attempting a voyce of deprecation, but by reading and repeating the same in the inward parts. The second species is fasting and praying, for the praying man God heareth. The third species is chastity; he that would operate in this Art, let him be clean and chast by the space of nine dayes at least; and before you begin, it is necessary that you know the time of the ☽ for in the prime of the ☽ it is proper to operate in this Art: and when you begin so sacred an Art, have a care to abstain from all mortal sins, at least while you are proceeding in this work until it be finished and compleated: and when you begin to operate, say this verse kneeling:

Lift up the light of thy Countenance upon me, Oh Lord my God, and forsake not me thy servant N. that trusts in thee:

Then say three times *Pater Noster*, etc. And assert that thou wilt never commit wilfull perjury, but always persevere in faith and hope. This being done, with bended knees in the place wherein thou wilt operate, say,

Our help is in the Name of the Lord, who hath made Heaven and earth: And I will enter into the Invocation of the most high, unto him who enlightneth and purifieth my Soul and Conscience, which dwelleth under the help of the most high, and continueth under the protection of the God of Heaven: O Lord open and unfold the doubts of my Heart, and change me into a new man by thy love: be thou Oh Lord unto me true faith, the hope of my life, and perfect charity, to declare thy wonders. Let us pray:

Then say the Oration following:

Oh God my God, who from the beginning hast Created all things out of nothing, and reformest all things by thy Spirit; restore my Conscience, and heal my understanding, that I may glorify thee in all my thoughts, words and deeds; through him who liveth and reigneth with thee forever, Amen.

Now in the Name of *Christ*, on the first day of the Month, in which thou wouldst acquire Memory, Eloquence and Understanding, and stability thereof, with a perfect, good and contrite heart, and sorrow for thy sins committed; thou maist begin to pronounce these Orations following, which appertain to the obtaining of Memory and all Sciences, and which were composed and delivered by the Angel to *Solomon*, from the hand of God.

The first and last Oration of this art, is Alpha and Omega: *Oh God omnipotent*, &c.

This following is an Oration of four Languages, which is this:

Hely, Schemat, Azatan, honiel sichut, tam, imel, Iatatandema, Jetromiam, Theos: Oh Holy and strong God, Hamacha, mal, Gottneman, Alazaman, Actuaar, Secheahal, Salmazan, zay, zojeracim, Lam hay, Masaraman, grensi zamach, heliamat, seman, selmar, yetrosaman muchaer, vesar, hasarian Azaniz, Azamet, Amathemach, hersomini. And thou most Holy and just God, incomprehensible in all thy works, which are Holy just and good; Magol, Achelmetor, samalsace, yana, Eman, and cogige, maimegas, zemmail, Azanietan, illebatha sacraman, reonas, grome, zebaman, zeyhoman, zeonoma, melas, heman, hathoterma, yatarmam, semen, semetary, Amen.

This Oration ought to follow the first of the ten above written.

Lemegeton Clavicula Salomonis

To perform any work

This is to follow the third Oration above:

I confesse, O Theos hazamagielgezuzan, sazaman, Sathaman, getormantas, salathiel, nesomel, megal vuieghama, yazamir, zeyhaman, hamamal amna, nisza, deleth, hazamaloth, moy pamazathoran hanasuelnea, sacromomem, gegonoman, zaramacham Cades bachet girtassoman, gyseton palaphatos halathel Osachynan machay, Amen.

This is a true and approved experiment, to understand all Arts and secrets of the World, to find out and dig up minerals and treasure; this was revealed by the Heavenly Angel in this Notory Art. For this Art doth also declare things to come, and rendereth the sense capable of all arts in a short time, by the Divine use thereof.

We are to speak also of the time and place. First therefore, all these precepts are to be observed and kept; and the Operator ought to be clean, chaste, to repent of his sins, and earnestly desire to cease from sinning as much as may be; and so let him proceed, and every work shall be investigated into him, by the divine ministery.

When thou wilt operate in the new Moon, kneeling say this verse: *Lift up the light of thy Countenance upon us, Oh God, and forsake us not, Oh Lord our God.* Then say three times the *Pater Noster*. And afterwards let him vow unto God, that he will never commit wilfull perjury, but always persist in faith. This being done, at night say with bended knees before thy bed, *Our help is in the Name of the Lord*, etc. and this Psalm; *Whoso dwelleth under the shadow of the wings of the most high*, to the end; and the Lords Prayer, and the Prayer following.

Theos Pater vehemens; God of Angels, I Pray and invocate thee by thy most Holy Angels Eliphamasay, Gelomiros, Gedo bonay, Saranana, Elomnia, and by all thy Holy Names, by us not to be pronounced, which are these: de. el. x p n k h t li g y y. not to be spoken, or comprehended by humane sense; I beseech thee cleanse my Conscience with the Splendor of thy Name; illustrate and confirm my understanding with the sweet savour of thy Holy Spirit: O Lord Adorne my Soul, that I may understand and perfectly remember what I hear; reform my Heart, and restore my Heart, and restore my sense Oh Lord God, and heal my bowels: open my mouth most merciful God, and frame and temper my Tongue to the praise and glory of thy Name, by thy glorious and unspeakeable Name. O Lord, who art the Fountain of all goodness, and original of all piety, have patience with me, and give unto me a true understanding, to know whatsoever is fitting for me, and retain the same in Memory: thou who dost not presently Judge a sinner, but mercifully expectest repentance; I beseech thee, though unworthy, to wash away the filth of my sins and wickedness, and grant me my petitions, to the praise and glory of thy Holy Name; who livest and reignest one God in perfect Trinity, World without end, Amen.

Some other precepts to be observed in this work

Fast the day following with bread and water, and give Almes; if it be the Lord's day, then give double Almes; be clean in body and mind; both thy self, and put on clean Cloaths.

The processe follows

When thou wilt operate concerning any difficult Probleme or Question, with bended knees, before thy bed, make Confession unto God the Father; and having made thy Confession, say this Oration.

> *Send Oh Lord thy wisdome to assist me, that it may be with me, and labour with me, and that I may alwayes know what is acceptable before thee; and that unto me N. may be manifested the truth of this question or Art.*

This being done, Thrice in the day following, when thou risest, give thanks to God Almighty, saying, *Glory and honour, and benediction be unto him that sitteth on the Trone, and that liveth for ever and ever, Amen.* with bended knees and stretched out hands.

But if thou desirest to understand any book, ask of some that hath knowledge therein, what that book treateth of: This being done, open the book, and read in it; and operate as at first three times, and always when thou goest to sleep, write *Alpha and Omega,* and afterwards sleep on thy right side, putting the palme of thy hand under thy Ear, and thou shalt see in a dream all things thou desirest; and thou shalt hear the voyce of one informing and instructing thee in that book, or in any other faculty wherein thou wilt operate: And in the morning, open the book, and read therein; and thou shalt presently understand the same, as if thou hadst studied in it a long time: And always remember to give thanks to God, as aforesaid.

Afterwards on the first day say this Oration:

> *Oh Father, Maker of all Creatures; by thy unspeakeable power wherewith thou hast made all things, stir up the same power, and come and save me, and protect me from all adversity of Soul and Body, Amen. Of the Son say, O Christ, Son of the living God, who art the splendor and figure of light, with whom there is no alteration nor shaddow of change; Thou Word of God most high, thou wisdome of the Father; open unto me, thy unworthy servant N. the veins of thy saving Spirit, that I may wisely understand, retain in Memory, and declare all thy wonders: Oh wisdome, who proceedest out of the mouth of the most high, powerfully reaching from end to end, sweetly disposing of all things in the World, come and teach me the way of prudence and wisdome. Oh Lord which didst give thy Holy Spirit to thy Disciples, to teach and illuminate their Hearts, grant unto me thy unworthy servant N. the same Spirit, and that I may alwayes rejoyce in his consolation.*

Other precepts

Having finished these Orations, and given Almes, when thou entrest into thy Chamber, devoutly kneel down before thy bed, saying this Psalm: *Have mercy upon me, O God, according to the multitude of thy great mercies*, etc. and, *In thee Oh Lord have I trusted*, etc. Then rise up, and go to the wall, and stretch forth thy hands, having two nayles fixed, upon which thou maist stay up thy hands, and say this Prayer following with great devotion:

> *O God, who for us miserable sinners didst undergo the painful death upon the Crosse; to whom also Abraham offer'd up his son Isaac; I thy unworthy servant, a sinner perplexed with many evils, do this day offer up and Sacrifice unto thee my Soul and Body, that thou maist infuse into me thy Divine wisdom, and inspire me with the Spirit of Prophesy, wherewith thou didst inspire the Holy Prophets.*

Afterwards say this Psalm; *Oh Lord incline thine ears unto my words*, etc. and add:

> *The Lord is my shepherd, and nothing shall I want: he shall set me down in green pastures, his servant N. he shall lead me upon the waters of refreshment, he converteth my Soul, and leadeth me N. upon the paths of his righteousness for his Holy Name: Let my evening Prayer ascend upunto thee Oh Lord, and let thy mercy descend upon me thy unworthy servant N. protect, save, blesse, and sanctify me, that I may have a shield against all the wicked darts of my enemies: defend me Oh Lord by the price of the blood of the just One, wherewith thou hast redeemed me; who livest and reignest God, whose wisdom hath laid the foundation of the Heaven, and formed the Earth, and placed the Sea in her bounds: and by the going forth of thy Word hast made all Creatures, and hath formed man out of the dust of the Earth, according to his own image and likeness; who gave to Solomon the son of King David inestimable wisdome: hath given to his Prophets the Spirit of Prophesy, and infused into Philosophers wonderfull Philosophical knowledge, confirmed the Apostles with fortitude, comforted and strengthened the Martyrs, who exalteth his elect from eternity, and provideth for them; Multiply Oh Lord God, thy mercy upon me thy unworthy servant N. by giving me a teachable wit, and an understanding adorned with virture and knowledge, a firm and sound Memory, that I may accomplish and retain whatsoever I endeavour, through the greatness of thy wonderful Name; lift up, Oh Lord my God, the light of thy countenance upon me, that hope in thee: Come and teach me, Oh Lord God of virtues, and shew me thy face, and I shall be safe.*

Then add this Psalm: *Unto thee Oh Lord do I lift up my Soul: Oh my God in thee do I trust*; excepting that verse, *Confundantur*, etc.

Having fulfilled these things upon the wall, descend unto thy Bed, writing in thy right hand Alpha and Omega: then go to bed, and sleep on thy right side,

Ars Notoria

holding thy hand under thy right Ear, and thou shalt see the greatness of God as thou hast desired. And in the morning, on thy knees, before thy bed, give thanks unto God for those things he hath revealed to thee:

I give thanks unto thee, Oh great and wonderful God, who hast given Salvation and knowledge of Arts unto me thy unworthy servant N. and confirm this Oh God, which thou hast wrought in me, in preserving me. I give thanks unto thee, O powerful Lord God, who createdst me miserable sinner out of nothing, when I was not, and when I was utterly lost; not redeemed, but by the precious blood of thy Son our Lord Jesus Christ; and when I was ignorant thou hast given unto me learning and knowledge: grant unto me thy servant N. O Lord Jesus Christ, that through this knowledge, I may be always constant in thy Holy service, Amen.

These operations being devoutly compleated, give thanks daily with these last Orations. But when thou wouldst read, study, or dispute, say:

Remember thy word unto thy Servant, O Lord, in which thou hast given me hope; this is my comforter in humility. Then add these Orations: Remember me O Lord of Lords, put good words and speech into my mouth, that I may be heard efficaciously and and powerfully, to the praise, glory, and honour of thy glorious Name, which is Alpha and Omega, blessed for ever, World without end, Amen.

Then silently say these Orations:

O Lord God, that daily workest new signs and unchangeable wonders, fill me with the spirit of wisedome, understanding and Eloquence; make my mouth as a sharp Sword, and my Tongue as an arrow elected, & confirm the words of my mouth to all wisdome: mollify the Hearts of the hearers to understand what they desire, Elysenach, Tzacham, etc.

The manner of Consecrating the Figure of Memory

It ought to be consecrated with great faith, hope and charity; and being consecrated, to be kept and used in operation as followeth.

On the first day of the new Moon, having beheld the new Moon, put the Figure under your right Ear, and so consequently every other night, and seven times a day; the first hour of the morning saying this Psalm, *Qui habitat*, etc. throughout; and the Lords Prayer once, and this Oration *Theos Patyr* once in the first hour of the day: then say this Psalm, *Confitebor tibi Domine*, etc. and the Lords Prayer twice, and the Oration *Theos Patyr* twice.

In the third hour of the day the Psalm *Benedicat anima mea Dominum*, etc. the Lords Prayer thrice, and the Oration *Theos Patyr*.

In the sixth hour say this Psalm: *Appropinquet deprecatio mea in conspectu tuo Domine, secundum eloquium tuum.*

Grant unto me Memory, and hear my voyce according to thy great mercy, and according unto thy word grant Eloquence, and my lips shall shew forth thy majesty, when thou shalt teach me thy Glory: Gloria patri, etc, say the Lords Prayer nine times, and *Theos Patyr*.

In the nineth hour, say the Psalm *Beati immaculati in via*; the Lords Prayer 12 times, and *Theos Patyr*.

In the Evening say this Psalm, *Deus misereatur nostri*: the Lords Prayer 15 times, and *Theos Patyr* as often.

The last hour say this Psalm, *Deus Deus meus respice in me*, etc. and *Deus in adjutorium meum intende*, and *te Deum Laudamus*; the Lords Prayer once, and *Theos Patyr*: then say the Oration following twice.

O *God, who hast divided all things in number, weight, and measure, in hours, nights, and dayes; who countest the number of the Stars, give unto me constancy and virtue, that in the true knowledge of this Art N. I may love thee, who knows the gifts of thy goodness, who livest and reignest,* etc.

Four dayes the Figure of Memory ought to be consecrated
~ with these Orations.

O Father of all Creatures, of the Sun and Moon.

Then on the last day let him bath himself, and put on clean garments, and clean *Ornaments*, and in a clean place, suffumigate himself with Frankincense, and come in a convenient hour in the night with a light Kindled, but so that no man may see thee; and before the bed upon your knees say this Oration with great devotion.

O most great and most Holy Father, seven or nine times: then put the Figure with great reverence about your Head; and sleep in the Bed with clean linnen vestiments, and doubt not but you shall obtain whatsoever you desire for this hath been proved by many, to whom such coelestial secrets of the Heavenly Kingdome are granted, *Amen*.

Ars Notoria

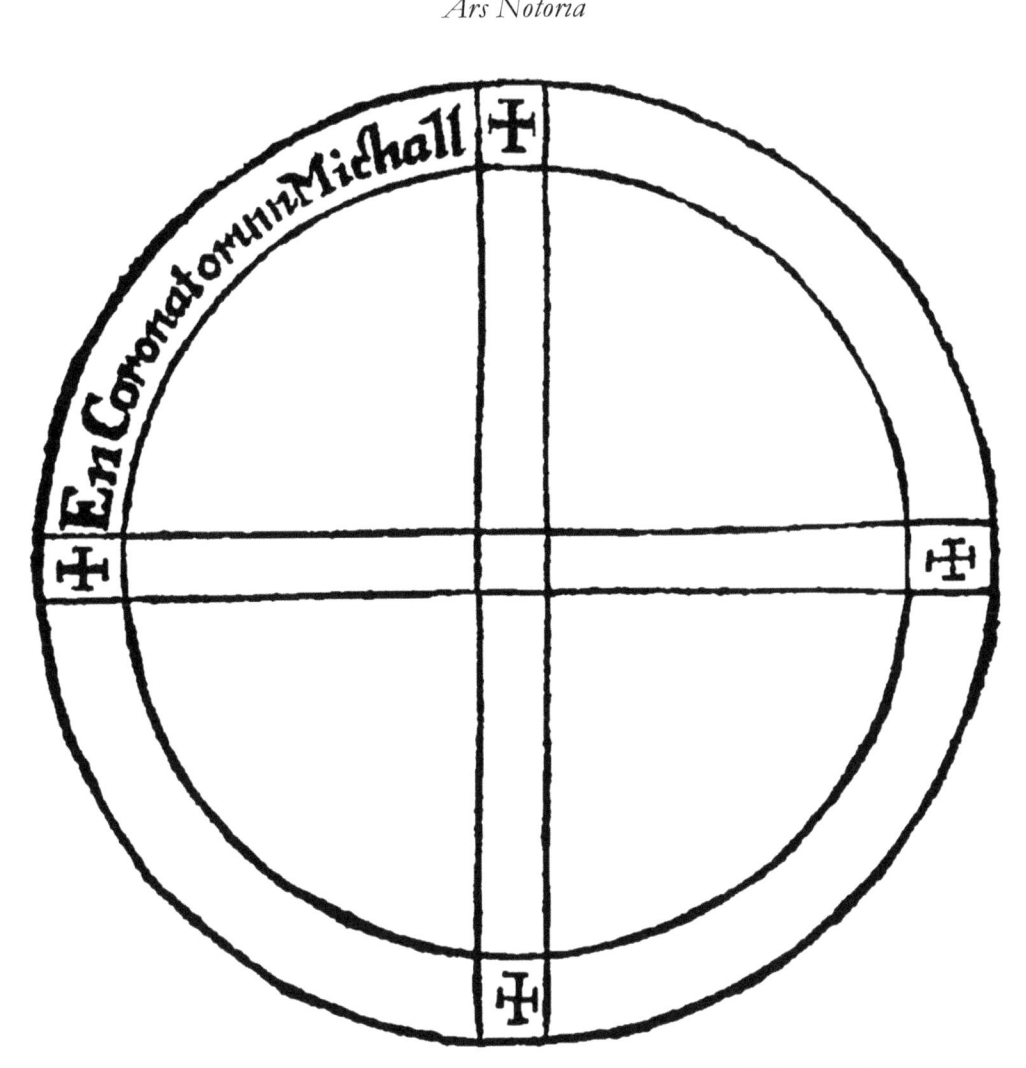

En Coronatorum Michall

O *great God, Holy Father, most Holy Sanctifier of all Saints, three and one, most high King of Kings, most powerful God Almighty, most glorious and most wise Dispensor, Moderator, and Governour of all Creatures, visible and invisible: O mighty God, whose terrible and most mighty Majesty is to be feared, whose omnipotency the Heaven, the Earth, the Sea, Hell, and all things that are therein, do admire, reverence, tremble at, and obey.*

O most powerful, most mighty, and most invincible Lord God of Sabaoth: O God incomprehensible; the wonderful Maker of all things, the Teacher of all learning, Arts and Sciences; who mercifully Instructest the humble and meek: O God of all wisdome and knowledge, In whom are all Treasures of wisdome, Arts and Sciences; who art able instantly to infuse Wisdome, Knowledg, and Learning into any man; whose Eye beholdeth all things past, present, and to come; who art the daily Searcher of all hearts; through whom we are, we live and dye; who sittest upon the Cherubins; who alone seest and rulest the bottomless pit: whose Word gives Law throughtout the universal World: I confess my self this day before thy Holy and glorious Majesty, and before the company of all Heavenly virtues and Potentates, praying thy glorious Majesty, invocating thy great Name, which is a Name wonderful, and above every Name, blessing thee O Lord my God: I also beseech thee, most high, most omnipotent Lord, who alone art to be adored; O thou great and dreadful God Adonay, wonderful Dispensator of all beatitudes, of all Dignities, and of all goodness; Giver of all things, to whomsoever thou wilt, mercifully, abundantly and permanently: send down upon me this day the gift of the grace of thy Holy Spirit. And now O most merciful God, who hast created Adam the first man, according to thy image and likeness; fortify the Temple of my body, and let thy Holy Spirit descend and dwell in my Heart, that I may shine forth the wonderful beams of thy Glory: as thou hast been pleased wonderfully to operate in thy faithful Saints; So O God, most wonderful King, and eternal glory, send forth from the seat of thy glorious Majesty, a seven-fold blessing of thy grace, the Spirit of Wisedome and Understanding, the Spirit of fortitude and Counsel, the Spirit of knowledge and Godliness, the Spirit of fear and love of thee, to understand thy wonderful Holy and occult mysteries, which thou art pleased to reveal, and which are fitting for thine to know, that I may comprehend the depth, goodness, and inestimable sweetness of thy most immense Mercy, Piety and Divinity. And now O most merciful Lord, who didst breath into the first Man the breath of life, be pleased this day to infuse into my Heart a true perfect perceiving, powerful and right understanding in all things; a quick, lasting, and indeficient Memory, and efficacious Eloquence; the sweet, quick and piercing Grace of thy Holy Spirit, and of the multitude of thy blessings, which thou bountifully bestowest: grant that I may despise all other things, and glorify, praise, adore, bless and magnify thee the King of Kings, and Lord of Lords; and alwayes set forth thy praise, mercy, and omnipotency: that thy praise may always be in my mouth, and my Soul may be inflamed with thy Glory for ever before thee. O thou who art God omnipotents, King of all things, the greatest peace and perfectest wisdom, ineffable and inestimable sweetness and delight, the unexpressible joy of all good, the desire of all the blessed, their life, comfort, and glorious end; who was from eternity, and is and ever shall be virtue invincible, without parts or passions; Splendor and glory unquenchable; benediction, honour, praise, and venerable glory before all Worlds, since and everlastingly time without end, Amen.

The following Oration hath power to expell all lusts

O Lord, Holy Father, omnipotent eternal God, of inestimable mercy and immense goodness; O most merciful Jesus Christ, repairer and restorer of mankind; O Holy Ghost, comforter and love of the faithful: who holdest all the Earth in thy fingers, and weighest all the Mountains and Hills in the World; who dost wonders past searching out, whose power there is nothing can resist, whose wayes are past finding out: defend my Soul, and deliver my Heart from the wicked cogitations of this World;

extinguish and repress in me by thy power all the sparks of lust and fornication, that I may more intentively love thy works, and that the virtue of thy Holy Spirit may be increased in me, among the saving gifts of thy faithful, to the comfort and salvation of my Heart, Soul, and Body. O most great and most Holy God, Maker, Redeemer, and Restorer of mankind, I am thy servant, the Son of thy hand-maid, and the work of thy hands: O most merciful God and Redeemer, I cry and sigh before the sight of thy great Majesty, beseeching thee, with my whole Heart, to restore me a miserable sinner, and receive me to thy great mercy; give me Eloquence, Learning, and Knowledge, that those that shall hear my words, they may be mellifluous in their Hearts; that seeing and hearing thy wisdom, the proud may be made humble, and hear and understand my words with great humility, and consider the greatness and goodness of thy blessings, who livest and reignest now and for ever, Amen.

Note, that if you desire to know any thing that you are ignorant of, especially of any Science, read this Oration: I co*nfess my self to thee this day, O God the Father of Heaven and Earth,* three times; and in the end express for what you desire to be heard; afterwards, in the Evening when you go to Bed, say the Oration *Theos* throughout, and the Psalm *Qui Habitat*, with this versicle, *Emitte Spiritum*; and go to sleep, and take the Figure for this purpose, and put it under the right Ear: and about the second or third hour of the night, thou shalt see thy desires, and know without doubt that which thou desirest to find out: and write in thy right hand Alpha and Omega, with the sign of the Cross, and put that hand under thy right Ear, and fast the day before; only once eating such meat as is used on fasting dayes.

The End of the Books of Solomon.

For Theft

The Mighty Oration

By the Great and most mighty power of Alpha and Omega, Jehovah and Emmanuel, and by him that divided the Red S and by that power which turned all the waters and rivers in Egypt into blood, and turned all the dust into lice and blains and by that great power that brought forth frogs over all the land of Egypt, and entered into the King's palaces and chambers and by that great power, that that terrible thunder and lightning and hailstones mixed with fire, and did send locusts which did devour all green things in the whole land of Egypt, and by the great power that did destroy all the first born in the land of Egypt, both of man and beast, and by that great power which divided the hard rocks, and rivers of water issued out of the same in the wilderness, and by that great power which led the children of Israel into the land of Canaan, and by that great power which did destroy Sanacrib's great host and by that great and almighty power of him that walked on the sea, as on dry land, and by that great and almighty power that raised dead Lazarus out of his grave, and by that almighty power of the Blessed Holy and glorious Trinity, that did cast the devil and all disobedient Spirits out of Heaven into Hell, that thou thief return immediately and restore the goods again that thou hast stolen away, therefore in and by the names of the almighty God before rehearsed, I charge thee thou thief to restore the goods again immediately, or else the wrath of God may fall upon thee, and cause thee to come immediately. Amen.

For Love

In the day of Venus (Friday) and in the hour thereof make a circle stretching forth thy hand and thy face towards the South say, I conjure you Spirit Ragarad, Sathan, and Iscaroth, By the great God the father; by the great God the Son ☩, and by the great God the Holy Ghost ☩ and by the most blessed Virgin Mary, and by the warfare of Heaven, and by the dreadful day of Judgement I conjure you Spirits of ♀, and by the figure of Venus which here is, so by the flowing of blood from the side of Christ Jesus, and by the rent of the veil of the temple at the passion of our Lord Jesus Christ, and by the virginity and fruitfulness of blessed Mary, the Mother of God, and by all the names of Jesus Christ and by that unutterable name ☩ Tetragrammaton ☩, which is graven upon my rod, and is upon my ring, that you make haste and go to the woman or maid N_ and that you make her so to burn in my love, that neither sleeping nor waking she may be at rest until I obtain what I desire of her, and to perform my will with her God permitting who liveth and reigneth for ever and ever Amen.

Or else, in this way: So far forth as in you lay bring hither such a woman the daughter of – and without vain vision or counterfeiting, or other diabolical transformation, without delay or deceit or gain, saying, year, convey her hither to me truly cause her to enter into this chamber, without hurt or any annoyance, even unto my bed, through our Lord Jesus Christ the Son of God, who liveth and reigneth for ever and ever, Amen.

But if the Spirit will not appear repeat it 3 times, and he will come.

Make an Image of virgin wax in the forehead whereof write her name and on the right front, Venus, and in the left, Saturn, and in the back, Jupiter, then take red thorns and make a fire and say, I conjure thee image by virtue of the Father, Son, and Holy Ghost that as thou dost waste, so may this woman's love waste from all other men except me, and I conjure thee image and planets whose names are written in thee by the virtue of God and of the Holy Saints, that you tempt this woman whose form and name thou art made for, that she shall not sleep nor rest in any place, neither standing or walking, or sleeping or doing anything else, but that she comes to me with all speed to fulfil my will and desire.

Always work in the day and hour of Venus.

Appendix A
Divine Names of the Magic Circle of the Goetia

Within the *Ars Goetia* portion of Raphael's *The Little Key of Rabbi Solomon*, the illustration given for the Magic Circle resembles closely that given later by Arthur Edward Waite in *The Book of Ceremonial Magic*, particularly in the arrangement of the divine Names, with differences, however, such as the absence of tau crosses at the centre of the four 'candle' pentagrams. Absent also is the placement of *Restchich, Hagalgalim, Geburah, Seraphim, Camael,* and *Madim* which, in the Waite example, are arranged to the north, north-east, south-east, south, south-west and north-west respectively.

Within both the 'Raphael' manuscript and Arthur Edward Waite's example, the Names are arranged within the Magic Circle as two complete and concentric 'rings.'

Immediately following the illustration of the Magic Circle, the arrangement of Names employed within another, unidentified manuscript is given. For further comparative purposes I give here also the Names employed within the Magic Circle of the *Ars Goetia*, based upon the Sloane manuscript 3825. Here, the Names are arranged as a spiral – beginning at the Eastern edge of the circle, and spiralling inwards:

Ehyeh Kether Chaioth Ha-Qadesh Metatron Rashith Ha-Galgalim PM [Sphere of the Premium Mobile] Iah Iehovah Chokmah Ophanim Jophiel Masloth SZ [Sphere of the Zodiac] Iehovah Elohim Binah Aralim Zaphkiel Sabbathai S♄ [Sphere of Saturn] El Chesed Hasmalim Zadkiel S♃ [Sphere of Jupiter] Elohim Gibor Geburah Seraphim Camael Madim S♂ [Sphere of Mars] Eloah Tiphereth Malakhim Raphael Shemesh Masloth S☉ [Sphere of the Sun] Tzabaoth Netzach Elohim Haniel Nogah S♀ [Sphere of Venus] Elohim Tzabaoth Hod Beni Elohim Michael Cochab S☿ [Sphere of Mercury] Shaddai Iesod Cherubim Gabriel Levanah S☽ [Sphere of the Moon]

The Names employed within the Magic Circle in the Mathers/Crowley edition, written in Hebrew, also spiral inward from the circle's outer edge and are arranged thus within the form of a serpent. The order of the names translated from the Hebrew are given as follows:

✠ Ehyeh Kether Metatron Chaioth Ha-Qadesh Rashith Ha-Galgalim S.P.M (for 'Sphere of the Primum Mobile') ✠ Iah Chokmah Ratziel Auphanim Masloth

175

S.S.F. (for 'Sphere of the Fixed Stars,' or S.Z. for 'Sphere of the Zodiac') ✠ Iehovah Elohim Binah Tzaphquiel Aralim Shabbathai S. (for 'Sphere') of Saturn ✠ El Chesed Tzadquiel Chaschmalim Tzedeq S. Jupiter ✠ Elohim Gibor Geburah Kamael Seraphim Madim S. of Mars ✠ Iehovah Eloah Va-Daäth Tiphereth Raphaël Malakim Shemesh S. of the Sun ✠ Iehovah Tzabaoth Netzach Haniel Elohim Nogah S. of Venus. ✠ Elohim Tzabaoth Hod Michaël Beni Elohim Kokav S. of Mercury ✠ Shaddaï El Chai Iesod Gabriel Cherubim Levanah S. of the Moon ✠

Appendix B

The Proper Times to Make the Invocations of the Art Armadel

These instructions are absent from the Ars Armadel portion of the 'Raphael' manuscript. The instructions are given here as they appear in the Sloane Manuscript 3825: "Nota: There are 12 princes rulling besides those in the 4 Altitudes, and they distribute their offices amongst themselves, every one rulling 30 days every yeare, now it will be in vain to call any of those Angells unless it be those that then governeth, For every Chora or Altitude, hath its limited time according to the 12 signs of the Zodiack and in that signe the Sunn is in. That Angell or those angells that belong to that signe have the government: as for Example; suppose I would call the 2 first of those 5 that belong to the first Chora, Then chuse the first Sunday on March: that is after the Sun is entred ♈, and then I make my Experiment; and so doe the like if you will the next Sunday after againe; But if you will call the 2 second that belong to ye first Chora,16 Then you must take the Sundays that are in Aprill, after the ☉ is entered ♉. But if you call the last of the 5th Then you must take those Sundays that are in May after the ☉ is entered ♊; to make your Experiment in; doe the like in the other Altitudes, for they have all one way of working: But the Altitudes have a Name formed severally in the substance of heaven even as a Character, for when the Angells hear the names of god that are attributed to them they hear it by the vertue of that carecter. Therefore it is in vain to call any angell or spirit unless you knew what names of god to call them by; Therefore observe the forme of this Following conjuration, or Invocation etc.

FINIS.

www.ingramcontent.com/pod-product-compliance
Ingram Content Group UK Ltd.
Pitfield, Milton Keynes, MK11 3LW, UK
UKHW051532130425
457270UK00004B/16